Apostle Arnold

Apostle Arnold

The Life and Death of
Arnold Toynbee 1852–1883

Alon Kadish

Duke University Press 1986

© 1986 Duke University Press
All rights reserved
Printed in the United States of America
Library of Congress Cataloging in Publication Data
appear on the last printed page of this book.
Frontispiece: The Toynbee Memorial Medallion
Balliol College, Oxford

To absent friends.

Contents

Preface

Arnold Toynbee died at the age of thirty. The story of his short life consists of a number of seemingly unrelated and somewhat ineffective endeavors. In addition to his academic work he was active in the promotion of church reform, in an effort to start a national system of adult education, in Oxford municipal politics, and, perhaps most significant, in an almost frantic attempt to salvage the crumbling alliance of the working classes and liberalism. At the same time he tried, desperately at times, to update the Liberal party creed so as to provide guidelines for the solution of current problems in a manner acceptable to both the middle class and the workers.

It is through this last aspect of his work that his life's story assumes some cohesion. Toynbee is representative of a confused and deeply troubled generation of Victorian middle-class, intellectual liberals. The old accepted fiats of liberal orthodoxy were proving less and less applicable to the political and social problems of the 1870s and the Great Depression. At the same time liberalism was losing its hold on the working classes. The class cooperation of the reform agitation was being eroded by growing working-class disenchantment. At first the course of change was unclear. There were some indications of the possible success of Tory populism as evinced in the 1874 general election and the ensuing Tory government's social legislation. There were fears of a growing popularity of High Church ritualism—at the time still identified with political reaction—in working-class parishes and a growing concern for the potential of a Tory party organization capable of successfully competing with Liberal party caucuses on their own ground.

By the early 1880s the trend was clearer. Henry George's popularity and the growing militancy of the new unionism indicated a working-class tendency to adopt an independent and dangerously radical political course. Toynbee's commitment to liberalism involved him in a simultaneous effort on two fronts: an attempt to define the precepts of a new liberal creed and a struggle to convince working-class audiences to abandon revolutionary doctrines in favor of the, as yet, only partly worked out liberal alternative.

The origin of Toynbee's views can be largely traced to his religious convictions. With the help of T. H. Green and R. L. Nettleship he had emerged from an adolescent spiritual crisis with a strong sense of mission aimed at the realization of a moral, Christian commonwealth. With the church's dogma, which he found unpalatable, safely separated from faith, and with faith expressed, and thereby defined, by duty and service, Toynbee approached the problems of modern industrial society with the confidence of a missionary. With a number of close friends he embarked on a search for spheres of action in which they might fulfill their sense of duty. The initial principles of their work had been laid down largely by T. H. Green in the course of his own civic activities. It was in essence a combination of liberal orthodoxy modified, somewhat hesitantly, by the growing awareness of the multiplicity of problems whose solution could not be left simply to self-help and free competition. Toynbee and Green joined an attempt to revive an interest in church reform aimed at transforming the Church of England into a truly national church, the spiritual embodiment of the national community. Some years later, following Green's death, Toynbee entered Oxford municipal politics, unsuccessfully attempting to save the last Liberal city council seat in Green's old ward. In both instances Toynbee tried to infuse old struggles with new concepts and in both his efforts were thwarted by the inherent conservatism of the church establishment and the Oxford electorate.

In his early campaigning for church reform Toynbee's faith in democracy and in the common sense of the common man had led him to demand a change in the rules of the game. He wished the issue of church reform to be placed before the people rather than left to the clergy and to politicians. He was confident that the people would not fail to adopt his point of view and thus, by their involvement in the campaign, a significant part of its purpose would be achieved. In municipal politics he had wished to introduce general ideological principles and national issues, thereby stimulating in the local electorate a greater awareness of, and consequently, an involvement in, civic activity on both the local and national level. In both campaigns his approach proved too radical, but Toynbee never doubted that his vision of democracy could be realized.

Democracy, for Toynbee, was an empty concept without active working-class participation. Initial fears of a Tory attempt to bribe the working class into an acceptance of paternalism were replaced by fears of the threat to democracy from the militant left. Toynbee's interest in economics, in questions of consumption and distribution, combined a moral point of departure with what was gradually becoming a political, rather than a philanthropic, issue. He felt that orthodox theory had neglected these matters, although his initial views demonstrated a primary faith in free trade, free competition, and self-help. He did not doubt the adequacy of economic theory as a means for the analysis of reality or the validity and applicability of its conclusions, so long as they confirmed his moral view of the world. Hence, in his first attempts to popularize political economy (by means of addresses to audiences in northern industrial centers), economic arguments were employed as proof of his view of the underlying harmony of all aspects of social behavior. Facts were collected and used in order to demonstrate the validity of his theory.

It was only with the submission of his views to the criticism of "proper" orthodox economists that Toynbee began to realize the difficulties of the simple application of economic theories. He soon found that in order to substantiate his hypotheses concerning the nature of progress he would have to provide his own theories based on his own research. Having found economic theory inadequate he increasingly turned to the use of historical data as advocated by Cliffe Leslie and other positivists. Historians had long insisted that the study of the past was the key to comprehension of the present. The positivists went one step beyond traditional historiography by extending the scope of historical research to areas other than political and constitutional history and by attempting to derive from history general laws of progress rather than just simple analogies and precedents. Influenced by the Oxford school of historians, Toynbee turned to the history of economic and social conditions in his search for scientific confirmation of his concept of moral progress through material change. Possessed with an absolute faith in scientific reasoning and in its ability to produce clear and unambiguous conclusions, Toynbee embarked upon his inquiries; their nature is only imperfectly expressed by his Industrial Revolution lectures. The main obstacle to his academic work was the tendency of events to outstrip his research. New problems and new unscientific theories emerged at a rate faster than his ability to work out the scientific principles to deal with them. Consequently, he was constantly deflected from his initial course of inquiry leaving us with only an outline of a research program and some initial findings.

Through the complexity of historical evidence Toynbee began to realize the similar complexity of the issues of the day he wished to analyze. He had gradually lost his faith in the doctrinaire liberalism of free trade and free competition. He found that his faith in the ends of progress was not a sufficient means for the explanation of the various stages of progress. Yet he remained confident that it was possible to produce a consistent and comprehensive program of social and economic reform that, despite its inevitable complexity, would preserve a unity of purpose. At no point was Toynbee prepared to admit that the construction of such a program was beyond his powers. Despite an attempt to distribute the work among a number of friends he felt compelled to deal with each new development as it came along. Consequently, one could argue that, in view of his indifferent health, he in effect drove himself to his eventual breakdown and death.

In this book, the development of Toynbee's thought is described in considerable detail. This is done for a number of reasons, the least of which is that much of the material has been virtually ignored by the editors of his published work. It is felt that the process by which he reached his final, although not finalized, positions is of interest on two counts. First, this volume is a biographical study of the development of Toynbee's economic, social, and historical thought, described and analyzed chronologically rather than under subject headings. The convoluted and tortuous nature of the development of his views on subjects such as state intervention provide a valuable demonstration of some of the problems inherent in the transition from orthodox to new liberalism (including the not uncommon disparities between fact and theory evident in Toynbee's experiences with the cooperative movement, in municipal politics, and finally in his attempt to convert a crowd of radical Londoners to his brand of liberalism). Second, the detailed analysis of Toynbee's intellectual development demonstrates the various strata of his weltanschauung, of interest to historians of late nineteenth century liberalism. Religion, in this respect, is as important a component as new methodological and scientific fashions.

Toynbee did not develop his ideas in a vacuum. His views as well as his position among his peers are of importance in the understanding of the development of economic and historical thought at Oxford and elsewhere. Indeed, a number of his contemporaries came to regard him as their spokesman, if not their mentor. His work is of particular interest to the student of the development of economic history and its relation to the study of history and economic theory. The story of this process is yet to be written but it is clear that Toynbee's direct and indirect (e.g., through the work of W. J. Ashley) influence is of major importance. His scientific reputation in relation to a number of standard issues (e.g., his contribution to the "pessimists'" view) is considered in detail, but it is his concept of the industrial revolution as a unique historical development that has helped to establish the study of economic history as an autonomous branch of history rather than as a merely supplementary one.

It is with considerable pleasure that I record my gratitude to all those who have contributed in various ways to this work: to E. Sidon and J. Lipschitz who provided the initial incentive; to Professor Y. Elkana through whom I first became interested in Toynbee; to Professor Peter Mathias who kept my interest from flagging and who, with Professor A. W. Coats, offered invaluable feedback and unwavering support; and to I. Asquith whose idea this biography was. I am especially grateful to Margaret Toynbee for her help in tracing the Toynbee family history and in piecing together Toynbee's early years and to S. Brown and B. J. Fehr who lent a sympathetic ear to my amateurish efforts at reconstructing Toynbee's personality.

At various times I have profited greatly from conversations with, and suggestions from, numerous friends, teachers, and colleagues in England and in Israel. I am especially indebted in this respect to Avner Offer, to J. R. Symonds, and to Milner's biographer, Terence H. O'Brien.

Research for this book was greatly facilitated by the patience and efficiency of the Bodleian librarians. Special thanks are due to my friend V. Quinn and to P. Bulloch of Balliol College, to Mrs. Macdonald of Oriel College Library, to A. Raspin of the British Library of Political and Economic Science, and to J. J. Fewster of the Department of Palaeography and Diplomatic of the University of Durham. I am grateful to B. Halpern for her many helpful suggestions and to Mr. and Mrs. C. A. Brodie and to E. Rendel for their helpfulness and generous hospitality. Thank you also to P. V. W. Gell and M. P. Thompson for their kind permission to study their families' papers.

Finally, I would like to thank the Hebrew University for financial help in preparing the manuscript for print and S. Farhi for valiantly struggling with the various drafts.

Alon Kadish
The Hebrew University of Jerusalem
Mount Scopus   June 1985

1. Family

On 23 August 1852 Harriet Toynbee bore her fourth child and second son. Her husband, Joseph Toynbee, named him Arnold after Dr. Arnold of Rugby.[1] The family had recently moved to Savile Row, London, following Joseph Toynbee's election to the position of aural surgeon to the charity and lecturer on the diseases of the ear at the newly founded Saint Mary's Hospital. Two years later the family moved again, this time to Wimbledon where Joseph Toynbee purchased a country house, Beech Holme. It was at Wimbledon that Arnold spent the happiest years of his childhood and it was to Wimbledon that he was brought to die and where he was laid to rest beside his father's grave.

Joseph's father, George Toynbee (1786–1865), a tenant farmer, worked a farm of some six hundred acres between Swinshead and Heckington in the Lincolnshire fens. His first wife, Elizabeth Cullen, bore him seven children of whom it was remarked that they seem to "have produced brains, but have not made much money."[2] Following her death in 1820, George Toynbee married Sarah Obbinson; they had another eight children, a large family by any standards.

The size of the family meant that a private education could not be simply a "nursery operation." Fortunately, George Toynbee's wealth (upon his death in 1865 each child was left £1,000) allowed the conversion of one of the barns into a schoolroom and the hiring of a schoolmaster. Some of the boys were sent to a boarding school in King's Lynn and they were all given the opportunity to enter the liberal professions and thus move away from farming and from Lincolnshire.

George and Elizabeth's first child, George (born 1812), revealed a bent toward scholarly work and the promise of a career that may have inspired his brother Joseph (born 1815). In 1833 George spent some time in Bonn studying languages in the course of which he attended A. W. Schlegel's lectures on German literature.[3] Upon his return to England he settled in London where he combined some literary work with medical studies (in which he was helped by his younger brother Joseph). Both became members of the Royal College of Surgeons, but George's career was terminated by his premature death at the age of twenty-nine.

As for the rest of George and Elizabeth's children, Elizabeth (1813–85) married a clergyman, William (1814–47) became a farmer in Jamaica, Charles (1817–65) remained a farmer with his father, John (1818–41) became a missionary in India, and Henry ("Harry") (1819–1909) went to sea at the age of fourteen.

At seventeen Joseph left for London to begin medical training as an apprentice to William Wade of the Westminster general dispensary in Gerrard Street, Soho. He studied anatomy under George Derby Dermott at the Windmill Street school of medicine where he acquired an enthusiasm for surgery. He next attended the practice of Saint George's and University College Hospital and in 1838 was admitted a member of the College of Surgeons of England, having already decided to specialize in aural studies.[4]

While in London, Joseph and his older brother George befriended Mazzini and helped him to set up a school for Italian organ boys in Hatton Garden.[5] In later years Arnold Toynbee would proclaim Mazzini "the true teacher of our age," claiming *The Duties of Man* to be more important than the work of Adam Smith and Carlyle.[6]

The member of the family with whom ties seem to have been strongest was Joseph's youngest brother, Henry, who retired from the merchant navy in 1866, the year of Joseph's death. Upon retiring, Henry, who had married one of the daughters of Admiral W. H. Smyth, settled in London as a marine superintendent in the Meteorological Office.[7] During his years at sea he had developed an especially fiery brand of Low Church evangelicalism. The Toynbees as a rule disliked religious intolerance and were, on the whole, devoid of any strong feelings on religious dogma. Henry, on the other hand, was a convinced antipapist who regarded High Church ritualism as "the great enemy's most successful plan of attack on God's Church."[8] The only Toynbee brother (except for the missionary, John) to possess strong religious convictions, he took an interest in his nephew's religious development.[9]

However, Henry's influence on Arnold seems to have been minimal and at best it may be said that Arnold's love of Bible reading when at Oxford may have owed something to his uncle's influence; on other matters they clearly disagreed. For example, on social reform Henry Toynbee expressed views common among missionaries. He held a poor opinion of all forms of secular social work while stating that "there is however always hope that these workers will grasp the fact that Christ would not have died on the Cross if anything less would have done the work, and that the greatest relief to a worldly-distressed or sin-troubled mind lies in a simple truth or two about Christ."[10] The solution to most, if not all, the troubles of the human race could be found in daily readings of the Bible, Henry thought, and while Arnold was to derive great comfort and inspiration from such daily readings his view of society's maladies and their cures was far more complex.

Joseph Toynbee's choice of aural studies for specialization was extremely fortunate as the field had been long neglected, dominated by quackery. He began his surgical career as an assistant to Richard Owen and was soon elected surgeon to the Saint James and Saint George's Dispensary where he established a Samaritan fund. In 1842 he was elected to the Royal Society (to which he was presented by Sir Benjamin Brodie) and in 1843 he was elected a Fellow of the Royal College of Surgeons (FRCS). At roughly the same time he started a successful private practice; he was the first aural practitioner to charge for consultations two guineas rather than one.[11] As a result he could afford to move the family from Argyll Place, first to Savile Row and later to Wimbledon.

In August 1846, with his career and practice well established, Joseph Toynbee married Harriet, daughter of Harriet and Nathaniel Reynolds Holmes. The Holmeses, who were far from affluent, came from a line of merchants dealing mainly in cheese and leather.[12] Nathaniel Holmes (1764–1840), father of Nathaniel Reynolds Holmes, had been a liveryman in the Leathersellers' Company, Rochester. Having retired (c. 1810), he moved to Derby where his son,

Nathaniel Reynolds, settled and raised his family. Of the twelve children Harriet and Nathaniel Reynolds had, only five survived infancy. In them, as in the family in general, a tendency toward upward mobility is discernible. Nathaniel Reynolds's brother, John Holmes (1800–1854), became an assistant in the Department of Manuscripts of the British Museum. One of Nathaniel Reynolds's sons, Nathaniel Holmes, became an electrical inventor and another, Richard Jackson Holmes, joined the East India Company as a cadet.

Following her marriage to Joseph Toynbee, Harriet's ties with her family remained strong so that the Holmes's family fortunes are of some relevance to Arnold Toynbee's background. John Holmes had married Mary Anne Rivington, of the wealthy booksellers' family. Yet, despite their wealth, John's death in 1854 presented his widow with the serious financial problem of providing for their children's education. The eldest, Charles Rivington Holmes, who had matriculated at Clare Hall, Cambridge, in 1852, was informed that he would have to terminate his studies in order to enable a younger brother, Herbert, to complete his training as a naval cadet. With the help of some money lent by friends, Charles was allowed to complete his education, but his family's misfortunes seem to have severely undermined his performance in the tripos.[13]

After his graduation, Charles spent two years in France as a private tutor and then took Holy Orders in December 1857. Convinced that his calling lay in serving in the East End of London, he became a curate at Saint John's, Limehouse. During a period of dedicated work Charles contracted smallpox (1861) and then tuberculosis (1867). The miserable conditions in which he served and his selfless indifference to his own welfare eventually cost him his life; he died a relatively young man in 1873.

Joseph and Harriet had nine children, the choice of whose names seems mostly to reflect their father's taste. Gertrude, born in 1848, was followed by William (1849), named after William Wordsworth, and Lucy (1850). Arnold (1852), named after Dr. Arnold of Rugby, was followed by Rachel Russell Everard (1853) and Paget Jackson (1855), named after Joseph's friend, John Jackson (1811–85), then bishop of Lincoln and the future bishop of London. Next came Mary Hakewell (1856), Grace Coleridge (1858), named after the poet, and, finally, Harry Valpy (1861), named after another of Joseph's friends, R. A. Valpy, a barrister and philanthropist active in the Bloomsbury district.

Harriet was a stern mother and it was said that the Toynbee children and their descendants could be clearly divided into the "jolly" ones who took after Joseph and Arnold and those who took after Harriet. Her grandson, A. J. Toynbee, wrote of her, "Like many other mothers of large Victorian families my grandmother was a minor replica of Queen Victoria herself and one had to be careful to treat her with the deference that she expected of one, as of right."[14]

Since well before his marriage, Joseph Toynbee had been interested in applying his medical knowledge to the problem of sanitation in urban working-class districts. He had helped Edwin Chadwick and Lord Morpeth in their efforts to appoint officers of health as part of the Health of Towns bill.[15] For a number of years Joseph Toynbee considered a career as an officer of health and, having suffered a deterioration in his health during the year following his marriage, he had set his hopes on such an appointment. An anticipated income of £800 per year would allow him to live outside London which, he felt, "pulls me down and makes me ill," while commuting to it daily. Although the appointment never materialized, he eventually moved the family to Wimbledon and commuted to his practice in Savile Row.

Joseph Toynbee's view of the problem of the lower classes was the reverse of his brother Harry's and was characteristic of a school of thought that had been gradually gaining currency among social reformers. It set environment before religion and body before spirit as the main targets of the assault on poverty. It was Toynbee's contention that "there never was a sound mind in an unsound body" and, accordingly, that the lower classes' spirits could not be elevated unless their environment was made more wholesome and their physical health improved. Toynbee regarded poverty as the social equivalent of clinical disease. Neither were inflicted by fate, nature, or God as part of a universal order of things and therefore their presence was not inevitable if one understood their cause. It was his view that "in disease Nature is always attempting to remedy an injury, that sometimes without, but often with, the aid of art, her purpose is accomplished, the injury is removed, and the disease ceases. Sometimes the injury is too great to be remedied even by nature and art combined; and life is lost in the contest."[16]

Thus the task of the medical doctor, as well as of the social reformer, was "to seek to ascertain what Nature is endeavouring to accomplish by the so-called diseased processes, what local or general injury she is attempting to overcome" and to help to remove them.[17] Once the physical environment of the lower classes showed signs of improvement, emphasis might shift toward their spiritual and cultural elevation. It was the opinion of Joseph's eldest daughter, Gertrude, that "Mazzini's principle that the people should claim liberty not as a right, but as a means for doing their duty, was the keynote of my father's efforts in Social Reform. He deplored the physical degradation of the masses of the people and he always strove to remove it, but to raise them to a consciousness of their dignity as immortal souls was his ultimate aim."[18]

Ideally the solution for the social problems of the lower classes would be found through self-help. However, Joseph Toynbee realized that self-help must first be stimulated and guided by members of the more fortunate classes if it were to affect the lives of the working classes. In a lecture delivered at Mazzini's school in 1841, he stated that while he regarded "with delight" the formation of schools for the education of the poor, he was much more impressed by voluntary association of the working classes "in order to redress and improve themselves by the best instruction which is placed within their reach." He regarded self-help of this sort as "one of the most encouraging signs of a social reformation. . . . It carries with it a repeal of the sentence of degradation which has for ages been inflicted upon the greater part of the human race. In their hunger and thirst for knowledge it is proclaimed that the spirit of man is not always to be weighted down by toil for animal life, and by the appetite for sensual indulgences."[19]

Through his dealings with the problems of poverty and social reform, Joseph Toynbee came to attach considerable importance to closer contact between the classes. While basically an optimist, he regarded the gulf between the classes as distinctly unhealthy. The poor required the help of the more affluent classes, and closer contact between the two "nations" would elevate both.

It appears to me that the mental and physical ills from which the poor in all nations are suffering cannot be much alleviated, without the existence of more intimate social relations between the two great classes of Society, the Rich and the Poor; or rather the educated and the uneducated. Between these classes at present there exists an awful chasm. They have no knowledge of each other; scarcely any sympathy with each other. The old bonds of society still continue. The true tie, which is mutual respect calling for the mutual neverfailing acts of kindness is as yet little known.

Having reduced the class problem to a question of education, Joseph Toynbee could not help wondering why the problem was so slow in solving itself. In a manner not much different in its simplistic view of society from his brother Harry's, he wrote to his daughter in 1860, "It seems strange that the working people cannot afford to educate their children, provide themselves with proper homes or pay for medical attendance without assistance from the rich. But, doubtless, the kindly feeling this induces is a boon to both rich and poor."[20]

The practical expression of Toynbee's view of cultural elevation may be found in his philanthropic activities in Wimbledon, where the conditions of local working-class life were presumably relatively wholesome and therefore did not require major changes as in the East End. He was instrumental in starting the Wimbledon Village Club and was elected its treasurer. The club was to serve the dual purpose of providing for the proper recreational wants of the working classes while bringing all classes of the community into closer and friendlier intercourse.[21] His intention was for the club to contain a small local museum that would help "to develop and foster in the minds of all classes of people, an interest in the common objects of Nature which surround them." The recreation the club's committee had in mind consisted mainly of penny lectures of usually not more than thirty minutes, penny readings, musical evenings, and the demonstration of various scientific instruments and experiments.

The lectures were something of a family affair; the Toynbee children, including Arnold, were brought along to help with the scientific experiments and demonstrations.[22] It was Joseph's view that such recreational centers could and should be founded in every village and in every urban parish, providing "the masses of the people additional sources of improvement, healthy recreation and worthy occupation." Local museums would introduce the people to scientific knowledge as well as produce insight, as vague as it might be, into "the designs of the Great Farmer of all things."[23] Bringing the working classes to a state in which they might be induced to lift their eyes from their bleak and sordid surroundings and cast them toward higher things had always been considered a significant and valuable step in their amelioration; in this instance science replaced the Bible as the means of achieving a change in perception.

Joseph Toynbee shared the literary tastes of most middle-class Victorians. He demonstrated his admiration of Wordsworth and Coleridge by naming two of his children after them and in his letters he often quoted from Keats. In addition he had cultivated a taste for art which he also regarded as an educational aid.[24]

Although the Toynbee household contained a nurse and a governess, the children's upbringing was not left entirely in their hands. Joseph seems to have been closer to them than most Victorian fathers or, for that matter, than Harriet Toynbee. He shared most of his interests with them: reading to them from his favorite works and taking them to picture galleries, plays, and popular scientific lectures. His letters to them are full of warmth and gentle humor and are not unduly moralistic or sanctimonious.

Gertrude Toynbee, in her memoir of her father, portrays him lovingly as a tall, slight, and erect person with a face "singularly beautiful," "a fine bearing and very gracious manners," often surrounded by a swarm of small adoring children, patiently introducing them to the mysteries and beauty of nature, literature, poetry, and art. Nowhere in these descriptions does Gertrude's mother, Harriet, appear. One might imagine her in the background, always distant and perhaps slightly disapproving, an impression strengthened by Arnold's subsequent attitude.

Joseph Toynbee strove to bring up his children in the light of his social ideals, encouraging them to help in his various philanthropic activities and to share his interests in social matters. In a letter to his eldest son, William, dated 27 Feb. 1866, he wrote, "Geddy, Arnold and I rode to see Tooting Common yesterday; the enclosure by Mr. T. is outrageous. If the landowners persist in enclosing commons the *people* will be without a country. Arnold has made a sketch of the British people viewing their native land by means of ladders planted against the walls of the great landowners' parks!"[25]

It was Arnold Toynbee's wife's retrospective view that young Arnold "had remained untaught in religion to a curious extent."[26] This was a misconception partly caused by the peculiarities of Arnold's mental process and partly due to the fact that, although the family's routine included daily prayers and church attendance, Joseph Toynbee attached relatively little significance to the formal aspects of religion. Once Arnold turned his mind to religious matters his views came to closely resemble his father's and there can be little doubt that Joseph was a deeply religious person.[27] He was greatly preoccupied with reconciling his fundamental faith in the possibility of realizing "heaven on earth" with his knowledge of sorrow and pain. Such a reconciliation, he believed, was possible through faith, which allowed one to prepare to meet and master pain without changing one's view of the world. The strengthening of one's faith in anticipation of future trials was a process each individual must go through alone, and it was his hope that the education his children had received at home had encouraged and prepared them to undergo such a process.[28]

These views explain Joseph Toynbee's fascination with the work of his friend and fellow aural surgeon James Hinton (1822–75), who, following Joseph's death, took up his practice in Savile Row.[29] One of the last books Joseph read was Hinton's *The Mystery of Pain: A Book for the Sorrowful* (1866), copies of which Joseph sent to Benjamin Jowett and to F. W. Farrar (then at Harrow). Hinton argued that knowledge could alter an individual's perception of the world and, accordingly, that knowledge of the nature and purpose of pain should transform the individual's attitude toward it. It was Hinton's contention that pain was an indispensable part of the order of the world and that "things that we call painful, that are painful in our ordinary state, are essential conditions of our highest good."[30] Without pain there is no sacrifice and without sacrifice the higher forms of love and happiness are unattainable. Without pain people would be unable to express the full essence of their existence, since "the necessity for sacrifice is built into the structure of our being, it is the birthright, the inalienable inheritance of life."[31] Pain, however, Hinton said, should not be confused with sacrifice as the highest expression of an individual's existence and therefore should not be sought for its own sake. Pain is mastered by shifting one's focus from the presence of pain to the function it serves in allowing sacrifice.

Joseph seems to have found in Hinton's work an expression of many of his own views and it is therefore not surprising that when Arnold began to develop his own religious views he started by considering Hinton's book.

2. Childhood and Adolescence

The Toynbee children were raised with the help of a nanny, Elizabeth Sheppard, and a governess, a Miss Wanustrocht. Nanny Sheppard, who was first employed when Gertrude, the eldest child, was quite young, saw all the nine children through their nursery days. She was a simple, uneducated country woman (probably from Hampshire), blessed with a warm and outgoing nature. The Toynbee children and later their own children were all devoted to her,[1] and in a revealing passage Gertrude Toynbee confessed that nanny Sheppard "was like a mother to us," thus demonstrating the basic difference between Joseph and Harriet in their role as parents.[2] Harriet, despite her large family, lacked nanny Sheppard's warmth and affection in dealing with children. From the nursery she seemed a distant and cold figure; the children's concept of the world of adults seems to have been dominated by nanny Sheppard and Joseph Toynbee.

Arnold's letters to his mother are, accordingly, cold, dutiful, and dryly informative. Their contents demonstrate his mindfulness of his duties as a son while displaying no affection or heartfelt concern; his language is impersonal and formal. The letters open with a distant "My dear Mother" and end with the standard "Ever your affectionate son." On the other hand, his letters to nanny Sheppard are much more childish, containing rambling expressions of the deepest love and devotion. A letter to Arnold's mother dated November 1872 contains as an afterthought: "I am sorry to hear you have been ill, but glad to hear you are well again now."[3] In contrast a letter to nanny Sheppard from February 1871 contains the following passage: "I miss very much your constant love; and I often look at your dear old face in the not very bright photograph which stands on my chimney-piece." It ends with:

With much love to you, dear nurse, and the hope that you may at no distant time find a more peaceful home with some one of us than you now possess.

I am, yours ever lovingly,

A.T.

Ask Lucy to read this letter to you alone.[4]

It is evident that Arnold's devotion to his nanny did not abate after his leaving home. According to Gertrude, "Arnold was very good to her; once a year he would take her to the Grand Military Tournament, which was the greatest treat she could have, and he always gave her a new cap on her birthday."[5] It is not clear whether this was by design or by accident but it is interesting that nanny's "greatest treat" coincided with Arnold's fascination with the military.

Clearly, nanny Sheppard and not his mother was the recipient of Arnold's love as a child, though she had little if any impact on his intellectual development. It was under the influence of Joseph Toynbee that all the children developed an interest in art and drawing, a love of nature, and an interest in literature.

His father is said to have spoken of Arnold, when the latter was only four years old, as his child of promise. Not surprisingly, Arnold's fondest childhood memories were linked with the memory of his father, including "those rambles over Wimbledon Common on which his father would take out a volume of poetry and as they rested in pleasant spots here and there read aloud such passages as a child could feel at least, if not understand."[6]

Arnold as a child was remembered by his elder sister "as a lovely little boy with beautiful light brown curls and a winning smile," an image borne out by a photograph of the young Arnold seated, clasping his hands, dressed, as was then fashionable with small boys posing for the camera, in girl's clothes.[7]

From an early age he displayed at times a fixity of purpose that could border on obsession. Once he set his mind on a certain matter, persuading him to change it or allow for diversity of interest proved extremely difficult, and attempts to do so were often met by temperamental outbursts. In the schoolroom, "he had fits of violent temper, which were almost ungovernable," and at one time Gertrude was encouraged by Joseph Toynbee to try to moderate Arnold's temper with "a little talk privately now and then."[8] These must have had a very limited effect since, as he was about to enter his first school, his sister's fears for the possible consequences of his temper led her "to taking him into a room alone and praying with him and giving him a little textbook."[9]

The positive expression of this purposefulness was Arnold's ability to become completely absorbed in whatever caught his interest. One such boyish interest was in all things military. At play "his favourite amusement was the construction of forts in the garden of his house, but with a characteristic which always belonged to him, he built them with unusual thoroughness, with as much scientific accuracy as possible and mounted them with the largest cannon procurable."[10] This interest found expression in early aspirations toward a military career and an interest in military history; at Oxford he joined for a short while the Oxford University Rifles.[11] Mrs. Barnett's memory of their first meeting in 1875 contained an impression of his "passionate interest in war, it's tactics and traditions."[12]

While high-spirited and playful the young Arnold suffered from indifferent health. Being somewhat self-conscious, he was determined to overcome his physical frailty in a characteristic, although occasionally absurd, manner. Determined to stand up to the hardships of school life as well as anyone and anxious not to lose face, he insisted at the age of eight that in preparation for his first schooling outside home nanny Sheppard should soundly cane him one or two nights in succession before he left home. This way he might know how it felt and if flogged at school he would not be taken unawares and cry out.[13]

Once at school, the Reverend Cowley Powles's in Blackheath, his obsession with holding his own combined with his natural alacrity to make him a leader of boys, some of whom were older than himself. He readily joined in traditional boys' pranks with characteristic abandon. In one instance, having "planned a joke upon a master which was to be executed by a roomful of boys to whom the master's back was turned, he was so intent on carrying out the project that he remained perfectly unaware of the entrance of another master by an opposite door wh[ich] had been perceived in this by all other boys and these had resumed their seats, leaving him standing alone in front still caricaturing."[14] He consequently became the sole recipient of the inevitable punishment.

His schoolwork further demonstrated his inability to divide his attention so as to handle all subjects regardless of his interest in them. He did poorly in languages and mathematics while excelling at history and literature. In addition, his health remained poor necessitating periods of absence from school while convalescing at home. On such occasions his father "made a special companion of Arnold . . . and looked after his health very tenderly."[15]

Toward the end of Arnold's stay at Blackheath, various possibilities were discussed concerning his next school. It was felt that if he chose to pursue his earlier fascination with the military, his scholarly ability provided him with a good chance of entering Woolwich.[16] In addition, having already sent (in 1863) the older William to Harrow, Joseph Toynbee raised the possibility of Arnold going to Haileybury or Rugby.[17] It seems that by early 1865 definite plans were made for Arnold to enter Rugby by February 1866 only to be thwarted by a serious deterioration of his health.[18] As he would recall some years later, "When I was between 13 or 14 I had a fall from my pony, striking the back of my head against the ground; I was ill and out of sorts for a few months and have been subject to bad headaches there ever since."[19]

As plans for Rugby were dropped, at least for the moment, Arnold entered, as a temporary solution, Rev. J. M. Brackenbury's school in Wimbledon while still residing at home.[20] In the long run he was never to recover completely from the effect of the accident. Slow in the acquisition and assimilation of new knowledge,[21] he now had to confine his daily reading to not more than a few hours for fear of recurrent migraines.[22] However, it is unknown to what extent the accident's long-term consequences were perceived during the months immediately following it. It is not clear whether new plans were made for Arnold's schooling once his health improved, but as late as July 1866 he was still quite weak.

By 1866 Joseph Toynbee was at the height of his professional career. In 1864 he had been sent for by the queen "on account of deafness and noises in the head which had, in spite of all treatments, much increased as to cause great discomfort."[23] Within half an hour the queen was cured; later the same year Joseph Toynbee was presented at court.[24] Having established a thriving private practice, he

resigned that year his position at Saint Mary's Hospital and took up
the posts of aural surgeon to the Earlswood Asylum for Idiots and
consulting aural surgeon to the Asylum for the Deaf and Dumb.
This left him with sufficient time to resume research in connection
with his old interest, surgery. During an experiment with chloroform
as an anesthetic an accidental overinhalation led to his death on
7 July 1866.

Upon being informed of the tragic news, Arnold rushed home
from school. "He threw himself on the sofa in impassioned grief,
crying, 'It can't be true, it can't be true.' "[25] In their grief the Toynbee
children were drawn even more closely together, seeking compensation for their loss in each other's company. This was especially true
of Arnold and Gertrude. In 1875 he was to describe their mutual
emotional dependency as "a strong bond of love. . . . I talk over
nearly all my work to her, indeed I hardly do or say anything that I
don't tell her—our lives are almost one."[26] Beyond its emotional impact, Joseph's death also meant a loss of guidance. Arnold had seemed
quite content to follow his father's advice concerning his schooling,
but Joseph's accidental death left Arnold with no clear sense of direction. Plans for Rugby were now definitely dropped. Harriet Toynbee, possibly influenced by the memory of the circumstances of the
death of her uncle, John Holmes, decided that the family could not
afford to spend as much as it had on education. William left Harrow
and Arnold, in accordance with his own childhood ambition, entered
an army prep school where fees were lower than at Rugby. In addition, Harriet and the rest of the children moved into a smaller house,
Newlands, also in Wimbledon.

As his character was already considerably formed, Arnold went
through two years of military prep school without its making much
of a positive impression on his development other than convincing
him that he was unsuited for a military career. While at school, his
poor health forced him to give up games thereby compelling him to
take his health more seriously in planning his future.[27] He continued
to develop his interest in history, however. In time, Arnold came to
look down on the intellectual standard of the school as inferior to
his own and left it at his own request in 1868.

Having abandoned his childhood visions of an army career and
without his father to guide him, Arnold was left with no clear plans
for the future. For the following two years he resided at home spending most of his time reading alone in his room, attending classes at

King's College, and working on his own in the London Library.[28] The lack of regular tutoring and the absence of any scholarly guidance in his studies led to the development of a certain lack of academic modesty. At the military school Arnold had considered himself at least equal to his masters. Having chosen to work alone, his confidence in his own ability became boundless. "He hoped to write a great book on the Philosophy of History, and he wished to write it in a very perfect style. He was very intolerant of the misuse of words, and he had an idea that he would perhaps have to make a sort of dictionary to explain the exact sense in which he used them."[29] Another grandiose project conceived at the time was a study of the life of Cardinal Wolsey, "deeming that his character had never been adequately portrayed."[30] In this instance he went beyond collecting material and had actually begun writing parts of it before abandoning the project.

Upon leaving the military school, Arnold's first plan was to prepare for the Civil Service examinations. This was soon dropped and replaced by an ambition to read for the bar. However, his mother, still fearful of the family's financial future, felt that they could not afford the expense. Joseph had left each child some money to be handed over to them only after reaching the age of twenty-one. Until then Harriet was in control of all family finances and she seems to have considered Paget's going to Haileybury (in 1869) more important than Arnold's new plan. The result was a clash between two strong-willed personalities, adding an element of bitterness to a relationship that, to begin with, had hardly been affectionate. Although eventually Arnold's sense of duty prevailed, he found his mother's addiction to gossip and her general manner frivolous, lacking both depth and warmth.

In his dejection over the lack of monetary support Arnold withdrew from Newlands, choosing to spend most of his time reading on his own in various remote villages. His ultimate aim was to enter Oxford once he came into his inheritance money. It was a period characterized by long spells of melancholy and introspection; he would write Gertrude letters in which "he would chafe against the littlenesses and limitations that marred such a great part of daily life and speak of his loneliness, and he would yearn for the life beyond the grave when he looked forward to meeting the great spirits of all ages."[31]

It was F. C. Montague's judgment that at this point in his life Arnold himself did not fully understand his own restlessness:

The youth of thoughtful persons is often racked with pains which they cannot express and which are not the less real, because their elders can prescribe nothing better than platitudes. The suffering of middle and later life bear no more analogy to these pains than does the anguish of a toothache to the torture of cutting one's teeth. Whilst the surface-current of Toynbee's mind set now towards this, now towards that profession, the undercurrent set more and more steadily towards the pursuit of truth.[32]

Arnold's reading was dictated by various interests as the fancy took him rather than by any definite plan. His method of reading is reflected in advice he gave at the end of this period to his younger sister, Rachel. "Take up any book or any subject at all interesting to you and . . . read it carefully through, making notes in a common-place book of anything that struck you or of any thoughts that came. . . . any book really thoroughly read through does one a great deal of good in more ways than one. . . . Only stick to one book and get through it, making notes of what you know and don't know—what you don't agree with and what you like. . . . Don't read it too fast, but think over it as you go on."[33]

Having developed the habit of concentrating on one author at a time his knowledge, although limited in scope, was considerably detailed. His favorite authors included Elizabethan poets, Milton, Gibbon, Burke, Keats, Shelley, Scott, Thackeray, Wordsworth, Shakespeare, Bolingbroke, and Macaulay, with all of whom "he lived on terms of no ordinary intimacy, and such converse unconsciously affected his own utterance."[34] Some of the subjects that attracted his attention included Plato's Republic (possibly using Jowett's translation first published in February 1871) and an inquiry into the cause of the absence of landscape painting among the Greeks.[35]

In 1871 Arnold took lodgings in East Lulworth on the Dorset coast. (He also returned in 1872 and in 1873.) His love of nature, his solitude, and the drama of the coastal scenery combined to produce a strong and lasting impression on him. Images of sea and sky often found their way into his later work.[36]

As 1871 ended Arnold's attention turned more and more toward religion. Determined to work out for himself the fundamentals of religion, he turned first to Hinton's Mystery of Pain. Despite some initial misgivings, it made a strong impression on him. Not satisfied with merely reading the book, he sent Hinton a list of questions and criticisms to which he received a long and detailed reply.[37] From Hinton's answers, it appears that one of Toynbee's criticisms concerned the validity and strength of Hinton's main arguments in that they were based on moral and spiritual observations rather than on scientifically collected empirical data. The nature of Toynbee's question supports an impression derived from his letters and his reading list: his self-compiled study program had not included any modern continental philosophy, certainly not Kant. His plans for a study of the philosophy of history seem to have been confined to English works: Gibbon, Bolingbroke, Macaulay. Appropriately, Hinton's replies contained some Kantian arguments thereby providing something of an introduction to modern moral philosophy, more of which Toynbee would encounter at Oxford.

Hinton argued that basing an argument on nonsensory observations did not necessarily rob it of its validity.

I do consider the main thought of the little book—that in all pain we are serving and serving man's redemption *proved*; that is proved by the proof that is appropriate to the case. . . . A need for moral sensibility as essential to feeling the evidence of a fact, does not render the evidence less conclusive. Why is intellectual constitution to be held to give proof and our moral constitution not? . . . Science has no other "proof" than man's reason; and I venture to say his conscience and his heart are just as good for proof as that.

Although Hinton did not elaborate on how he established the objective validity of conclusions based on nonsensory observations, it is clear that he himself did not doubt their universality. "No heart that is human, when once it has received the thought that its pain might serve others' good will be satisfied if it be not so."

Another Kantian argument employed by Hinton concerned the existence of an extrasensory reality as established by reason, although he seemed to go beyond the mere statement of its existence. "By faith . . . I mean a thing not *furnished*, but absolutely demanded by reason. I mean the taking into account that which we cannot see; but then reason demands this, for it proves there is and must be more than we can see. . . . By faith here I mean perhaps the practical conviction and assurance that that is, which though it is not within our direct perception, the intellectual and moral evidence give us reason to be sure must be."

In the course of his letter to Toynbee, Hinton came close to stating a more traditionalist justification for the existence of pain. "How should man ever even discover the hidden selfishness of his heart if it were not for the woes and degradations of his fellows which make him see: 'why it was myself I was thinking about all this time.' . . . *Others' pain,* I should say, has wrought all the true life man hast." At the same time the tone of the letter seemed to emphasize that the knowledge of pain should bear significance for the individual rather than be used to justify universal misery.

Elsewhere in his letter, Hinton admitted that his concentration on the knowledge of pain could have been misleading since it "does not do justice to pleasure. . . . I no more mean to say that pleasure is not true good. . . . Pleasure taken not for self, or pleasure's sake, but for service also, is the perfect good, is the means and instrument of love, the condition of its perfectness." In this instance Hinton's terminology seems to suggest that in some cases "service" is inter-changeable with "sacrifice," without fundamentally altering his pre-scription for individual moral behavior. Although, in certain cases, service may not entail sacrifice (and therefore pain), it still may be prescribed for individual moral action.

Finally, Hinton stated that he was inclined "more and more to think of all good as coming to man on this earth," a view that Joseph Toynbee had associated with Ruskin and one that Arnold whole-heartedly adopted.[38]

At the time, Hinton's views made a profound impression on Toyn-bee. At one point, according to Gertrude, following his return to Wimbledon from one of his periods of solitary study in the country, "he quietly took my hand under the table as we all sat at supper and whispered, 'I have learnt the secret of self-sacrifice now, Geddy'; and then he added, 'I feel there is so little self left to conquer.' In his quiet days of lonely thought and meditation in the country, this idea of self-sacrifice had taken possession of his whole being as a revela-tion and filled him with calm joy."[39] In a reply to Hinton he stated that he was

determined to devote my life, and such power as I possess, to the study of the philosophy of history. With this object in view I have no inclination to enter any profession. . . . To this pursuit I wish to give my *whole* life. . . . I do not care to spend my life in acquiring material benefits which might have an evil, and which at any rate, could not have a good effect on me. These ideas . . . are not the result of mere ambition or of any desire for fame in itself, or for the rewards with which it is accompanied. My sole and, as far as it can be so, unallowed motive is the pursuit of truth; and for truth, I feel I would willingly sacrifice prospects of the most dazzling renown. I do not even think myself capable of accomplishing any work of importance. If my labours merely serve to assist another in the great cause I shall be satisfied.[40]

Having for some time sought a clear path away from the agony of uncertainty and restlessness, Toynbee seems to have latched onto the first definite system that succeeded in striking a chord in him. He wholeheartedly adopted the concept of sacrifice and wove it into his previously conceived intent to concentrate on the philosophy of history. This produced a vision of his own future revealing lack of experience, intellectual conceit, and uncertainty of purpose, coupled with a determination to base his life on moral principles, vague though they may be. His vision left no room for uncertainty and doubt, nor did it provide for possible changes due to future experience or study.

Arnold Toynbee's religious contemplation did not end with Hinton. He now turned more and more to the Bible, seeking a way in which he could combine all previously formed and half-formed notions into a system that would help provide a clearer sense of direction and purpose. At an age at which contemporaries usually took for granted maxims acquired through a standard religious education or else rejected them, Toynbee was turning almost desperately to the fundamental principles and texts. His earnestness stood out in the company of young men of his age. One of his Oxford friends is supposed to have commented in a half-baffled, half-amused, manner, "Why Toynbee doesn't read his Bible as the rest of us do, because it is the right thing—I do believe he reads it because he likes it."[41]

His fascination with the Bible and with works such as the *Imitation* and Thomas Browne's *Religio Medici* lasted a number of years, during which they provided him with a much needed spiritual anchor.[42] During his first year at Oxford, he wrote to a friend, "I am perfectly spellbound by parts of the Old Testament histories. . . . I agree with what you say about principles, and I recognize easily in a spirit of very deep emotions there would be an instinctive love of principle. We struggle on bit by bit, and now every day I try to beat the *devil* in detail. I want to get drenched in the spirit of that wonderful *Imitation*."[43]

Obviously the Bible, the *Imitation,* and *Religio Medici* provided an expression of certain emotions Toynbee had felt deeply but had been unable to articulate himself. "Two things the Bible speaks to our hearts most unmistakably are the unfathomable longing for God, and the forgiveness of sins; and these are the utterances that fill up an aching void in my secular religion—a religion which is slowly breaking to pieces under me."

Browne's *Religio Medici* also provided Toynbee with an aesthetic model. According to his wife, "The ring of its eloquent passages delighted him as well as the beauty of its image clothed thoughts. . . . It is not too much to say that for a while he principally educated himself and his style upon this favourite book; his copy of it is scored and re-scored. . . . A part of its fascination to him was due to his great fastidiousness of taste, he never [could] get help [from] an elevated sentiment or a moral exhortation unless it was clothed in worthy and dignified language."[44]

One can almost sense the relief Arnold must have felt in discovering these texts for himself; one also senses his determination to extract from them all that he could although, at the same time, the *Religio Medici* could not provide him with a comprehensive system. It is clear that Arnold derived much comfort from finding many of his own moral and spiritual notions expressed in such sublime prose. Browne's love of nature, "the Art of God" (1:16); his loyalty to the Church of England (1:15); his tolerance of all other forms of Christian dogma in the conviction that beyond all formal differences "there is between us one common name and appellation, one faith, and necessary body of principles common to us both" (1:3); his confidence in his ability to express his faith by use of reason (1:9–10); his insistence on the joy present in temporal life (1:45); and his faith in the resurrection (1:47) are all echoed in Toynbee's letters of the period. Browne's statement, "I study not for my owne sake onely, but for theirs that study not for themselves," may have inspired Toynbee's similar statement in his letter to Hinton (2:3).

Browne's assertions, "wee are happier with death than we should have beene without it" and "the heart of man is the place the deveil dwels in" may also have inspired Toynbee when writing some of the letters quoted above (1:44, 51). Yet some of Browne's views, for example, his superstitions and his intolerance of non-Christian monotheistic religions, have no parallels in Toynbee's writings.

One curious example of what Toynbee might have found both acceptable and unacceptable in Browne's views was his position on charity. On the one hand, Browne emphasized the selfless nature of charity: "to love God for himselfe, and our neighbour for God" (2:14), a view coinciding with Toynbee's ideal of sacrifice. On the other hand, Browne maintained that "statists that labour to contrive a Commonwealth without poverty take away the object of charity not understanding only the Common wealth of a Christian, but forgetting the prophecy of Christ" (1:14), a position contrary to Toynbee's future social philosophy.

Despite Toynbee's own claim, religion did not at the time replace a comprehensive secular philosophy. It is doubtful whether he indeed possessed any such comprehensive system of ideas, and, although religion constituted an important step in his intellectual development, it cannot be seen as providing at this stage a complete weltanschauung. Toynbee may have been determined to dedicate his life to the search for truth, but he seemed, at best, vague about what this truth was or how he was to go about finding it.

Religion also seems to have had a marked effect on the development of Toynbee's character. His determination to lead a selfless life helped to soften some of the rougher edges of his personality. Whereas long periods of introspection might have otherwise resulted in a certain selfish attitude toward society, religion helped to transform his stubbornness and fixity of purpose into a resolution to lead a life of self-sacrifice. One of the first consequences of this resolution seems to have been a determined effort to improve his relations with his mother.

Ever since his father's death, Arnold had accepted no idea or advice on the basis of its advocate's authority. Each concept and each position was considered on its own merit and it was either rejected or adopted only after a slow process of intellectual and mental digestion. One result of this process was that, although Toynbee received ideas from many people, he never came to consider the originators of any adopted views as his masters. He had neither a closed mind nor an outstandingly original one but he insisted on working out each idea for himself. Another consequence was the power of conviction with which he held ideas since they were acquired through a process that, at times, came close to revelation. In one such instance a friend recalled that "as we were coming down the side of a mountain once in the Lake country, suddenly, as though he had struck on some momentous thought, as indeed it was, he broke out with the unexpected sentence: 'Yes! seek ye first the

Kingdom of God and His righteousness!' That's what we've got to do, and nothing else really much matters."[45]

The absence of authority did not mean refusal to accept any. Toynbee had not resented his father's guidance; it was principally the low standard of his masters at the military school and the lack of regular schooling that had led him to seek his own counsel. With the approach of his twenty-first birthday and limited financial independence, Toynbee realized that if he were to make it to Oxford he would require some regular tutoring. Such a tutor was found in Alfred G. Beavan, a recent graduate of Pembroke College, Oxford, and a future (1874) headmaster of Preston Grammar School where, by coincidence, he taught the young Charles John Holmes, son of the Reverend Charles Rivington Holmes, Harriet Toynbee's first cousin. Beavan left a lasting impression on Holmes: "With his dark beard, beetling brow, eyeglass screwed tight into his right eye and his reputation for flogging, Mr. Beavan was a memorable figure."[46]

An outspoken man with a passion for classics, Beavan briefly became the first firm authoritative figure in Toynbee's life since his father's death. His influence is all the more striking since it led Toynbee to choose a college and a subject that he would come to consider as serious mistakes. (His choice of college was also approved by his father's friend, Bishop Jackson,[47] and its having been Thomas Browne's college may have added to its attractions.) In a letter to his mother sent from Worcester, where he studied with Beavan, Toynbee explained his plans, "I have chosen Pembroke College because it is a small one with good 'Dons', especially in classics, and inexpensive, and also because it was Mr. Beavan's college. I knew he would like me to go to his own college, and as I owe absolutely everything I know in classics to him, I did not hesitate to go there."[48] Arnold decided to read for an honors degree in classics and to compete for the Brackenbury scholarship at Balliol although he felt far from confident about his prospects.

While studying with Beavan, Toynbee was confronted with some of the disadvantages that had resulted from his method of self-education. One obvious problem was his lack of training in classics.

With most boys you see classics are with their earliest entrance at school the main subject, and even if they are lazy, the work which is forced from them and the influence to which they are subjected leaves them, perhaps in spite of themselves when they leave school, with a tolerable knowledge at any rate of classics, or with an acquaintance which a little labour could improve into knowledge. With me it has been different; I left off classics at fourteen, just at the age when a boy begins to know a little, and since that time . . . my studies have been desultory in the extreme.

I would not have had this otherwise; indeed, I suppose that at the time my neglect of classics was greatly owing to my own desire. I see my mistake now, and feel the consequences for which I am only willing to blame myself.[49]

For the first time a note of academic humility figured in Toynbee's plans. Although his faith in his own intellectual powers did not diminish, he came to realize that he could not obtain an adequate standard of learning on his own. The necessary instruction, he felt certain, would be provided by Oxford. In addition, Toynbee became aware of the lack of social contact with his contemporaries. He found himself looking forward to associating with young men of his own age and determined to fulfill his resolutions concerning his future. "The chief benefit of my going to Oxford will be the intercourse I hope to have there. . . . You need not doubt, I hope, that I shall do well in verity; that I shall gain immensely in knowledge and experience . . . and above all, that I shall try at least to become a better boy, more loving and more humble, and more than that, less selfish in my life."

Toynbee was beginning to realize the narrowness of his own intellectual endeavors. It is F. C. Montague's judgment that before entering Oxford "he imagined himself to have gone deeper and further than was really the case."[50] Montague was probably right in arguing that had it not been for his entering Oxford—and, one might add, his mental and intellectual receptivity—Toynbee's intellectual development would have been of little interest to the world.

3. A Balliol Man

In January 1873 Arnold Toynbee entered Pembroke College, Oxford. Away from Alfred Beavan's influence he soon came to regret his choice of college. In the course of the term he passed "Smalls" which he described to his sister as "a miserable, easy, disagreeable exam."[1] He planned spending the summer in London reading for the Brackenbury which, if he won, would allow him to transfer from Pembroke to Balliol by Michaelmas 1873.

While he seems to have made few, if any, friends at Pembroke he did not remain in social isolation long. He was "discovered" by W. M. Hardinge who had met him "years before at a tutor's."[2] Hardinge, having found Toynbee "panting" to transfer to Balliol, introduced him to a set of Balliol undergraduates. The occasion was a luncheon organized by Hardinge, in the course of which Toynbee met Alfred Milner and Leonard Montefiore who were to become two of his closest Balliol friends.[3]

At the time Toynbee had already acquired a somewhat enigmatic reputation. Milner had heard of him within two months or so of both of them coming up. He was to recall that "it was not so much admiration which Toynbee's personality inspired as veneration. His friends spoke of him with affection, certainly but also with a kind of awe . . . which was not without real significance. When, therefore . . . I first came across him . . . I was fully prepared to meet a personage. My attitude, as well as I remember, was one of intense interest, not without a touch of defiance."[4] It took some getting used to, but after a few meetings Milner was to write to Philip Lyttleton Gell, a close friend from their days at King's College, "I have seen a great deal of Toynbee lately and I am getting more and more impressed by the fact that he is a 'true bill.' His vagueness, and vague he often is, seems rather a fault of language than of thought. I have given up my old notion that he thinks loosely. On the contrary he seems accurate in pure speculation and wonderfully restless—a good sign, for he is never satisfied with his own ideas, however true he thinks them."[5]

Part of Toynbee's charm seems to have been due to the unique quality of his conversation, especially when discussing his views concerning matters on which he had dwelt during his periods of solitary contemplation. On such matters his thought must have been refreshingly unorthodox, free from the intellectual confines of a public school education. Indeed, having had little intercourse with young men of his age, his whole style of conversation was noticeably different. He had never mastered the art of small talk and, although he spoke with considerable eloquence, he did not exactly converse. His habit of concentrating for long periods on a limited number of subjects with complete dedication led him, whenever discussing these matters, to pronounce his views with utmost confidence and unusual enthusiasm. At Oxford he discovered in himself a style of delivery and a power of persuasion of which he had been previously unaware.

The faces of listeners supplied him with the stimulus which his sensitive temperament and weak body required. . . . Although he spoke rapidly and copiously, he never was betrayed into a vulgar phrase or slovenly construction; he spoke as one to whom idiomatic utterance is natural, correctly and forcibly, without the cant phrases of the undergraduate or the studied negligence of the college tutor. Nor did he, like so many other exuberant speakers, suggest to those who heard him that he spoke out of a passion for display. If he talked much it was because he forgot himself in his subject.[6]

His eloquence, the complete earnestness with which he tackled each subject, and a noticeable lack of self-consciousness produced a startling effect on listeners expecting from an Oxford undergraduate the usual style of clever conversation. His future wife was to recall that whereas when they had first met she had regarded him only "as a bright young Oxford undergraduate," her view changed "when in the course of an ordinary walk and talk on a country hillside, he said 'the spirituality of life is what we have got to teach man'—'seek ye first the kingdom of God and His righteousness—that's what we've got to do'—with an unconsciousness that it might seem unusual to be so simply possessed by such desires which almost startled by its vivid reality."[7]

The years of solitary contemplation had left their mark on his overall bearing. Generally speaking, he was "very unexcitable in the ordinary sense, and unemotional, markedly quiet and callous in manner."[8] His expression in repose was rather cold and inanimate, an impression strengthened by his grey and somewhat inexpressive eyes.[9] Yet, when in conversation, his whole countenance was transformed revealing something of his true nature. It was, Montague wrote, as if he was lighted up by "a brilliant yet soft irradiation, which charmed the beholder and can never be forgotten by those who knew him well. Together with his winning countenance he had a manner singularly frank, open and animated . . . neither shy nor slow nor abstracted nor languid, but always prompt and lively."[10]

The forceful impression his conversation had on his listeners was strengthened further by his physical appearance. As a child much had been made of his beauty.[11] Those who knew him in later years tended to describe his features as classic: "a face of almost Greek regularity of feature, but with a height of brow and a certain touch of aggressive force about the mouth, which distinguished it from the conventional Greek type."[12] This impression was reflected in the memorial medallion commissioned by his friends after his death and kept at Balliol. His physical appearance was complemented by a "singularly melodious voice" and a winning smile.[13]

In conversation his true nature, concealed by the deceptively cool exterior, asserted itself. It is therefore not surprising that his friends' reminiscences often recall him in conversation. C. E. Vaughan wrote that Toynbee "had the hot temper and aggressive spirit that often goes with genius, and I have to confess that our talks more than once ended . . . in a violent explosion."[14] Not everyone found Toynbee as irresistible as his friends did. When Frederick Rogers, a bookbinder and an East End activist, first met him, he was impressed by Toynbee's courtesy but, on the whole, he concluded, "We neither of us cared for each other."[15] This was especially the case during his bouts of physical and mental exhaustion when " 'his light was low' and his speech ineffectual."[16] A Balliol contemporary who first met him in such a state described him as slipping "about the quad as a forlorn stranger."[17]

Toynbee was aware of his inability to strike a balance between his physical frailty and his consuming enthusiasms which resulted in recurring periods of near total exhaustion. In a letter to a friend who had remonstrated him for not taking his work more lightly, he wrote, "You see I am like a bad pen, I can't write without a splutter and my anxiety is to prove to myself that I gain by the splutter; remember it is not so much excitement *about* my work as the excitement *of* it that I speak of, and really I'm afraid I can't get rid of what is an element of my mental nature."[18]

Toynbee's intensity of commitment to his views did not result in his being either humorless or unusually somber. He retained a pronounced playfulness that found expression in outbursts of animated high spirits and, in the words of his wife, "many a furious 'bally rigging' in which he was always the inciter and the most desperate combatant."[19] Although he did not become an active participant in any of the usual undergraduate sporting activities he did not adopt Ruskin's disapproving attitude toward such forms of leisure.

Little is known of Toynbee's intellectual development during his terms at Pembroke although Milner's letter quoted above indicates the beginning of an Oxford influence on Toynbee's religious views. In it Milner described a conversation with Toynbee in the course of which he found that

Toynbee rather modifies his original tone on that subject [religion] and as far as I understand him now, I thoroughly coincide with his views. Theology, he seems to say, is neither false nor absolutely true. It is the outward and visible sign, by which men have interpreted the real but undefinable grace which we call religion. It is true, as long as it makes these truths of religion as clear to men as they can be at any particular age. It is false when it obscures those truths or comes to be mistaken for them. Such is the case with much of our present Xian theology. But what we hope to do is not to attack theology but to insist on the essentials of religion and where these are fully appreciated the veil will of itself pass away. This is a sort of crude resumé of a Toynbee-Milner philosophy of practical religion.[20]

These views may reflect the influence of a number of Oxford contemporaries, including R. L. Nettleship who had met Toynbee during the latter's terms at Pembroke.[21] Their friendship was based, according to Milner, on the dissimilarity of their characters.[22] "Each found in the other qualities that were a supplement to his own. Toynbee admired Nettleship's scholarship, the subtlety of his intellect, his fine faculty of speculation. Nettleship felt the need of a stimulus such as Toynbee's intensity of conviction and missionary zeal supplied."[23]

Whatever the origins of the views expressed by Toynbee in his conversation with Milner, they indicate the beginning of an important development in his intellectual outlook. Progressing beyond the purely personal dimension of his religious experiences, he began to express his views in a more philosophical form. Having adopted a relativist view of dogma, reducing it to a means forged by, and in the service of, the particular age in which it was formulated, Toynbee proceeded, through the widening of his intellectual horizons, to apply the same principle to other doctrines in other spheres of knowledge. A relativist and instrumental approach to religious doctrine provided a philosophic principle that, in turn, lent cohesion to his various intellectual pursuits; it is possible to see in his approach the beginning of a comprehensive weltanschauung. At the same time, previously held views were not discarded. Arnold's new approach to religion incorporated both Joseph Toynbee's dislike of dogma as well as Thomas Browne's catholicity in dealing with the value of the religious practices of the various Christian churches.

Unhappy with his choices of both college and subject, Toynbee set his hopes on winning the Brackenbury, the preparation for which earned him an exemption from college lectures.[24] In sitting for the Brackenbury he was to compete with one of his new Balliol friends, Philip Gell. In the course of the examination (November 1873) Toynbee's lack of training in producing commonplace essays to demonstrate a command of standard scholarship, became obvious. To his disgust he was informed by one of his examiners that his failure was partly due to his having picked up his ideas "from hearing the clever talk of London society" and having then written them "just as you would talk."[25] It seems that his essays, rather than furnish proof of adequate scholarship, expressed his personal views in an argumentative manner. His annoyance with his performance was partly due to his mistake, as he put it half-jokingly, in assuming that "the examiners could take off the top of my head and look at the contents within."[26] Later, Toynbee came to realize that the examiners' criticism demonstrated the deficiencies of his training and perhaps the

crudity of some of his self-formed ideas. While he did not lose his
faith in the validity and importance of the knowledge he had acquired,[27] the examination results dealt a telling blow to his confidence in the adequacy of the scope of his intellectual attainments. It
also helped to rid him of some of his contempt for ideas not his own
as well as his delusion that his intellect and resolve would always let
him realize whatever goal he chose.[28]

Beyond the disappointment of his failure, the strain of the examination proved too much for Toynbee. Following the ordeal, "I could
not get to sleep till 4 in the morning . . . and my brain was in such
an excited state that it got beyond my control and *would* think and
do just as it pleased in spite of my efforts. So I fled [Oxford] leaving
all my baggage behind."[29] For two days he remained in a feverish
state and it was some weeks, during which he was looked after by
William and Gertrude, before he recovered. His breakdown seems
to have scared him momentarily into a resolution to avoid at all costs
its repetition. "The exam[ination] brought on a fierce attack which
warns me never to go in again for one like that at any rate. I can no
more help my brain getting excited under such circumstances than a
man inclined to sea-sickness can help being sick on a rough sea and
I have no ambition to paint the moral of over competition by going
mad—just yet at any rate."[30]

According to Hardinge, Toynbee had been introduced to Jowett
while still at Pembroke and it is possible that his father's name as
well as the probable intercession of Bishop Jackson, visitor of Balliol, helped to bring Arnold to Jowett's attention.[31] Jowett had offered Toynbee rooms at Balliol, an offer that may have been made
quite innocently in reply to a query by Toynbee preceding the
examination concerning the possibility of allocating college rooms
to the winner of the Brackenbury after the term had already begun.[32] Toynbee was desperate to change colleges, and Jowett, impressed by the originality of Toynbee's performance despite his
failure, did not withdraw his offer, even though it was quite irregular.

Apparently Toynbee was completely ignorant of the problem of
migrating from one college to another. It must have seemed to him
to require no more than the assent of the master of the college to
which he wished to transfer, whereas migrations were normally possible only when an undergraduate obtained a scholarship or an ex-
hibition at another college. Unaware of the principle involved,

Toynbee, still convalescent at Wimbledon, asked his younger brother, Paget, a Balliol freshman, to inform Dr. Evans, the Master of Pembroke, that he had accepted Jowett's offer of rooms. Dr. Evans's incensed response was a flat rejection.[33]

It is obvious that Toynbee did not consult Jowett prior to the move, and it is to Jowett's credit that, despite the awkwardness of the situation, which he probably had no intention of creating, he chose to confront the Master of Pembroke rather than withdraw an offer made to a dark horse. Nevertheless there was little Jowett could do. He pointed out to Toynbee that Dr. Evans was well within his rights in refusing to sanction the transfer. His advice was that, unless Toynbee managed to obtain Dr. Evans's permission, he should return to Pembroke and either read for another attempt to win the scholarship or submit a formal request for permission to migrate at the end of the year.[34]

In his reply to Jowett's letters of advice Toynbee described his plans for the future, altered by his physician's advice: "If I come to Balliol I should be able to work quietly on for 3 or 4 years by which time I hope I should be strong enough to do well in the final schools of philosophy and history [? probably Greats]; but I should be obliged to keep myself as free as possible from brain excitement during that time."[35]

Prolonging his stay at Oxford for four more years would mean a serious strain on Toynbee's limited private means. This, in turn, led him to believe that in any event he would be unable to afford to remain at Pembroke, where he would require private tutoring in classics. He informed Jowett that if his request to transfer could not be granted, he would ask to become an unattached student (thereby saving college fees). Jowett, in reply, supported his decision and offered him to attend Balliol lectures for a year as an unattached student, free of charge, after which he could officially migrate to Balliol.[36]

A detailed letter from Toynbee to Evans containing a profuse apology managed to modify slightly the tone but not the substance of Evans's refusal to allow the transfer.[37] In his view the matter was really between himself and Jowett. Balliol was denounced for being "a kidnapping college—they wish to have not only the first rate men and the second rate men, but even the third rate men and the fourth rate men,"[38] thereby revealing his view of Toynbee's potential. Toynbee finally petitioned the chancellor, Lord Salisbury, but from the latter's reply it became clear that whatever the circumstances it was felt that the university could not afford the precedent.[39] By then, however, a solution had been found. On Jowett's advice, Toynbee, who, in any event, was still convalescing (now in Brighton), took his name off the books. When his health allowed, he came up to Oxford for the rest of the year, nominally as Jowett's guest at Balliol.[40] After a year off the books Toynbee was able to matriculate again in Hilary Term 1875 at Balliol.

Thus Jowett became a prime mover in shaping Toynbee's development. It was his insistence and advice that got Toynbee into Balliol and that later allowed him to spend his time there reading for a "Pass" degree rather than for Honors. In the final analysis Jowett's action on Toynbee's behalf must be attributed to his having detected in Toynbee a uniqueness justifying exceptional treatment. Yet it should be noted that while allowing a promising student to settle for a pass degree was not quite usual, it was not unheard of. Jowett himself had, in the past, allowed exceptions on similar grounds.[41]

Toynbee, in turn, would remain grateful to Jowett for the rest of his life. Typically, he held Jowett in deep affection rather than in awe as so many other Balliol undergraduates did. With his characteristic tendency to regard acceptable authority as a form of paternal guidance, Jowett's patronage was received with gratitude and affection rather than with unquestioning deference. Toynbee succeeded in breaking through Jowett's shyness and natural reserve by means of his unorthodox approach. According to one account, "after dinner [Toynbee] would jump up and say, just as a son might say of his father 'I think I must just look in on that dear old gentleman. I expect he's all alone, and I'm sure he would like it,' and like it he did."[42]

What Toynbee's unusual attitude toward Jowett meant to the latter is revealed in a curiously touching passage in Jowett's memoir of Toynbee. "Among older persons may be found someone who will value the aspirations of such a man as Arnold Toynbee above the great and successful careers of others; who will desire in later life to be revisited by the dreams of their youth, without inquiring too curiously into the possibility of their accomplishment in the brief period of human existence; who will pray, even in declining years, that 'they may have more of a spirit like his.' "[43] Thus, Toynbee's almost filial love of Jowett was answered by the paternal affection of the elderly Master detecting in the younger man something of his own lost youthful spirit. Upon Toynbee's death, his wife noted that Jowett "has lost one more like a son to him than any one he ever had—he said he mourned as for a son. . . . the College must grieve really also for the dear old gentleman who is much alone."[44]

Balliol provided Toynbee with a rich social life, devoted friends, and inspiring teachers, a form of existence that came closest to his vaguely formed ideals. In a letter to a friend describing life at college one detects a joy as well as a sense of relief at having finally found such a perfect haven.

The garden quadrangle at Balliol is where one walks at night, and listens to the wind in the trees, and weaves the stars into the web of one's thoughts; where one gazes from the pale inhuman moon to the ruddy light of the windows, and hears broken notes of music and laughter and the complaining murmurs of the railroads in the distance. . . . The life here is very sweet and full of joy; at Oxford, after all, one's ideal of happy life is nearer being realized than anywhere else—I mean the ideal of gentle, equable, intellectual intercourse, with something of a prophetic glow about it, glancing brightly into the future, yet always embalming itself in the memory as a resting-place for the soul in a future that may be dark and troubled after all, with little in it but disastrous failure.[45]

Shortly after his return to Oxford as Jowett's "guest," Toynbee became involved in Ruskin's North Hinksey road project, in the course of which he was to reveal qualities of leadership. It would be difficult to overestimate Ruskin's position as cultural hero at Oxford in the 1870s. His lectures drew crowds the size and composition of which were rarely seen at professors' classes. "Before the hour appointed for his lectures in the museum every corner of the theatre was crammed, and this not being only by the young men who would most naturally have been expected to be there, but by a medley of men who would have been found on the running path or in their college barges—men of whom Philistia might have been proud and glad."[46] Ruskin's reputation was based largely on his work on art and the fame of his controversial condemnations of industrial society and laissez-faire political economy. Yet despite the enormous appeal of his "performances," they were received with considerable skepticism. He had gathered about him a small circle of undergraduate disciples for whom he would hold intimate dinners in his rooms at Corpus Christi College and to whom his art collection was open. But beyond this small body of followers his tirades were of a limited effect. One of his listeners, Alexander MacEwen, a Balliol undergraduate, described one of his lectures as delivered in "a despairing tone, a wail against our material prosperity and iron development. As a matter of fact, he talks utter if not complete nonsense; but then the nonsense is very very eloquent, and he is a beautiful man." In another letter he added, "I have been going regularly to hear Ruskin this week. He is utterly mad."[47]

Early in 1874 Ruskin asked one of his followers, J. R. Anderson, to bring MacEwen, a fellow Scot, to take tea with him. Although MacEwen was unable to take most of Ruskin's social theories seriously, he found Ruskin's charm irresistible: "The evening was devoted to my entertainment, and though our host is slightly insane he succeeded to perfection. He has a childlike simplicity and beauty of manner, and is withal so unlike anyone else, so honest and gentle and unaffected, that one's admiration very soon turns into affection for him."[48]

In the course of the evening, Ruskin divulged his major current concern as well as the conceptual outlines of a plan that would serve to demonstrate his point. "Ruskin's great vexation just now is the amount of energy which men waste up here in boating and gymnastics. He is making an effort to get men to turn their physique to some practical end, such as gardening or landscape improving." This idea soon found expression in Ruskin's lectures. He argued that it was a pity "that men could not see the worth of adding to the joy of gainning health of body the gladness of health of mind, which would assuredly come to them, if they would put their muscles to some work of benevolence for the nation,"[49] such as helping to satisfy the need for good rural roads or possibly helping to improve a village green, thereby creating for the villagers a more wholesome environment.

Eventually Ruskin developed a scheme to improve a road leading through the village of North Hinksey, the site of one of his favorite walks. The road that ran along the edge of the village green had become, through faulty irrigation, too deeply rutted to be of any use. Consequently the villagers had been driving their wagons, carts, and livestock through the village green, rendering it unusable for any recreational purposes. Through his friend, H. Acland, Ruskin obtained the permission of Sir W. Harcourt, owner of the land, to improve the road's irrigation and beautify it by planting wild flowers on its banks.[50] Execution of his scheme by Oxford undergraduates would serve to demonstrate his argument by making them discover through personal experience what the work of a laborer was like, while bringing them, through some practical toil, into closer contact with rural reality. The main goal was the project's hoped-for effect on its participants so that, although Ruskin sincerely intended to improve the villagers' environment, no serious attempt was made in advance to determine the best route for the road.

MacEwen is probably right in arguing that Ruskin may not have been entirely serious at first.[51] He knew little if anything about road digging and in any event had planned to leave Oxford for Italy at the end of Hilary Term for the rest of the academic year. However, the enthusiasm with which the scheme was met by Ruskin's followers encouraged him to proceed. Rather than change his travel plans—having been assured by his closest disciples that his presence on the site was not required—Ruskin summoned his Brentwood gardener, David Downs, to Oxford to take charge of the technical supervision of the work.

The first phase of the project required the excavation of a new course that would offer better irrigation. The workers were mainly Balliol undergraduates organized by Anderson and MacEwen. A core of about twelve Balliol men met with Ruskin on 16 March and were given the full details of the scheme following which they "swore their allegiance."[52] After some delay due to Ruskin's absence from Oxford, the "diggers" met with Downs in Anderson's rooms where the project was finally launched. Ruskin's original plan, which was quite ambitious in scope, was modified to deal just with the stretch of road along two sides of the village green, running between the green and the cottages facing it. The organizers managed to assemble a work force of some eighty students who were divided into groups of twenty. Each group spent two days a week during the summer term handling, for two hours at a time, pick, barrow, and spade under Downs's supervision.[53]

The project attracted wide notice within the university and it was soon commented on in the national press. To most it was an object of ridicule and for a while going down to Hinksey to watch the diggers became quite a popular pastime for Oxford cynics. The diggers' lack of technical experience must have added to the spectators' entertainment: "clumsy we were at the business, few knowing on which side of a spade the foot should rest, and many digging with a vehemence which fagged them in ten minutes." As for the spectators, an observer marked upon the contrast offered by "the numbers of athletic men, followers of all kinds of sports, who were sitting smoking in the shade of the hedge watching the efforts of men who were, by comparison, but puny and feeble specimens of their race."[54]

One such "puny and feeble" specimen was Toynbee. Ruskin had been one of his father's favorite authors and Toynbee's own interest in art must have made him eager to meet Ruskin. One way for younger men to enter Ruskin's immediate circle was to join the diggers and, as the work was largely a Balliol project, Toynbee soon joined one of the work parties along with many of his friends including Milner, Montefiore, and Hardinge.

Once the road's new course was dug all work ceased. The main core of diggers were in their last year and were preparing to sit for their finals during Michaelmas Term 1874.[55] Therefore, if work were to proceed and the road undergo surfacing, a new generation of diggers would have to take over. In the course of the initial excavation Toynbee's enthusiasm and single-mindedness had won him the position of foreman of one of the work parties. As the work proceeded, Ruskin had been corresponding with his disciples instructing them in the aesthetics of the project and elaborating on the significance of their selfless dedication in the service of mankind.[56] By May, Toynbee was added to the circle of correspondents. Apparently Toynbee had written to Ruskin suggesting that the latter should have tried to reach Oxford men beyond the confines of his immediate circle. In response Ruskin admitted his mistake and vowed rectification, "I hope when I return to Oxford, that we may have little councils of friends both old and young in my rooms at Corpus, which will be pleasanter for us than formal lectures, and will reach many other, or perhaps pause at many *nearer,* needs of thought than any connected with the arts."[57]

Upon Ruskin's return to Oxford in the autumn of 1874, work was resumed as were the "councils," breakfast parties held every Tuesday in Ruskin's rooms.[58] Meeting Ruskin and an invitation to join the "councils" proved sufficiently attractive to guarantee a steady stream of recruits—some of whom lasted no more than one outing. In order to supervise the road's surfacing Ruskin had observed the work of a stonecutter on the London Road.[59] Confident in his fitness to instruct the diggers in the art, Ruskin joined them regularly, with the result that walking with him to and from the site was added to the project's attractions.[60] However, despite his confidence, the surfacing as well as the excavating lacked adequate planning, and the Oxford oolite used for the surfacing soon proved too soft to keep the road firm. Thus, although the surfacing was completed in 1875, the project did not in fact result in any lasting improvement; the road was soon abandoned in favor of the open common.

Much has been made by Ruskin's admirers of the lasting effects of the lessons taught by the North Hinksey project. It has been argued that the gospel of labor as taught by Ruskin and demonstrated by the road digging found later expression in the introduction of manual labor as part of the training in some of the public schools (e.g., Bedales, Clayesmore, Shrewsbury, Sedbergh, and Bath College).[61] It has also been maintained that Ruskin's expressed hope that the diggers would form a sort of brotherhood that would extend the North Hinksey ideal to work among the poor of the great cities was realized in the university settlements.[62]

Be that as it may, most of the undergraduates who took part in the digging were unable to take Ruskin's gospel altogether seriously. Milner, for one, saw nothing incongruous in writing during the course of the digging, "I have not been on the river the last day or two, but have been digging instead—Ruskin's plan, you know! It is good exercise too and it does not matter much what exercise you take, so long as you get some."[63] He added two weeks later, "I go to the digging and the river on alternate days."[64] In later years he was to dismiss "the Ruskin roadmaking craze" as an expression of young men's eccentricities, not to say absurdities.[65]

Toynbee was certainly much less dismissing of his experience as a digger. His zeal at the time was genuine and in his enthusiasm he managed to overcome his physical handicap. But, although he regarded Ruskin with reverence and affection, he was not, strictly speaking, a disciple. However, it is quite likely that Ruskin was at least partly responsible for stimulating Toynbee's interest in political economy, which dates from about 1875,[66] an interest that from the outset was closely linked to Toynbee's religious and social views. Toynbee's work in political economy was directed mainly at examining the economic implications of modern industrialization and their social, moral, and political consequences. He was to reject the economics of laissez-faire, but here as elsewhere his reasoning was fundamentally different from Ruskin's. Unlike Ruskin, Toynbee was a firm believer in the liberal concept of continuous progress—expressed politically in the form of democracy—an essentially optimistic view of history. Like most liberals of his generation, his social outlook included as a premise the belief that individual and class self-help were the main driving forces of progress. State action was required in order to dismantle obstacles in the way of such progress thereby offering equal opportunity to all. All forms of civic action had one purpose: to support and encourage self-help. Toynbee would still believe this even after he allowed for a greater measure of state intervention. In the final analysis he believed that progress was conditional upon conscious action aimed at self-amelioration.

Ruskin, in comparison, had a fundamentally paternalistic and undemocratic vision of society. In his preface to *Unto This Last* (1862) he put forward a scheme for state education and state enterprise on a national scale. The state, in his view, should set up training schools, workshops, and factories to ensure that every child received full vocational and moral training and, eventually, a guaranteed, secure job. State factories, whose workers were fairly paid and the superior quality of whose products was guaranteed by the state, would inevitably lead to the disappearance of private enterprise. Finally, in order to complete the state's supervision of human economic activity, it should provide pensions on which workers could retire with dignity. Ruskin left no room for any kind of self-help. All wants were to be provided for by the state, which in turn would gradually come to control supply and distribution. His vision was of a total solution accomplished at one fell swoop through a central initiative, an approach to the solution of social problems categorically rejected by Toynbee.

In particular, Toynbee differed from Ruskin in his understanding of what constituted a viable solution to an economic problem. Ruskin contended that wherever change was required it must be preceded by a transformation in moral attitudes if it were to have more than a superficial effect. Society as a whole, including its economic activities, could, and should, be transformed by such a moral conversion. In discussing wages Ruskin argued that their rate should be determined not by the supply of, and demand for, labor but by the amount of labor invested. A just wage should enable the laborer to purchase "at least as much labour as he has given, rather more than less," a concept avowedly "wholly independent of any reference to the number of men who are willing to do the work" or of the demand for and supply of their product or of a product they wish to purchase.[67] The precise rate could be determined by the amount of time, skill, and effort invested by each laborer. Thus, if an employer were to be approached by two workers seeking employment, it was his moral and social duty to employ one of them and pay him a just wage, rather than allow them to compete for the job by bidding lower wages against each other. The moral attitude of the employers was crucial, in Ruskin's view, in determining the continuance or abolition of competition in the labor market. Short of adopting his scheme for state intervention, a moral conversion of society meant in effect the moral transformation of employers through which a sense of moral and social duty would transcend narrow self-interest.

Ruskin's economic views were confined to a very simple and elementary model in which all the factors determining price in exchange could be reduced to the amount of work expended in producing an item and to the amount of work the procurer could be expected to give in return.[68] The amount of labor invested in producing any single item could be computed with relative ease by reducing the process of production to the time and labor expended. Ruskin was inspired by, and in turn sought to inspire Oxford undergraduates with, a vision of a "dreamland of simpler lives to which he had sought . . . to make us wish to return."[69] Like Carlyle he idealized the guild system, raising it to the level of a model for future society.

Toynbee on the other hand did not condemn industrialization as a perversion of natural economic and social relations. He did not denounce it as destroyer of all beauty, culture, and spirit but accepted it as an essential stage in the great march of progress. He did not seek the abolition of industrial society but rather its further development so that by developing some of its inherent characteristics and by changing others it would overcome its own faults. He rejected the "golden age" argument that called for the restoration of a bygone system.

Toynbee's analysis of industrial society differs from Ruskin's in its details as well as in its overall concept. On wages he is much more elaborate: where Ruskin hoped for the employers' moral conversion, Toynbee suggested the organization of labor in trades unions that, in turn, would raise laborers to a position approaching equality in wage bargaining and allow them to enforce a "fair wage" principle.[70] Nevertheless, he did envisage a probable future change in moral attitudes that would affect the very nature of wage negotiations. In addition, some of his fundamental concepts of the nature of political economy may be regarded as attempts to redefine the boundaries and contents of the study of economics so as to provide an answer to Ruskin's condemnation of the "dismal science" as the only instance in history "of a nation's establishing a systematic disobedience of the first principles of its professed religion."[71] In introducing his subject to an audience in Bradford, Toynbee stated that political economy "assumed an end, and framed precepts for the attainment of that end, the end assumed by political economy being identical with the end assumed by morality and religion."[72] It is only in this not-unimportant aspect that Toynbee might be described, through his work, as a disciple of Ruskin's.[73]

Whereas the North Hinksey road was, at best, an illustration of a somewhat hazy concept, most of the members of Toynbee's set at Balliol became involved in a much more concrete form of social work. In 1873 Leonard Montefiore began regularly visiting the local workhouse, with the permission of the Poor Law Guardians, where he would spend an afternoon with the older inmates amusing them with stories and an occasional lecture on a popular subject.[74] During the autumn of 1874 T. H. Green approached the headmaster of the Oxford Wesleyan Boys' School, whose pupils were to take the Board of Education qualification examination as teacher-trainees, with an offer to help to prepare the school's top form pupils for the examination. The offer was readily accepted, and Green recruited Montefiore to teach English Literature, C. E. Vaughan to teach Latin, and A. Milner to teach History.[75] A. F. Hoare and Toynbee were later added.[76] Work entailed teaching a weekly class that, in Milner's case, consisted of ten pupils. Milner found that on the whole they were "a civil and intelligent lot, ages between 19 and 15, looks in the main not remarkable. If I can get them to be at all interested in the subject I shall be very well satisfied."[77]

Toynbee's participation in the teacher-trainees' tutoring indicates a change of influences from Ruskin's to T. H. Green's. Green's influence was crucial to the final shaping of Toynbee's basic weltanschauung, and it was later said that "if there was any one among his older acquaintances to whom Toynbee especially looked up as a guide and master, it was Green."[78] Green's impact on Toynbee's intellectual development is mainly noticeable in the transformation of various vague spiritual and intellectual notions into a coherent system of ideas on the basis of which Toynbee was to decide upon concrete courses of future action. Their close association lasted until Green's death in 1882.

The personal influence of T. H. Green on the majority of Balliol students—who did not choose to specialize in philosophy—should be distinguished from the influence of his philosophy on the Oxford idealists. Few of his students could claim to have mastered his system, including some of those who brought him essays. One of the latter recalled the tutorials at Green's home during which Green "used to sit over the fire, 'tying himself into knots.' He beat his music out with some difficulty, and the music itself was not an obvious melody. I once said that I was afraid some phrase of mine was not very clear. 'I am afraid,' he said, with a rueful smile, 'that in philosophy clearness of thought is often in inverse proportion to clearness of expression.' "[79]

Another student, looking back on his undergraduate days, confessed that he could not remember "a single definite phrase or judgement . . . except a vague impression as of one running unceasingly round the same lamp-post and never advancing."[80] Nevertheless both students were greatly impressed by Green regardless of whether or not they fully grasped the substance of his philosophy. This generally felt mixture of incomprehension and affection was expressed at the time in one of the Masque of Balliol rhymes.

> I'm the self-distinguishing
> consciousness in everything;
> the synthetic unity
> one in multiplicity,
> the unseen nexus of the seen,
> sometimes known as Tommy Green.[81]

Green's was mostly a moral influence. Many of his students felt that the essence of his teaching, hence the essence of his influence, was in providing a guide to personal conduct. "A good man is a good man, and a bad man is a bad man; and this is the ultimate mystery of the universe which cannot be twisted into anything else. To be a good man was to live in the spirit in which Mr. Green lived. That was all, but it was also everything."[82] Yet, despite most students' incomprehension, the nature of Green's moral influence was in fact part of his philosophical system. "To him metaphysics were not only the basis of theology, but also the basis of politics. Everything was to converge on the free life of the individual in a free state; rational faith and reason inspired by emotion were to have their perfect work in making the good citizen."[83]

Thus one might remain ignorant of most of Green's philosophical system and yet, by following the principle that all culminated in the individual's conduct as a citizen, use as little as a single strand of Green's reasoning as the theoretical basis of a position on social matters.[84] Furthermore, as in the instance of the teacher-trainees, Green suggested to his closest students, often through personal example, means by which they might realize the principle of individual civic duty. There was nothing vague about many of his political and social positions when expressed in practical and immediate terms. This shortcut approach seems to have been consciously accepted by Green who, in Jowett's view, "seemed to acknowledge that his teaching was not equally suited to everybody" and that the truth, therefore, "must be adopted to the capacity of the hearer."[85]

Green provided Toynbee, still greatly preoccupied with religion, with sorely wanted spiritual guidance. Having succeeded in defining his religious beliefs Toynbee still seemed unable to fit them into a wider world outlook from which he could proceed with some confidence in planning his future. Action based on instinct and partly conscious sympathies, some of which may well have originated in Joseph Toynbee's influence, became the logical conclusion of newly defined convictions. The direction did not change but it was given a clear rationale it had not previously possessed.

The substance of Green's religious position may be derived from his two lay sermons, "The Witness of God" and "Faith," which he left in his will for Toynbee to prepare for publication.[86] Green had been the first layman to fill the office of college tutor at Balliol. Having been entrusted with the moral guidance of his students, he followed the existing custom of discussing with them a religious subject on the evening before the administration of Holy Communion. The sermons were based on two such discussions, during the second of which, held in 1878, Toynbee had been present. They may be described as Broad Church in tone, with a strong emphasis on the moral precepts of religion.

Religion, according to Green, was in essence a God-seeking morality. Dogma, on the other hand, was a theory originating in the miraculous and aiming at explaining it or deducing certain lessons from it. As dogma was based on the acceptance of the supernatural, it was fundamentally opposed to scientific reason. True faith emanated from beyond scientific reason and therefore could not be contradicted by it. This did not in any way weaken the certainty of the believers' knowledge of faith. It also meant that, if it were to survive rather than remain a passive knowledge, faith must become an active form of knowledge (analogous, perhaps, to scientific knowledge and scientific activity). Faith and an active moral life were, therefore, the two complementary characteristics of religious conviction. One was meaningless or false without the other. Since religion was definable as a moral life "neither the prayer nor the life is a means to anything beyond itself. Each has its value simply as the expression or realization of the Divine principle which renders each possible." Hence, "you cannot find a verification of the idea of God or duty; you can only make it." The individual, rather than concentrate on seeking proof for his convictions, should ascertain the adequacy of his modes of expressing them. It is in this respect that faith may be said to depend on reason, the understanding of the meaning of faith and the realization of it in a conscious way.

A God-seeking morality was essentially a life of selfless dedication to the service of society. "Our very self-consciousness, crucified with Him, must cease to be our own. Only then can our work, as being of God that worketh in us, work out the true salvation, the deliverance from self seeking self. Thus we gain a righteousness which . . . instead of exalting men in concert against each other, blends all in a common society of the redeemed. Thus finally we are sanctified. Bearing each other's burden." Once the principle was admitted, the individual was left with the need to seek for himself the best manner in which he might serve society.

For Toynbee it was as if pieces of a monumental puzzle which had been acquired one at a time fell into place, eliminating much perplexity concerning its final shape and meaning. To his immense relief religion had indeed provided the clue he sought for determining how religious convictions could be expressed in the sort of secular life toward which he was inclined. Green had showed him a way in which he might reduce religion to the concept of duty and finally overcome the doubts he had expressed in his questions to Hinton concerning the reconciliation of empirical (i.e., scientific) knowledge with spiritual certainty. In October 1875 he could, at last, write with confidence:

It seemed to me that the primary end of all Religion is the faith that the *end* for which the whole universe of sense and thought, from the Milky Way to the lowest form of animal life—the *end* for which everything came into existence, is that the dim idea of perfect holiness which is found in the mind of man might be realized; that this idea is God Eternal and the only reality; that the relation between this idea which is God and each individual man is Religion—the consciousness of the relation creating the *Duty* of perfect purity of inner life or *being,* and the duty of living for others, that they too may be perfectly pure in thought and action; and, lastly, that the world is so *ordered* that the triumph of righteousness is not impossible through the efforts of the individual will, in relation to Eternal existence.[87]

Thus, two important principles were firmly established: that individual action emanating from a sense of duty must aim at raising the spiritual level of others and that such action may be undertaken with the certainty that an individual's action can contribute directly to the "triumph of righteousness." An individual's search for the Kingdom of God would be replaced by an effort to realize it.

Toynbee had finally succeeded in combining his faith in the unshakable validity of his religious convictions with an adequate rationale. That the task was of paramount personal importance may be deducted from his declaration that "if I did not believe that the moral law was eternal I should die."[88] By adopting T. H. Green's position the certainty and the meaning of faith were established in a manner unshakable by scientific criticism. The elements that were vulnerable to such criticism—miracles and dogma—were eliminated (partly with the help of relativism applied to doctrine). Science and faith became complementary spheres of human consciousness. Furthermore, Toynbee appears to have felt that if a component of religious doctrine could be shaken by scientific criticism it was, by definition, nonexpressive of the essence of faith, the "correct interpretation of man's spiritual character" through the comprehension of the ideal Christ.[89]

Whereas science only apparently contradicted faith, there were two significant intellectual trends that actively challenged the moral concept of the individual's civic duty, as held by Toynbee, and its importance in ensuring human progress: materialism, which perverted ethics, and positivism, which under the banner of humanism reduced religion to an intellectual abstraction. Green had argued that these two creeds reduced Christian morality to a state of triviality and were therefore more dangerous than dogmatism, scientific criticism, or even doubt.[90] Having conquered doubt, and tackled dogmatism and scientific criticism to his own satisfaction, Toynbee confronted materialism and positivism as the main intellectual obstacles in the way of progress. While both seemed at first equally dangerous, Toynbee gradually concentrated on disputing materialism while positivism became a relatively minor concern.

Having achieved a degree of religious certainty and having established that faith entailed helping others to find that certainty, Toynbee's first instinct was to try and convert others to his way of thinking. However, in time he came to realize that under the current circumstances direct preaching was relatively ineffective. Consequently he came to concentrate on the means by which circumstances could be altered, thereby allowing society and the working classes in particular to progress to a higher level of spirituality. The means in themselves would have to express the ideal they were to help realize lest they be confused for the ends. The nature of the means became as important as their effectiveness, in as much as it was believed that if the means were not modeled on the ends neither would be their results. Thus, while concentrating on the problem of realizing a moral ideal, Toynbee moved from preaching to the realm of practical reform.

During the 1870s education had become one of the main targets of liberal reform. Middle-class liberals sought, as a rule, to bring culture, as they understood it, to the working classes. At the same time they did not regard working-class education as a preliminary step on the path toward a classless society (a state precluded by their faith in the indispensability of a division of labor and its rewards, determined by the unequal distribution of individual natural talents and ability). Due to this inherent inequality equal opportunity was not seen as leading to the working classes transforming themselves economically and professionally and joining the middle class. Those who could rise above their class should be allowed to do so; those unable to should be helped to lead a better life, materially, culturally, and spiritually. These objectives were described in a straightforward manner by Green in an address to the boys of the Oxford Wesleyan School. "The first object of education was not to help them to rise in the world. . . . It was much more important that they should teach the people to respect themselves and to respect each other without rising in the world, and to appreciate those true pleasures which were not to be bought for money."[91] Toynbee seems to have held a similar view of education at least until the summer of 1875, and, although he went beyond Green's concept of working-class progress, he still retained his faith in the possibility of reconciling a class-structured society and the vision of national moral progress and social harmony.

During Eights week of 1875 the Reverend and Mrs. Samuel Barnett of Saint Jude's, Whitechapel, were invited to join a party at Oxford, organized by Gertrude Toynbee, an old school friend of Mrs. Barnett.[92] The party consisted of the two older Toynbee sisters, Gertrude and Rachel, and most of Toynbee's Balliol and Oxford friends (including R. L. Nettleship, A. L. Smith, and W. H. Forbes, all of whom were Balliol Fellows, A. Milner, P. L. Gell, L. Montefiore, A. F. Hoare, G. E. Underhill, R. Whitehead, S. Ball, then at Oriel College, and John Falk of New College, Rachel Toynbee's future husband). In the course of their stay the Barnetts succeeded in interesting some of their hosts in their East End work. At one point it was arranged for Barnett to address an audience of Balliol undergraduates in their common room on the problems of the East End. Not having provided for the size of the crowd that unexpectedly turned up, permission was hastily obtained from the Fellows present—Smith, Green, and Forbes—to move the meeting to the hall. To the organizers' surprise and initial horror Jowett unexpectedly showed up only to express his total approval of their initiative, thereby providing the future cooperation between Balliol and the Barnetts with something approaching official sanction. Barnett's words influenced Toynbee to the extent that he decided to spend at least part of the long vacation in the East End and to study conditions there at first hand.

During the long vacation of 1875 Toynbee took two unfurnished rooms in a lodging house situated above the Charity Organization Society (cos) offices in Commercial Road, Whitechapel.[93] He placed himself at the Reverend Barnett's disposal and helped in various parish activities as well as acting as a visitor for the cos. It is not clear for how long Toynbee intended to stay in the East End; by mid-July he had joined some of his brothers and sisters for a vacation in the Lake District which had probably been planned in advance.[94] In any event, the shock of his direct encounter with the squalor and destitution of the East End had, as was often the case with him, both a spiritual and physical effect. And, although he was to return to the East End quite often, he never returned with the intention of remaining in residence for a prolonged period.

The force of the impact made on him by East End conditions was partly due to his choice of lodgings. There he was directly and constantly exposed to the sounds and sights of life around him. "At night I used to feel an intense pity as I listened fr[om] my window to the broken pieces of talk, oaths, jests, [and] blasphemy that came up fr[om] the crowded street lit with only one gas. Our delicate impalpable sorrows, our aching darling emotions, how strange almost unreal they seem by the side of the gross mass of filthy misery that dogs the life of great cities."[95] During his stay Toynbee avoided the West End. The only time he abandoned his lodgings was in order to help a battered wife seeking refuge in the middle of the night from her husband, an incident that ended with his appearance in a police court the next day as a witness. The only form of escapism he "indulged" in were short visits to the National Gallery, a choice of recreation that would have pleased his father.[96]

In an attempt to achieve direct contact with his East End neighbors Toynbee became a paying member of the Tower Hamlets Radical Club, situated in a back street on the south side of Mile End Street. The club provided a venue for one of the East End's most popular forms of recreation: political debates, usually held on Sundays. In addition, it contained a reading room with newspapers available for members, a stall selling radical newspapers and political pamphlets, a bar, and a hall that was used for various forms of locally provided entertainment, in addition to the debates. The hall, which was built by the members, had a seating capacity of five hundred. A typical hall audience was described as

of a mixed character, many were decent looking workmen of respectable appearance, but many were dirty, unshaven, and, if appearance might be trusted, would by the time the meeting was ended be none too sober . . . the conditions . . . were the reverse of elevating—the atmosphere reeking with the smoke of a hundred pipes, the tremendous consumption of beer, the "beery" look that was gradually creeping over the faces of a large portion of the audience, the noise of pots and glasses, the unwashed and unshaven men—all combined to make a scene at once depressing and saddening.[97]

The standard form of the club's political debates was described disapprovingly by Walter Besant as calling for the abolition of the "Crown, Church, the House of Lords, . . . landlordism, lawyers, established armies, pauperdom, Divesdom, taxes, and all kinds of things which the hateful Tory or that pitiful creature the moderate Liberal considers necessary for the welfare of the State. . . . Here . . . was a body of men, old and young, all firmly persuaded that things were wrong, that things might be made better, yet casting about blindly for a remedy."[98] It was in the course of one such debate that Toynbee addressed for the first time a crowd of any size with his recently formulated beliefs.

Toynbee had been asked to take part in a debate on religion and politics in the presence of an audience known to consider religion as completely divorced from, and adverse to, radical politics.[99] With his newly strengthened confidence in his religion and its direct bearing on all aspects of life, Toynbee addressed the crowd for some forty minutes on religious duty and God. According to a friend who was present:

His whole soul was in his face, his whole heart set on breathing into his hearers the same spiritual fervour that consumed himself. It would be rash to say that he convinced them. But it is quite certain that they were touched, more perhaps than they would have cared to own, by his transparent sincerity and that many of them left the room "almost persuaded" to think there might be something in the faith which shone in the countenance and palpably irradiated the life of the beardless youth to whom they had listened.[100]

With a sense of exhilaration Toynbee wrote the next day, "I feel as if I had discovered a new power to do God's word with; though I am still doubtful naturally about it; it drains my energy, I must use it sparingly, but I hope always in God's service."[101] He had sensed within himself a power for reaching working men, for bridging the gap between the two nations, and would henceforth seek opportunities to employ it. The cos and the Reverend Mr. Barnett may have provided him with information and positions on various subjects, but he had come to believe that the most effective way in which he as an individual could contribute to progress, and thereby fulfil his social duty, would be to address directly working men on their problems. Toynbee had acquired a firm belief in democracy and in the capability of the lower classes to determine their own future. He believed that change must emanate from below but that the working classes would have to be carefully and gently coached in the nature and means of progress and democracy. In this Toynbee found his calling.

The ties with the Barnetts and the East End proved lasting and the same was true of most of the other members of the Toynbee set. Leonard Montefiore had begun his East End work by helping the Barnetts to organize a flower show. Upon leaving Oxford he became increasingly active in East End work, and in the autumn of 1877 he cofounded the Tower Hamlets branch of the London Society for University Extension, becoming the branch's first secretary. One of the branch's first lecturers was James Bonar, also of Balliol, who, in April 1879, helped organize weekly meetings for some members of his political economy class. They were held during the summer for the purpose of discussing the subjects dealt with during the winter lectures.[102] A year later the same group provided the core of the Adam Smith Club, with Bonar as president and Toynbee as vice president. Founded with the primary intention of concentrating on the study of *The Wealth of Nations,* the club soon expanded its scope of study by going "beyond our teacher [A. Smith] to the point where our teacher would have himself arrived, if he had lived in our own times. The habit of reasoning in the ways he follows, but from premises unknown to him, is his best lesson to us. . . . In these times Political Economy is developing with society and with the changes in public opinion." Members of the club regarded themselves as "a community of spiritual aim" whose special intellectual goal was "the discovery of the truth about the causes of poverty and wealth." Although the club's official position was one of political neutrality, most of its members were dedicated members of the Liberal party who were in general agreement as to the desirability of replacing "the Great Capitalists" with productive cooperatives, thereby effecting a fundamental change in the socioeconomic structure of society.

The purpose and nature of the Adam Smith Club coincided with the next major development in Toynbee's intellectual and ideological outlook. He was clearly shaken by what he saw of East End conditions. The spiritual and moral attitude of the lower classes became a cause for considerable concern, while material and environmental changes were considered prerequisites if moral progress was to be achieved. By October 1875 Toynbee stated confidently that "social and religious reform is my ideal purpose."[103] Like many of his contemporaries he was fully confident of the existence of a direct and tangible relation between the morally desirable and the practicably attainable; scientific analysis based on moral precepts could not fail to discover that relation. This attitude explains how it could be said that "for the sake of religion he had become a social reformer; for the sake of social reform he became an economist."[104] Moral principles, social ideology, and economic analysis could and must combine to form a coherent and harmonious picture of reality, reflecting both in its harmony and its complexity the nature of society. Thus, to a certain extent, proof of validity was in the theories' harmony, a built-in source of future consternation whenever thought failed to wed fact.

Toynbee's determination to master the problems of social reform through the study and application of political economy was followed by a prolonged period of reading and study with little, if any, formal instruction. Despite his previous resolution he intended to read for an honors degree in Greats (Literae Humaniores), a school that did not set a paper in political economy.[105] He planned, upon leaving Oxford, to seek a teaching position in political economy although it would be some time before he was to express any independent views on the subject.

Toynbee spent part of the Christmas vacation of 1875 at Jowett's house in Malvern as a member of a reading party. Despite his ill health and inability to keep up with the rest of the party in working into the night, Toynbee saw no reason to change his plans. However, within a few months his health once again deteriorated with a recurrence of headaches and spells of giddiness.[106] These persisted, causing him to abandon plans to join Milner at Tübingen during the summer and, more important, to abandon any thought of taking an Honours degree. Instead he took a Pass, requiring less work but including a paper in political economy for which the basic texts were Adam Smith's *Wealth of Nations* and J. S. Mill's *Principles of Political Economy*. His method of study did not change and, although he may have eventually received some formal instruction in the subject, he spent very little of the following year at Oxford.

By the time of his decision to take a Pass Toynbee's personal life had undergone a significant change. In 1873 he had met his future wife, Charlotte Maria Atwood, more than eleven years his senior.[107]

Both her parents were of landowners' stock. Her father, a clerk in the Foreign Office, was said to have belonged to a secret branch that, apparently, made use of his ability as a linguist. He was an accomplished equestrian and a lover of dogs; it was at a hunt in Hampshire that he had met his wife, Charlotte Maria's mother. Atwood was a restless man who moved his family frequently before settling at Wimbledon where his daughter met Toynbee. Charlotte was not especially beautiful. Those who knew her in her later years described her as "slight in person as of stature, of the most admirable carriage. . . . Without any regular beauty, and without any sort of conscious attention to dress . . . she could make herself look very attractive, especially in the evenings, always in low toned clothes and generally with some white arrangement at her neck. She had a beautiful low voice and a rather deliberate habit of speech."[108] Her nephew described her as kind-hearted although "her personality was commanding, and her manner was sometimes imperious." Her "gifts of cleverness" he described as "not great but exceedingly well assimilated." Her view of the world was *aristocratic pur-sang* with some of the quiet old-fashioned prejudices of the caste." Toynbee himself described her as having "a strong intellect but quite unlike mine. Great perception and comprehension, but little originality or creative power." Her relationship with Arnold Toynbee, while obviously affectionate, had its peculiarities; the most noticeable one was the appearance of mutual detachment. At times Toynbee seemed to act as if his marriage was of secondary importance in his life, while Charlotte, possibly due to the age and class differences between them, appeared occasionally remarkably detached in judging her husband's character and abilities, often in sharp contrast with the idealization of his friends. Not surprisingly, perhaps, she seemed to get along with Harriet Toynbee better than Arnold did.

As the relationship developed, Toynbee came to be accepted by Mrs. Atwood as a member of the family. He often preferred to spend his vacations at the Atwoods' rather than at his mother's.[109] Hence, when his health once again deteriorated he chose to convalesce at the Atwoods'.

By the autumn of 1876 Toynbee's health still had not improved. He spent at least part of Michaelmas term in Margate where he was joined by Mary and William.[110] In December he visited a Balliol friend, V. W. Calmady Hamlyn, at his home at the edge of Dartmoor. As his health remained indifferent Toynbee left England in

January 1877 for the sunshine of Capri. On his way there he managed a number of short excursions in Paris, Florence, Rome, and
Naples before settling in the Hotel Tiberio in Capri. There he was
joined by M. G. Glazebrook, a Balliol friend reading for his finals
in Greats. Toynbee and Glazebrook soon established a routine allowing Toynbee three hours of work a day while the rest was spent
in short walks and the occasional game of badminton.[111]

In his letters Toynbee set out to tackle the problem of nature descriptions, a common Victorian preoccupation. Nature had long
been a source of fascination for him and he chose to use his letters as
deliberate experiments, trying to reduce natural scenery to words
without becoming meaningless or trivial. After some attempts he
finally reached the conclusion that a satisfactory description of nature must be one of two types. Either it must be detailed and accurate reducing nature to "a strict topographical account of a place,
noting down the relative heights and distances, character of the
vegetation, conformation of the rocks, in such a way that you piece
together the details into an accurate outline." Or it must be a gener-
alized description "carefully eliminating all local details, and retaining only the general effect of the scene, of its character and colours,
on [the author's] mind at the time."[112] The second type seems to
conform with his previous notions, whereas the first was largely due
to his "interest in surface geology and physical geography . . .
sharpened by the study of political economy." On the whole he
found that the best description combined both types. The combination of an accurate and detailed survey of particulars and a general-
ized view of the subject transcending its components was, in his
view, the only way in which any form of reality could be adequately
described. Toynbee did not place the two types of description in a
causal relation. They were, rather, two distinct and valid approaches,
each representing a different dimension of reality. Toynbee's reference to political economy suggests that his generalization concerning the aspects of reality could be applied to the study of society as
well as nature. If so, it allowed for the formulation of generaliza-
tions that were not narrowly based on factual analysis, similar to the
ones concerning the moral dimension of social or economic activity.
At the same time he had come to realize the importance of factual
analysis where previously a general philosophy seemed to suffice.

Toynbee approached political economy with typical enthusiasm,
declaring, in a letter to Falk (29 December 1876), "I am going to

devote my life to political economy." He wrote that, as soon as he took his degree, "my life as a political economist and social agitator and philanthropist begins. . . . I do really hope then to be a good soldier of Christ." As in his early attempts in philosophy he tried to apply relatively sketchy knowledge to the analysis of complex problems that might have daunted another beginner. In a letter from Capri to his youngest brother, Harry, he considered the problems of Italian paper currency and the dangers of using any form of currency that is not a precious metal but, rather, a promise to exchange it for an amount of such metal on demand. Toynbee argued that whenever confidence in the issuing bank or government was shaken the notes' value was bound to suffer a drastic drop, a view neither original nor exhaustive, aptly remarked upon by Toynbee himself: "Perhaps this is not clear, after all."[113]

In April Toynbee returned to England, traveling overland to southern Italy and the rest of the way by sea. He spent the summer of 1877 first in Derbyshire and then in Cromer on the Norfolk coast; by autumn he was back in Oxford for his final year. He initially hoped to complete his examinations by the end of Michaelmas but he was eventually left with three papers which he could not take until summer of 1878.[114] The small amount of capital left to him by his father was nearly exhausted and future prospects were far from clear. Jowett arranged for him to tutor Lord Herbrand Arthur Russell, second son of the ninth Duke of Bedford (and the future eleventh Duke), in history and political economy for a period of up to two years for a fee of £300 per annum. However, his future was finally determined by the College Committee on Lectures for 1878–79 (consisting of Jowett, T. H. Green, Nettleship, Strachan-Davidson, and E. Abbott) which, on 15 June 1878, recommended to the General Meeting that Toynbee be appointed tutor to the probationers of the Indian Civil Service (ics) with an initial salary of £100 per annum plus tutorial fees.[115] The committee's recommendation was certainly unusual (suggesting for the job a student who had not yet completed his examinations for a Pass degree) and, like Jowett's initial decision to help Toynbee to migrate to Balliol, it was based more on personal knowledge of Toynbee's potential than on actual academic accomplishments.

Balliol had decided in 1875 to accept annually some ten ics probationers who were to be given the same status as other undergraduates. The probationers had their own two-year curriculum of

Indian languages, law, and political economy and were exempt from college and university examinations. Their studies were supervised by college tutors with the aid of the university lecturers entrusted with their instruction. Socially they came to constitute a separate set within Balliol and the university, and were regarded by other undergraduates as "birds of passage,"[116] not quite up to the academic and social standards of the public school sets, a view that Toynbee resented.[117] In accordance with his students' status as regular college undergraduates Toynbee's was a standard college appointment. In 1879 his annual stipend was raised to £200, and in 1881 he received an additional £50 per annum in consideration of the increase in the number of LCS probationers. Later in 1881 he was appointed Senior Bursar with an additional annual salary of £125, and it was generally assumed that he would shortly be elected Fellow. By then his income from tuition fees had reached £83.6.8 per term; in sum, his salary was considered sufficient for the needs of a young lecturer.[118]

With his future relatively secured, Toynbee's engagement to Charlotte was announced in November 1878, and they were married on 24 June 1879. In a letter to Mrs. Barnett he described the future Mrs. Toynbee: "That silent, unnoticed little lady about whom you could learn nothing is the wisest and most lovable human being it has ever been my lot to know; I love her with all my heart and soul; without her I know not how my life would end; with her I know all will be well with me."[119] Yet, despite the obvious sincerity of his feelings, as the date of the wedding approached Toynbee became increasingly occupied with other matters. A story was told at the time that in reply to a friend who wished to consult him on some matter he said, "You must come and see me about it tomorrow. Oh! no, I forgot, I am going to be married tomorrow."[120]

4. The "Regeneration of Humanity"

From the outset Toynbee had had great expectations of what he and his Oxford friends would accomplish in life. Never content with discussions alone, he endeavored from the earliest days of his association with Milner and Gell to direct their conversations toward a commitment to action. Writing to Gell after the collapse caused by the Brackenbury examination Toynbee informed him, "I had got one or two plans about things I think both you and Milner have at heart; they are not eccentric or wild; on the contrary quite sober and tame being much influenced by my recent hints as to the science of common place. Will talk them over at the beginning of next term if you and Milner agree."[1] In a later letter he confessed to Gell that "I find the sense of working with men like Milner and yourself in a cause the most noble we can think of, [it] helps me very much to do right and to fling away all 'meaner things.' "[2]

The precise nature of these schemes is not clear, but it is obvious they were all aimed at the fulfillment of the ideal of duty.[3] That this should be done in collaboration with friends such as Milner and Gell was an additional source of enthusiasm. Having discovered friendship, it quickly became an indispensable component of Toynbee's plans for the future. When Gell moved to digs outside college Toynbee wrote to him, "Now you are out of College we shall be able to know each other more and talk more about our work. That, I'm sure, will bring us together of itself. I feel it has already ennobled me, and will slowly drive out of me all that prevents our coming together in enthusiasm for it, as the only object worthy of us. The thing must be clear and we will do it; there is no hurry, we need not be impatient, we are very young."[4]

By 1879 all of Toynbee's Balliol contemporaries had graduated. He continued to maintain close contact with Milner and Gell, now mostly in London, as well as with some of the other members of his undergraduate set who remained at Oxford, including D. G. Ritchie (at Jesus) and L. R. Phelps (at Saint Mary's and later at Oriel). New friendships replaced some old ones and a new set began to form that included J. D. Rogers, F. C. Montague, W. N. Bruce (second son of Baron Aberdare), E. T. Cook, and B. R. Wise.

During the early 1870s the various groups that constituted the Liberal party were on the lookout for a cause that, like the pre-1867 cry for a franchise reform, would unite the party around a platform acceptable to all of its components. A coalition of radicals, including Joseph Chamberlain and John Morley, Dissenters, and some High-Churchmen regarded the issue of the disestablishment of the Church of England as such a cause.

The Established Church represented, to radical secularists and to Dissenters, another stronghold of privilege, strengthened rather than weakened by W. E. Forster's Education Act of 1870 that allowed it to retain and, it was feared, to extend its hold on elementary education. In direct response to the act the National Education League, which had campaigned for universal, secular, and compulsory education, raised the cry of disestablishment. Dissenters and secularists were occasionally supported in their campaign by High-Churchmen (such as Canon Liddon), many of whom were apprehensive of parliamentary curtailment of sacerdotalism and High Church pageantry (very popular in working-class parishes). Disestablishment was largely opposed by Broad-Churchmen who, on the issue of education, were represented by the National Education Union.[5] However, an element within the Broad-Church party argued that a truly national church was the only alternative to disestablishment and that therefore the Established Church must purge itself of the abuses that had rendered it a target of its critics.[6]

Many of those who, in the 1870s, felt that opposition to disestablishment did not dispense with the need for internal reform had already in the 1860s urged such a reform, partly in anticipation of the subsequent attacks. In 1862 a Society for Church Reform had been formed with the aim of campaigning for a bill establishing church councils in parishes.[7] Each parish was to have a church council elected by all the residents of the parish, including Dissenters, which would share with the Church the responsibility for the running and supervision of local Church affairs. It had been hoped that parish councils would provide a model for popular, local self-government in which all residents of each parish would take part. It was argued by the Reverend William Henry Fremantle, then rector of Saint Mary's, Bryanston Square, London (where S. A. Barnett was at the time curate),[8] that "unless the Church of England becomes much more than it is now the Church of the people, its claim to be a National Church will be less and less allowed . . . its power of doing good will be lost through the cessation of its hold on the respect of the people."[9]

As all national institutions were to be transformed in the coming liberal age from aristocratic to democratic, the Church must reform itself if it were to keep up with the rest of the nation in its march toward progress and fulfill its duty in providing for the moral and spiritual amelioration of the people. It was Fremantle's belief that, rather than continue to govern over local Church affairs like an autocrat, the clergyman should be brought into closer contact with his parishioners. Better integration would enable the local clergyman to gauge more accurately his parishioners' feelings on religious matters, to avoid alienating them by adopting unpopular policies on matters that until then had been left entirely to his discretion (such as parts of the ritual), and to draw them, through greater active involvement, back into the Church.

At the core of the movement for internal reform was a small group of London clergymen, members of the Curates Clerical Club, some of whom had tried to start councils in their own parishes.[10] Membership of the club included Fremantle, Arthur Penrhyn Stanley, Frederick Denison Maurice, J. Llewellyn Davies, J. R. Green, and Brooke Lambert. Some of them were also followers of Maurice in the promotion of Christian socialism and, in particular, the London Working Men's College (of which Thomas Hughes was at the time principal and where John Robert Seeley gave occasional lectures).[11] Their association went beyond church reform, was not greatly dependent on it, and, therefore, did not dissolve when their legislative effort failed.

During 1870 the cause of parish councils was incorporated into a wider reform program promoted by the newly founded Church Reform Union (CRU).[12] Its platform, which contained a list of grievances concerning the state of the Church, was regarded as representative of the feelings of a wide body of opinion within the Church. "The laity have not their fair place and work in the Church system; there are certain obligations and restrictions in force, which occasion discontent and have no real value; the working machinery of the Church is clogged with various anomalies and abuses; and it is wanting in provisions for self-regulation in minor matters, so indispensable to an institution that would retain the affections of a great and varied population."[13] This sorry state, the CRU believed, could be rectified through reform in three directions: the admission of the laity—initially in parishes—to a defined share of power in Church matters, the removal of impolitic restraints on the clergy, and the promotion of practical improvements.

The first direction contained the parish councils scheme.[14] It was argued that, whatever problems might result from its adaptation, they were negligible compared with existing evils and would be relatively easy to bear in the light of the benefit derived from drawing the public closer to the Church. By adopting a gradual approach the scheme would ensure that councils would be awarded powers only after they had proved their value to the community. The CRU maintained that in any event the powers they proposed to award parishioners were relatively limited compared with the power the same people had as voters over Church matters through Parliament.

The second course of reform applied the principle, which had largely dominated liberal thought of the period, of removing constraints on freedom of action. The CRU suggested the abolition of clerical subscription, the removal of any legal hindrances by which those who had received Holy Orders were excluded from civil employment, the discontinuance of the use of the Athanasian Creed in the services of the Church, and that power be given to an incumbent to invite persons not in Anglican Holy Orders to preach, subject to the inhibition of the Ordinary.

Finally, the third course of reform was aimed at updating the organization and practices of the Church by adopting some positive measures that went beyond the mere lifting of constraints on the operation of its clergy. The CRU felt that some structural changes were required if the Church were to operate more efficiently and derive the full benefit from the other two courses of reform. The measures proposed included: a gradual subdivision of the larger dioceses, a modification of the forms of election and confirmation in the appointment of bishops, a rearrangement, by a royal commission, of the boundaries of parishes, a more efficient procedure in ecclesiastical matters, a plan for superannuation for the clergy, a revision of the translation of the Bible, more elastic arrangements of the church services, and some provision for securing the repair, or authorizing the disuse, of church fabrics.

The CRU deliberately concentrated on technical internal reform. It avoided adopting controversial causes such as the abolition of patronage and the revision of the Common Prayer Book. Hence it felt reasonably confident that "each of these proposals . . . might be accepted without a sacrifice of principle by all parties. If they were all carried together, it cannot be said that any party would have gained a party victory."

Unexpectedly, it was precisely the technical and catholic nature of the suggested reform that served to undermine much of its hoped-for popular appeal. Clergymen as a rule were naturally suspicious and would not commit themselves to a comprehensive and immediate reform. Working-class radicalism showed itself hostile to any attempt to defend the existing clerical establishment. Hence the two anticipated sources of popular pressure failed to adopt the cause of the CRU. Thomas Hughes found that working-class audiences that were otherwise enthusiastic supporters of radical reform, became hostile when he tried to win their support for the CRU.[15]

The active core of the CRU was not much different in composition from that of the earlier Society for Church Reform. Its council included the Reverend J. Llewellyn Davies, Thomas Hughes, Professor J. R. Seeley, the Reverend W. H. Fremantle, and two MPs, T. Salt and the Right Honorable W. Cowper-Temple, chairman of the council. Again, the reformers' burst of activity was relatively short-lived. Another failure of its legislative effort and a shift in parliamentary attention toward Irish and then imperial and foreign matters resulted in another prolonged period of inaction.[16] The initiative to revive it came toward the end of 1878 from Toynbee and his friends. Toynbee contacted Barnett on the matter and was, in turn, put in touch with Hughes; a meeting was set between Toynbee, Milner, and Hughes.[17]

Hughes was considerably elated by the meeting and the prospect of renewed activity. In a letter to J. Ll. Davies he conveyed his impression that Toynbee and Milner "represent that there is a great Liberal Church uprising ready to break out there, and that they want to see and consult such of the friends of Maurice as can be got at."[18] Hughes arranged for Davies to join his discussions with Milner and Toynbee and a meeting of the four took place sometime around mid-January 1879. According to Toynbee the meeting was dominated by a discussion between Davies and himself from which Toynbee emerged somewhat disillusioned. He seems to have expected from the veterans of the CRU an eagerness for action as powerful as his own. Instead he found that

Davies' views on the matter seemed to come to this—(i) The Established Church is in no immediate danger, nor is there much probability of danger for some time to come, (ii) The Dissenters are willing to be conciliated with the exception of a small political minority, (iii) it would be best to leave matters alone. He deprecated religious "excitement"—I told him that it was not "excitement" but something much deeper than that which was moving people's heads in this question—a profound conviction of the necessity of discussing the whole matter calmly while there was yet time, in the interests not of the church but of the whole religious life of the people.[19]

Finally, Davies defended Christian theology (the equivalent, in Toynbee's view, of dogma) as essential for the existence of the Church, clinching Toynbee's negative impression of the chances for cooperation with the veteran reformers.

As a result of his meeting with Davies, Toynbee resolved that it was best to start working on Church reform independently of existing organizations. His intention was to start at Oxford an independent society for reform consisting mainly of younger men. In his view such a body of men "may stimulate thought together with drawing together the older men again. But it is in the younger generation that our hopes must be fixed—in the younger generation not merely of ministers but of laymen whom we must bring to see the question in it[s] real vast importance."

Apparently the impression left by the discussion with Davies was assuaged by assurances that Davies's positions were not representative of the view of all of the veteran reformers. Fremantle promised to help by drawing up an updated version of the CRU's program to serve as a basis for discussion. Toynbee's view was that a practical program should be based on certain concepts.

The spiritualization of life in all its aspects, the obliteration of the vicious distinction between things spiritual and things secular, these are the principles of Church Reform. The abolition of clerical subscription, the increase of lay influence through the establishment of Church Councils and the admission of laymen to the pulpits, the conciliation of non-conformists by their admission to church pulpits, by this limitation in the power of the minister, by the permission and review of portions of the liturgy by the minister with the consent of his council, by abolition of the sales of benefices, by the abolition or modification of lay patronage—these measures or something like them affecting ministers, laymen and non-conformists are the practical steps.[20]

Toynbee now felt that an effort must be made to revive the CRU in order to launch a new campaign for Church reform. His main concern seems to have been the growing strength of the High Church party, which still retained an antiliberal image. It was feared that wherever the High Church gained control over a parish it would inevitably alienate the local working class. Disestablishment would only play into the hands of the High-Churchmen by allowing them greater freedom of action. If sacerdotalism were not stemmed it would lead to greater support for the separation of church from state due to the latter's inability to reform the former. The negative image of the Church must be changed, and the time was ripe; all the indications pointed toward success. "The set of thought if I mistake not is distinctly *for* organisation and against individualism, *for* pure religion and against dogmatic Theology, *for* the identification of the spiritual and secular, against their separation."

Toynbee's position on church reform seems to have been largely influenced by T. H. Green whose main concern in the matter was to prevent the alienation of the majority of the people from the Church. He found signs of such a process of alienation in the shying of competent men of true Christian spirit from taking orders or actively participating in Church affairs because of an aversion to inflexible dogma. Another disquieting phenomenon was the estrangement of many parishioners from their local churches caused by the clergy's lack of sympathy for their spiritual views and wants. Green had long been an admirer of Congregationalism. In addition to his promotion of the Oxford Boys' High School, which was built and financed mainly by the town's council, he actively supported local Congregational educational activity. He confessed to regarding Congregationalism as "an essential element in what he might call the higher life, especially of English towns" and Congregationalists as allies in the promotion of liberty and toleration within, as well as outside, the Church.[21]

Green used Congregationalism as a model of church reform, naming it accordingly, congregationalization.[22] His vision of a reformed national church combined Congregational principles of organization with the existing Established Church, forming a unity of nation and church. Thus, both the state and the church would become institutional expressions of national needs. Furthermore, when such a stage were reached, state and church would be one since the needs they provided for—material and spiritual—must not be kept separate.

While adopting the essence of Green's vision of a national church Toynbee tried to fit it into a more elaborate framework.[23] In a paper delivered at a private meeting in Balliol in the spring of 1879, Toynbee chose, possibly under Nettleship's influence, to compare his view of the relation between church and state to Plato's *Republic*.[24] He stated in his opening remarks that, since in Plato's ideal state church and state were one, he would examine whether that held true of the modern state. He repeated a similar remark in his conclusions, but, although some Platonic concepts crept into his arguments, his paper cannot be described as an essay on the application of Platonic philosophy. It is, rather, an attempt to combine his own religious convictions with the various moral and political philosophical views he had received from Green and Nettleship to produce a cohesive argument that would provide as conclusions principles for practical action. The same principles had already been enumerated in his letter to Barnett; the paper was designed to provide them with a philosophical rationale.

Toynbee argued that man's two basic wants were freedom and religion. Freedom he defined as "the power to do what I like," a power guaranteed by the state as the organized expression of its citizens. Religion he defined as "the desire to do what is right," which found its institutional expression in the church as teacher and guardian of the community's spiritual ideals. Whereas the state provided and guaranteed the means by which the individual could realize his power to act freely (while, at the same time, restraining him from harming himself and others), the church provided him, through education, with the moral end for such action.

Toynbee's main argument then was to establish that the moral expression of the people embodied in the church must by necessity be linked to the state. He rejected the dichotomy by which the state was solely concerned with the material welfare of its citizens, while the church looked after their souls. In adopting the concept of the state from Greek philosophy he argued that, since the state was meant to secure the "good life" of each citizen, its concern was with both his material and moral welfare. Therefore, since the end of the church should be part of the ends of the state there was no justification for the church's institutionally independent existence.

The issue of the efficiency of a state church suggested another line of argument. Assuming that the definition of the church as the necessary expression of the people as a moral and spiritual community was generally acceptable, even if one did not accept the previous argument concerning the ends of the state, it could still be maintained that the state was best adapted organizationally to provide for the most efficient church. Toynbee envisaged a state church as independent of the people and yet in close contact with them. It was to be independent in order "to lead the people . . . in advance of the people" and it was to be in close touch with them in order to check sacerdotalism in its various forms which, Toynbee believed, threatened to alienate "the greatest number and the most intellectual of the members of the State from religion altogether." A popular church on purely Congregational lines or a completely independent organization could not guarantee "a religion wise and rational, comprehensive and universal, recognising a progressive revelation of God, such as the State may provide." A true national church could only be a reformed Church of England, the embodiment of the people's historical religion, the peculiar expression of the morals and spirit of the English.

Toynbee's paper was less an elaboration on church reform than an attempt to repudiate the rationale for disestablishment. He did not develop his suggestions for practical measures for reform, but it is clear that in his view they were derivatives of his concept of the ideal church in its relations to the nation and the state. His arguments are relatively simple and straightforward, well within the boundaries of Nettleship's and Green's philosophies. But the paper also contains a proclamation of faith that is somewhat outside the structure of the general argument and that provides the link between it and Toynbee's religious convictions.

In the course of the paper Toynbee restated his fundamental notion of faith. Faith was the consciousness a person had of an ideal self which embodied all that was good, a concept encapsulated in the idea of God. The existence of such a notion was due to a basic instinct; thus awareness of it was an act of faith based on emotional rather than on sensory observation. The next step in man's spiritual ascent was man's constant endeavor to emulate the ideal self or to become like God, "to enact God in our own soul and in the world; and though man must needs fail, failure here is the only success."

This was the introspective way to God, the way in which Toynbee probably regarded his years of solitary meditation. However, there was another way. God could also be discovered through observation of the outside world. Through knowledge of human civilization and of nature the individual could proceed beyond the instinctive notion of faith and discover how "to make possible his love of God," how in the light of his knowledge he could "transform the world." In terms of his own personal experience, having discovered faith within himself, Toynbee sought through the study of the outside world an external way of realizing it that would supplement and strengthen its internal expression. "Action is the realization of our ideal, the love not of ourselves but of our fellow-men, the removal of sin and pain, the increase of knowledge and beauty, the binding together of the whole world in the bond of peace."

Having undertaken to start a revival of church reform in Oxford, Toynbee sought to ascertain the popularity of the cause among his Oxford contemporaries. In pursuit of potential activists he addressed the Palmerston Club early in May 1879. Founded in 1877, the club's aim was "the consolidation of the Liberal Party in the University of Oxford." In addition to its undergraduate membership it was supported by a number of honorary members, graduates of the university most of whom were still in residence. These included T. H. Green, Toynbee, Arthur Herbert Dyke Acland, then student of Christ Church, T. H. Warren, S. Ball, and A. Milner.[25]

Toynbee thought the reception awarded to his views encouraging. For some weeks he deliberated his next step. He may have realized that for most people support for church reform was part of a wider commitment to social and political reform on similar and complementary principles. He finally decided to choose a wider issue as a basis for action. Early in June 1879, less than a month before his marriage, he called six of his closest friends to a meeting with the intention of founding a society that would "endeavour to form a body of social and political principles which shall be our common basis of action in the future." Toynbee's initial intention was that the discussion

is to be informal but each will take some one branch of politics and work at that chiefly. We shall all be able either to speak or write—but we shall be in no hurry to commence. Some of us will remain in Oxford, others will be in London but there will be a vital connection between the life and thought and experience of us all. I shall give a rough sketch of our political ideals at our first meeting, touching on all points of social and spiritual importance. No one will know of our exisetence and we shall work on quietly until we are ready to strike in public. All of the men are in the right temper for discussion and high time it is that people of radical sympathies *did* organize themselves. Every one is organized from licensed victuallers to priests of the Roman Catholic Church. The men of wide thought and sympathies are scattered and helpless.[26]

Despite the somewhat adolescent tone produced by the reference to secrecy and the exaggerated sense of self-importance, Toynbee's initiative reflected a strongly felt need within liberal/radical circles during the late 1870s. His aims were clearly political and in Milner's view, "It was part of Toynbee's greatness that he, from the first, so clearly realised that need [for a system of principles] and foresaw the coming confusion, that his aim was always a *body of doctrine*, that he insisted, in a degree really marvellous in an enthusiast of his order, on the supreme value of study and science."[27] Toynbee may have even intended to act in the forthcoming general election. His hope, like that of many young radicals, was to push the Liberal party into a firm commitment to social and religious reform based on a comprehensive and detailed program. The society, it seems, was to work toward drawing up such a program.

The society, later referred to half-jokingly by Milner as the "Regeneration of Humanity,"[28] consisted at its inception of Milner and Gell (veterans of Toynbee's old set), D. G. Ritchie, F. C. Montague, J. O. Rogers, and W. N. Bruce.[29] At its first meeting Toynbee read a paper on the "Organisation of Consumption" in which he outlined some of the economic measures that in his view constituted an essential part of any program of reform. In describing his hopes for the society he wrote to Barnett:

We hope to formulate a body of principles which will guide us in our political and social action and enable us to deal with the great questions of our time. We propose to pick out the ablest of the younger men who come up to Oxford and join them to us from time to time. One great object we aim at is to maintain a vital relation in the growth of principles between men in Oxford and men in London, men with a peculiar and rather narrow experience labouring at problems in their most fundamental aspects and men with a wide and practical experience facing these problems in their more immediate and practical aspects. I believe we have reached the period for *construction*, and I also believe that I see my way to the principle of construction in Religion, politics, and the industrial sphere.[30]

The society was mainly held together by the power of Toynbee's personality. Montague was to remark that many of its members "differed from him on many points or were even remote from him in habits of thought, but who could, he thought, understand his aims and enter into his aspiration." Ritchie, for one, "had an instinctive antipathy to the English way of regarding political questions. Nor had he . . . much sympathy with Toynbee's peculiar temperament nor tendency to approach modern politics from his spiritual standpoint."[31] Beyond the binding power of Toynbee's personality the operation of the society was made possible by the allocation of special subjects to each member according to his preference. Thus Milner chose foreign relations and Ritchie chose education. The group met once or twice a term, sometimes in London but most often in Oxford in Ritchie's rooms at Jesus College. The meetings were always private and informal. A paper would usually be read by one of the members and a discussion would follow. With time and the development of their careers the members of the society increasingly drifted apart in their ideas and interests. Following Toynbee's death the society painlessly disintegrated.

It is evident that by the time of his marriage Toynbee had been almost entirely preoccupied with the society's activities and his own work. This state of affairs largely continued to dominate his married life. Yet there is no evidence that Charlotte Toynbee regarded her husband's preoccupation as an attempt to escape or to ignore his responsibilities toward her or that she interpreted it as a lack of love.[32]

It was generally agreed by their friends that the Toynbees were indeed a happy couple.[33] They established themselves first in east Oxford and early in 1881 moved to north Oxford to a house in Bevington Road, which soon became a meeting place for his many friends. That Toynbee was capable of love is not surprising for, although he had not enjoyed much affection from his mother, he had been brought up by a loving nanny and an adoring elder sister. Charlotte's age and general bearing must have added to the marriage's success. She regarded herself as an independent individual quite capable of looking after herself while young Toynbee was busy reforming the world. She had little interest in most of his projects and he did not seem to try to convert her to his way of thinking.[34] Following his death she was known to refer to him as a "poor young fellow."[35] She had loved him but had never been his disciple.

Despite his own growing interest in economic matters, Toynbee was initially of the opinion that the society should first concentrate on church reform. In a letter to Gell, who was similarly committed to church reform, he argued:

The *Church* seems to me to be by far the most difficult of all questions we have to deal with . . . I am very anxious that we should grapple resolutely with it at once. The *land,* it is true, is the immediate question; but for that very reason it is of less importance to *us* who are not yet prepared to influence public opinion—not yet a power either in parliament or the press—whatever we may be! Besides I think the question is well understood by those who ought to understand it, and is moreover compared with the *Church* a simple one.[36]

Toynbee may not have realized at first that most of the members of the society had at best a peripheral interest in the matter. The issue of the Irish land bill and its possible application to English rural conditions seemed much more pressing. Toynbee succeeded in keeping church reform on the society's agenda but by spring 1880 he was forced to admit that agricultural reform was assuming increasing importance and urgency as an election issue. The shift is evident from a report on one of the meetings sent by Milner to Gell:

At one "Regeneration of Humanity" meeting we rediscussed Church and then had a little all round fight about the Land Laws. We are all in seriousness thinking of writing a book to come out about the time of the elections, which shall explain to the Liberals the causes of their defeat which I take for granted using defeat in the sense of nonvictory, and point out to them how they are to strike out a new path in the future to regain public confidence. Of course it may never come off, but Toynbee and I at least are quite serious about it.[37]

It was becoming apparent that Toynbee's growing commitment to church reform had gone deeper and further than that of most members of the society, with the exception of Gell. Consequently, his work within the CRU continued independently of the society. In August 1880 Gell was appointed, with Toynbee's help, as a salaried secretary of the union.[38] It is indicative of Milner's attitude that, although he was anxious for Gell to find a job in England (there was a possibility of a professorship in New Zealand), he felt that Gell could do better than the secretaryship of the CRU.[39] At the same time he assured Gell that he was convinced that if anyone could make the CRU work it was Gell, to whom he offered his help and advice in making a success of it. When a branch of the CRU was started at Oxford it was organized by L. R. Phelps with Toynbee's help but without the participation of the remaining members of the society.

Apart from providing an initial stimulant it is difficult to assess the significance of Toynbee's meetings with Hughes and Davies in bringing the CRU back to life. In any event by May 1879 Hughes felt that it was time to revive a national campaign for church reform. Since such an effort was to culminate in parliamentary legislative action the creation of a lobby of MPs was essential. On 27 May 1879 he sent to Albert Grey, MP (and future fourth Earl Grey), a program and the first two (and only) annual reports of the old CRU. Hughes thought that the principles and methods of action laid down in the early 1870s were still valid and were readily adoptable as a current program. He also emphasized the link he had always conceived to exist between radical social reform and church reform, a position common to all church reformers with a Christian Socialist background. What was needed was for someone to take the first step and Grey seemed a likely candidate.

Will you take stroke one? [Hughes had stroked the Oxford crew in 1848.] . . . should you see your way to doing so I can promise cordial help from the old members and you will have got your work in life cut out for you. I doubt if you can find any worthier, especially if you combine with it (as you should do) the building up of healthy co-operation amongst our working people. The latter has been my more special work for near on 30 years, and it grows on one more and more every year as I get less able to pull my oar clear through. The two movements represent (to me at least) the great hope for the possible future of England, and I cannot tell you how anxiously I look for new recruits amongst those who "own the coming years."[40]

Following his appeal to Grey, Hughes prepared a draft of a report bringing up the CRU affairs to the present; this was read and approved by Fremantle.[41] The draft was circulated among some of the old CRU veterans and, finally, in the autumn of 1879, a meeting was convened at Hughes's house of a new self-appointed council of the CRU. The council consisted of most of the old members, including Davies, Fremantle, Seeley, Hughes, Cowper-Temple, Sir George Young, and T. Salt, MP. Another veteran Christian Socialist included was Brooke Lambert, and new members included Dean Stanley, T. H. Green, A. Robinson of New College, and, as secretaries, the Reverend J. R. Diggle, Albert Grey, and Arnold Toynbee.

Toynbee's comments on the first meeting of the council at Hughes's house were somewhat more tolerant than his reaction to his first meeting with Davies. He reported to Gell that his impression was that "they are not very bold, but then they know the ins and outs of the matter, and have had a wide experience. We shall learn much from them, and if we cannot persuade them to adopt a very decided position, we can at least work with them for they are on the right track."[42]

The revived CRU incorporated most of the old program with some minor changes in phrasing.[43] It laid greater emphasis on its conciliatory position toward "those who differ, on one point or another, from the Church as it is," thereby, in effect, recognizing the political power of Dissenters and trying not to alienate them. They may have further hoped that by advocating reforms similar to Congregational practices they might even weaken Dissent's support for disestablishment. To their list of reforms they added a greater flexibility of the burial services, a gradual move toward abolition of patronage, and, in rephrasing the earlier demand for more flexible services, they called for a gradual relaxation of the Act of Uniformity. The changes in the program reflected the accumulated experience of the old CRU campaigners inside and outside Parliament. Toynbee, on the other hand, found their deliberations maddening. With his immovable faith in democracy and the common sense of the English people he felt that all that was needed was a direct appeal to the English public. The people were bound to perceive the sense in their proposals and apply pressure on their representatives in Parliament to implement them. The CRU's careful deliberations, aimed at the avoidance of potential opposition and the fostering of alliances, were, he thought, a waste of valuable time and effort.

Toynbee expressed his exasperation in a letter dated 13 June 1880 to Albert Grey, who seems to have served as something of a lightning conductor.

This is an inspiriting letter, especially after the idle discussions of our last meeting. I don't want to speak harshly of our older & wiser colleagues but they are such languid, cautious, irrelevant colleagues! We are young men, of course, and impatient; we have not known disappointment & defeat; we are ignorant and hopeful;—all these things make it difficult for us to sympathize with the elaborate circumspection of a man like Davies—with his weighing of words & phrases, his insuperable difficulties in deciding whether the Society should be called a Union or a Committee. Still it doesn't require much sagacity to see that by such men nothing is ever accomplished, or by such discussions as took place last time. . . . Of course some such discussions as those last time are necessary, but did you ever hear anything more unbusiness like and irritating? And we younger men must sit by and chafe in silence.

I suppose we oughtn't to complain—but I can't forget what Seeley said to me—"Yes, I allowed my name to be put in the Council; but I think it is not the slightest good attempting to work with such men as Davies & Hughes (I think he said Hughes)—and Abbott thinks with me." That is Seeley tried to work with them ten years ago and found that it was [a] waste of time. Now this is no reason for parting company with Hughes and Davies, that would be fatal, but it is a reason for myself to push on as far as possible in independence of them, at any rate for not allowing ourselves to be held back [and] hampered by their exasperating caution and mismanagement.[44]

Confident of the effect of a bold and straightforward statement of principles Toynbee informed Grey of his intention to prepare one or two addresses containing such statements; he would be prepared to deliver them wherever required. Such an opportunity soon presented itself. In an attempt to overcome some of the resistance to reform from within the church the CRU organized a meeting at the Masonic Hall, Leicester, to coincide with (although not an official part of) the annual Church Congress of 1880.[45] The CRU was represented on the platform by Grey, Fremantle, Davies, Toynbee, Lambert, and George Harwood. The first resolution, moved by Grey and supported by Fremantle, called for the establishment of parochial councils. It was criticized by some of the clergymen present but was eventually carried by a large majority.

The next resolution, in favor of the abolition of clerical subscription, was moved by Toynbee. The issue was part of the CRU's program in which it was put forward with the mild argument that since subscription had already "lost whatever force it may once have had as a guarantee of conformity" its abolition would not serve to "increase the existing variety of opinion amongst the clergy" but rather help to clear the atmosphere in tackling the problem of pledges of opinion, mainly among candidates for Holy Orders. Toynbee adopted a somewhat more strident tone that may have offended some of the clergymen present. He argued that clerical tests

stood in the way of the simple law of religious developments, and made things fixed and rigid which ought to be expansive. Young men of 23 were compelled to subscribe to matters they had not fully considered, and the consequence was it created a spirit of suspicion as to their sincerity. These tests were the cause of deceit, hypocrisy, and unrighteous compromise. Political and educational tests had been abolished, and religious tests ought also to be done away with. They prevented good men from coming into the ministry, and without the Church [adapting] . . . herself to the spirit of civilization . . . she must necessarily lose ground.

The resolution was seconded by Davies and criticized by two clergymen from the floor. It was passed as was a third resolution in favor of the reform of patronage.

Milner, who was considerably less enthusiastic about church reform, appears to have shared some of Toynbee's misgivings concerning the veteran reformers. Gell, on the other hand, plunged into the thick of the reorganization of the CRU in an endeavor to influence its structure. While approving of his organizational concepts Milner gently reproached Gell for attaching too much importance to it. "Is it not ridiculous that *at this stage of the proceedings* you should feel disgusted and talk of striking because you don't see your way to a sound internal organization? Of course organization is a most important matter but never *the most* important in a *spiritual* movement."[46]

Toynbee shared Gell's impatience as well as Milner's misgivings concerning the CRU's priorities. The cool reaction their cause had received at the official Church Congress' meetings only served to strengthen his conviction that their choice of means was fundamentally wrong. In a letter to Grey he stressed that in his view

parliamentary action should follow and not precede our agitation for reform. I am not sure that it would be wise to bring in our bill at all until we had got more support from outside. . . . We do not intend to take advantage of any parliamentary support we can get and press forward a measure vitally affecting . . . [the ritualists'] position on the church, until we have appealed to the people. We will meet them fairly in the open field, and if they are really in the right and in possession of the true principle they will beat us and we shall fail to rouse the people. Nothing can be fairer than this—it is not an attempt of a little knot of politicians with no gospel of their own to strike a fatal blow through a parliament indifferent to gospels of all kinds at the only party in the church which has a gospel to preach; it is an unflinching appeal of a body of men who believe they have a gospel, to the people to decide between them and those whose gospel—however beautiful, however attractive it may be— they believe to be in a large measure false.[47]

Acting on the basis of his unshakable faith in a direct appeal to the people, Toynbee, with some help from Grey, wrote, for the use of the CRU, "Leaflets for Working Men. No. 1: The Church and the People."[48] The structure of Toynbee's argument, intended to convert working men to church reform, closely resembled his economic arguments aimed at the conversion of the working classes to gradual economic reform. He began by admitting the validity of what he believed to be the main grievances of the working class concerning the Church. It was "an episcopal sect," the "last obstinate remnant of a dead social system, . . . [an] institution of feudalism and fierce obstruction, . . . [a] church of dominant classes dark with memories of persecution and intolerance." At the same time, he stressed that religion (i.e., faith) was an indestructible part of humanity that cannot be eliminated or ignored. They were all united in their aim "to secure *a form of Christianity in harmony with progress, liberty, and knowledge.*" Rather than destroy the Church of England, which "combines more than any other church in existence freedom of thought with a hold on the people," reform, based on *"liberty of thought* and *popular government,"* would preserve its benefits while aligning it with progress. He concluded his appeal with his own credo as a church reformer: "first, a belief that without religion a man were better dead; secondly, a belief that a Church of England endowed with a principle of movement would become the purest witness to God and Christ the world has ever seen, and the most trusted staff of the people." Whatever the distribution of the leaflet, it was the only one produced under that title.

As for his personal contribution to the campaign, Toynbee chose to concentrate on local work.[49] Local branches had been organized in various localities including in the East End by Barnett, in Greenwich by Lambert, and in Oxford by L. R. Phelps.[50] Toynbee helped to organize meetings of the Oxford branch, some of which he addressed.[51] He also helped the cause by addressing a meeting at Cambridge of the Religious Equality Society held in Oscar Browning's rooms.[52] On the whole, Toynbee found that the small circles of Oxford and Cambridge dons and undergraduates were more receptive to his religious views than most audiences, including some of the veteran church reformers.

Despite that, Toynbee's faith in the power of the direct appeal to the people was not confined to church reform. With his newly acquired knowledge of the principles of economics and his confidence in his oratorical power he delivered in January 1880 a series of three lectures at the Bradford Mechanics' Institute, the expenses of which were covered by a local merchant. In his opening comments Toynbee made it clear that he regarded political economy as a combination of theory and practice. Beyond the objective theoretical analysis political economy "assumed a thing, and framed precepts for the attainment of that thing. . . . the thing assumed by political economy was identical with the thing assumed by morality and religion. The thing assumed by political economy was the development of man's life in all its aspects." Hence this "thing" could be described in various ways, depending on the aspect of human reality upon which one chose to concentrate. In the instance of political economy it was the endeavor "to secure the organization which should provide for the most efficient production and the most equitable distribution—. . . an industrial organisation in which wants of man should be satisfied with the least effort and the least antagonism of interests—. . . to establish an industrial organisation in which there should be an identity of interests, and a community of spirit."[53] The same could be said of any form of social and spiritual activity, that it aimed at realizing "a community of spirit." Any suggested change that could be shown to affect adversely the attainment of this end, for example, by fostering class antagonism, was inimical to progress.

Toynbee argued that a brief review of the development of economic theory revealed that each generation of economists chose to focus on different matters. Whereas Adam Smith's main interest was the production of wealth, present-day economists such as J. S. Mill emphasized the need to examine how the wealth ought to be distributed (rather than how it was distributed). This was in apparent contradiction to Ricardo. "Apparent" because Toynbee believed that political economy had been seriously distorted by phrases that were originally used to denote tendencies occurring under very particular conditions, now being made to stand for universal laws.[54] Therefore, although it was justifiable to criticize Ricardo for concentrating on the production of wealth rather than on the welfare of man, it was wrong to attribute to him the claim "that the existing arrangements of society were inevitable and just."

Toynbee, perhaps overoptimistically, felt that it was no longer possible to confuse political economy, which dealt with the study of human activity and aspirations, with the physical sciences. "The bitter controversy which lasted so long between human beings and economists had ended in the conversion of the economists."

Toynbee's first lecture was mainly an enthusiastic defense of free trade and free competition. He argued that it was to the credit of political economy that, despite its previously limited constructive role in society, it succeeded in setting free "the pent up energies of the people." It had helped society to take a major step in the course of progress. Toynbee considered the system that allowed complete economic freedom a great contribution to social harmony through economic means. "Separation of employment" (i.e., division of labor) meant that, in order to provide for his own wants, each individual was forced to provide for the wants of others. Competition, operating as an external stimulant, forced the mutual provision of wants to be carried out at minimum cost. Whenever the minimum cost could not be reached competition forced a further distribution of industry in order to make full use of local labor and natural resources. Thus fair-traders who attacked international free trade did so out of ignorance. Competition in itself was neither good nor bad, it was merely a force that could and should be carefully studied and controlled so that it could be used in the service of progress. Once controlled and used properly it was still no more than a tool. Society still needed religion and ethics in order to set the aims for which it would be used.

The necessity of a statement in the defense of free trade became apparent in the course of the discussion that followed Toynbee's address. Free trade was repeatedly attacked by members of the audience whose main grievance seems to have been the unilateral nature of England's commitment to a free trade policy compared with other countries' reluctance to follow suit. From his answers it emerged that Toynbee's views were based on relatively superficial research. In support of his argument he claimed that 90 percent of England's imports were raw materials.[55] When this was disputed Toynbee somewhat sheepishly admitted his ignorance and "disclaimed any original researches." It was obvious that, having adopted a policy that appeared to fit his general social outlook, Toynbee felt confident that the facts would bear him out. When this did not occur he confidently assured his audience that, whatever the facts were, a protective trade policy "would not only injure the consumer by increasing the cost to him, but the whole tone of the industrial system by excluding foreign competition. Foreign competition was more and more necessary to the industrial system. . . . The effect of keeping one industry alive at the expense of others was to diminish the productive power of the nation, and to cramp the industrial energies and activity of the people."

The passage of time between the first and second lectures gave Toynbee a chance to consider more closely the aspects of free trade to which his audience seemed to object most strongly. This was mainly the question of unfair competition due to unequal rates of wages. Since the second lecture was meant to deal with wages this was not too much of a digression (although it was omitted from a later version of the lecture delivered separately at Sheffield).[56] Toynbee pointed out that higher wages were a detrimental factor in industry and trade only if they did not entail higher productivity. If complaints of unfair competition relied on the higher wages paid to English labor, and if it were shown that English workers were proportionately more efficient than elsewhere, then the cause of commercial weakness might very well lie in the employers' insistence on making unreasonable profits. In those instances in which foreign products were cheaper because they were produced under worse labor conditions (e.g., longer hours), Toynbee was confident that the spread of the movement for the improvement of conditions of labor to other countries would eventually serve to equalize conditions. In a world "intimately connected" in bounds of commerce "it was impossible that one nation could be long alone in one great feature such as the shortening of the hours of labour."

Toynbee believed that, despite temporary fluctuations and localized crises due to the operation of competition in a free-trade system, the system as a whole was sound. It served the good of the community. The importation of cheaply produced foreign products served the interest of the consumer, that is, of each member of the community. If a local industry was unable to compete under these conditions it had no right to continue to exist at the expense of the consumer. Indeed, were it not in the consumer's interest to import cheaper goods the problem would not arise since all trade was dependent on demand. In the last analysis the collective interest of the community overrode the interests of any part of it employed in an uncompetitive industry.

The second lecture, which was delivered to a larger crowd despite adverse weather conditions, contained Toynbee's fullest exposition on wages.[57] His treatment of the subject demonstrated the importance he attached to the linkage between theory and practice and its relation to the methodological question of the use of induction and deduction (which he had so far ignored). The problem of the rate of wages was posed primarily by nontheoretical considerations. The material progress of the working class, expressed in terms of an increase in their real wages, was defined as essential to the moral and spiritual progress of society. Toynbee, a firm believer in progress, considered the existing system suitable to ensure the progress of all classes. It was therefore his moral responsibility to demonstrate how this could be done. In solving the problem both the means and the ends should correspond to moral criteria that transcended economic theory. The choice of analytical tools as such was relatively immaterial, merely a matter of technical preference. The appropriateness of an analytical method was determined by the actual case and, in this instance, Toynbee considered theory to be perfectly adequate.

In justification of the use of theory Toynbee began by emphasizing its moral neutrality. Theory explained how wealth was distributed; it did not thereby justify its findings. Political economy could be described as advocating the free operation of self-interest only when it promoted the good of the community. By objectively describing existing conditions it did not maintain "that there is no room for humanity or morality or religion in the world." Hence whenever in various instances (e.g., the American labor war of 1877, an arbitration case in the Durham coal trade, or a certain article in the *Times* on a strike), it was argued that a certain course of action was in keeping with, or contrary to, economic laws, these laws were erroneously awarded the validity of laws of nature. With a few exceptions laws of economics were "alterable by human endeavour." More often than not these laws were due to "existing human passions which could be modified in the progress of civilization by higher passions and higher ideals."

Toynbee's discussion of wages was aimed at providing an alternative to the wage fund theory. His argument followed Cliffe Leslie's 1868 article, "Political Economy and Emigration," and F. A. Walker's work on wages, which filled a gap in economic theory for those who rejected the wage fund theory. He also referred to Mill's approval of William T. Thornton's *On Labour* in his 1869 review in the *Fortnightly Review*. (Elsewhere Toynbee was to give Thornton joint credit, with Walker, for overthrowing the wage fund theory.)[58] Toynbee regarded wages as determined by four factors: the amount of produce, the price of the produce in the market, division of profit, and custom.

The amount of produce was determined by a variable, the efficiency of labor, and a constant, natural resources. Therefore, an increase in efficiency causing an increase in produce would effect an increase in wages. Efficiency of labor (and therefore the amount of produce) was determined by the physical strength and technical skill of the laborer, technology, climatic conditions (a constant), and the skill of management. On the latter Toynbee may have been influenced by Marshall's emphasis on the essential place of management in production.[59] He insisted that

it is a function at the present time of enormous importance. The employer scrutinises the natural resources of the country; he detects new possibilities; he creates a new industry out of the waste of old industries; he gathers together men in factories; he takes the whole risk of the business; he guarantees the wages of the workmen, and he studies the wants of the consumer. He must know where to buy his raw material; he must know how to buy it in the cheapest market, when to sell his goods, and when not to sell them. He must undertake operations which involve relations with all sorts of men, not only in his own country but in distant countries. Without him it is absolutely impossible, as long as the present industrial system lasts, for the workman to live.[60]

In addition to the demand for the product and the capital to cover costs of production until profits could take over, efficient management was one of the prerequisites of employment.

At the same time, Toynbee believed that, despite the employer's importance, his interests should be subservient to those of society as a whole. In the same way that workers risked their own redundancy if the demand for their produce fell, employers should face the possible consequences of free trade (i.e., their inability to withstand competition). In the course of the discussion following the lecture Toynbee's position was criticized by Mr. Lister, a local silk manufacturer, who stated the standard fair trade argument that, in the absence of protection, longer hours on the continent might force down English wages. In his answer Toynbee demonstrated a certain rhetorical flair.

Mr. Lister, they all knew, was a silk manufacturer. Mr. Lister wanted to know whether he could compete with a foreign silk manufacturer. (Hear, hear.) Let Mr. Lister compare the efficiency of his own labourers with the efficiency of the labourers on the Continent. (Applause.) In the next place let Mr. Lister compare the rate of wages in England in his own factory with the rate of wages in the factories on the Continent—(applause)—then let him compare the proportion between the efficiency of labour and the rate of wages. (A voice. "Mr. Lister has done all that. He knows what he's about, lad." Laughter.) Let them suppose for a moment that in England the efficiency of labour was double, but the rate of wages was more than double. Then he should say to Mr. Lister, "If you want to carry on this business in Bradford you must take lower profits; then you can undersell the foreign manufacturer. It is quite in your power to take lower profits if you are content with them. The real fact is, you want a certain rate of profit and you will find perhaps you won't get it in the silk industry. Then you may go to another industry." (Laughter and applause).[61]

In a system of free competition, in which products are sold for the lowest price at which they can be produced, the price of a product is evidently determined by the cost of production. In a system of monopoly the price of a product is determined by demand, that is, the highest price it can fetch. Hence the system of free competition is synonymous with the satisfaction of wants at a minimum cost. Workers could raise the price of their product by combining to limit production or to raise wages. The first course of action is legitimate only in case of a glut in production. However, if their aim is the consolidation of a monopoly, the result would be a small gain to the producers and a large loss to the consumers, creating a conflict of interests between a group of producers and the whole community. Such a conflict is fundamentally different from the conflict between the classes within the community over the just distribution of wealth. The former is adverse to the economic interests of the community and therefore condemnable on practical grounds.

Workers combining to raise wages would also cause a rise in prices. If the product was a "necessary," a rise in its price would diminish the purchasing power of most of the community. A small group would again benefit at the expense of the whole. If the product was not a "necessary," the rise in its price would result in a drop in demand causing job redundancies in its production. Hence, inasmuch as wages are a function of the cost of production, any attempt to tamper with them beyond ensuring complete free competition is bound to cause more harm than good.

Wages as a function of the division of profits are determined by the proportional division between the interest on capital, the earnings of management, and the wages of labor. Interest on capital is determined by circumstances external to the problem under consideration. The proper ratio between the earnings of management and wages has been a source of constant dispute. Both were determined by comparability and by supply and demand (i.e., by variables) that fixed the minimum rates of earnings and of wages. The labor market is not comparable to the commodity market. The individual laborer does not enjoy a position of equality with his employer in negotiating for his wages and is therefore liable to accept employment for wages that are unjustifiably low. This inequality is not compensated by the exposure of the employer to the dangers of competition. It was pointed out in the discussion that, despite the bonds formed by the expenditure of effort and time, "it was easier for the employer with his capital, with his brains, with his love of enterprise, with his energy, and with his knowledge of the world and of the conditions of industry in different countries to move and seek new fields of enterprise than it was for the employee with his wife and family, with little capital, and with ignorance, distress, and doubt."[62]

The inequality in wage bargaining could be rectified by trade unions that in their existence embodied the principle of voluntary

association by which the individual submitted to the collective interest. By amassing funds, trade unions could enable their members to
bargain with comparative freedom from care about provision for
their families during negotiations. Unions could, in addition, collect
information on market conditions that could be used in bargaining
and to aid labor mobility. Their function was to help raise wages to
the maximum acceptable within the economic confines of the trade.
At the same time unions had in their power the prevention of wild
bargaining of unorganized labor. However, with power came responsibility. Trade unions must not limit competition within the
labor market by excluding some workers from membership. They
should not abuse their power by obtaining wages that the industry
cannot afford. In both instances the abuse of power would eventually
result in impairing their own interests.

Toynbee envisaged that in following the principle of association
the organization of employers and of workers would serve to regulate
the struggle over the distribution of profits and transform it from a
direct confrontation to conciliation and arbitration. This course of
change could be aided by the fourth factor that determined the rate
of wages: custom, law, and public opinion. If the public was to be
properly educated so as to influence custom and legislation, it could
be made to force fair wage settlements and to prevent unnecessary
industrial confrontations. But not only attitudes were changeable,
human nature itself was pliable, especially toward "nobler ideas"
and "a truer sense of justice." Given time and the current course of
progress Toynbee was confident "that employers under the influence
of the wider and deeper conceptions . . . may be willing to forgo
the struggle for the division of wealth, some part of that share which
would come to them if they chose to exert their force without restraint." The future would see English employers and English workers acting "upon higher notions of duty and higher conceptions of
citizenship."

Toynbee had reduced wage settlements to three variables: efficiency, the power of labor to demand a better share of the profits
within certain parameters, and the power of public opinion to force
employers to accept such settlements. All three were to a large extent reducible in practical terms to trade unionism. Unions would
improve the workers' bargaining power, promote greater efficiency
through better organization, and help influence public opinion.
Thus, Toynbee hoped, he had succeeded in demonstrating how "the

economists of the most recent school" had changed their negative attitude toward unions. In addition he had aimed to provide an example of the proper use of political economy, while dispelling the misconceptions concerning the universality of most economic laws. The wage fund theory had been the main origin of these misconceptions. It had led economists to condemn all efforts by workers to improve their condition by raising their wages and was therefore responsible for their general mistrust of political economy. It ran contrary to facts. It strengthened the hands of the employer in wage bargaining by bringing public opinion to his side, the side that upheld the "laws of nature." Finally, it condemned the working classes to eternal poverty unless they could reduce their numbers.

Toynbee hoped that his demonstration of the nature of the new political economy and its attitude toward trade unionism would result in a corresponding change of attitude among workers toward economics. His aim was to convert the middle classes to support trade unionism while providing trade unions with the means of rectifying the imbalance in the distribution of wealth. However, although his message was aimed at both the middle and working classes his emphasis had been shifting toward the latter. He confessed that "if I have shown working men that they should study economic science, if they would understand within what limits they can raise wages under present social conditions, and taking human beings as they are—if I have succeeded in doing this, then also I shall be content."

Changing working-class attitudes toward political economy was only part of a wider educational goal aimed at the improvement of the workers' understanding of the moral implications of their newly acquired political power and their anticipated material wealth. "High wages are not an end in themselves. No one wants high wages in order that working men may indulge in mere sensual gratification. We want higher wages in order that an improved material condition, with less anxiety and less uncertainty as to the future, may enable the working man to enter on a purer and more worthy life." Hence Toynbee's work in political economy, his popular lectures, and his work on the behalf of church reform were all part of an effort to help the nation gain a moral sense of direction.

In the course of his lectures Toynbee made use of examples gleaned from contemporary social and economic developments. These were usually illustrations of points he made rather than premises on which his arguments were based. Consequently, whenever objections were raised by the audience concerning the accuracy of some of his facts Toynbee did not feel that their modification or qualification necessitated a revision of his arguments. His third lecture opened with a number of such qualifications. When describing the press as generally hostile to the trade unions he had meant the London rather than the provincial press. He did not wish to imply that the English laborer was uniformly more efficient than foreign labor. In some cases he merely enjoyed the advantage of richer natural resources (e.g., the northern miner). But otherwise his arguments remained unchanged.

The success of the first two lectures attracted a large audience "including many ladies" to the third one, which concluded the series.[63] In it Toynbee attempted to present the practical conclusion of his analysis. It was to consider "the future of England's industrial system in so far as it could be modified by human endeavour; and to show . . . how that system must be modified." He contrasted his approach with that of the "great Socialist writers" of the past fifty years, who had been "indefatigable in analysing the evils of the modern industrial system."[64] They had consistently pointed out how the system had wasted life, capital, and skill, how it had led to enormous inequalities in wealth, and how fluctuations in prices had "condemned a large mass of labourers to pauperism and demoralising dependence." They had insisted "that there was a permanent antagonism of interests between employers and workmen which they declared could never disappear under the existing system."

The modern economist, who Toynbee believed he was faithfully representing, chose a different approach. While no one could pretend that the present industrial system was perfect, "the age of criticism was past, and the age of construction had come. What the political economist had to do was to show how, by careful, painful, sustained effort, man could change his industrial conditions and get rid of those apparently inevitable evils of the system which had up to the present time prevailed." This could be done only on the basis of a thorough analysis of the industrial system as well as an understanding of the nature and course of progress in general.

Toynbee identified two progressive tendencies as consequential: the tendency toward voluntary association that Mazzini had described as the watchword of the future and the growing sense of duty to deal with suffering that was manifest in practical philanthropy and legislation "which expressed the moral determination of the people."

In his previous lecture Toynbee had discussed the significance of trade unions as forms of association. He now added cooperatives as further illustrations of the growing spirit of association. These had been obviously successful in organizing consumption and distribution but "an undoubted failure" in production. The failure of cooperative production seemed to indicate to Toynbee that, despite the importance of the principle of association in shaping the future of industrial society, it could not overcome the fundamental dependence on the division of labor. The abolition of the role of the employer was economically impractical. Association could improve the system but not change its structure. There was no way in which "the fact, the extreme sagacity, the determination, the foresight, the enterprise" of the employer could be replaced. "The employer must be a man who was not hampered by the control of a committee, but able to decide at once when to buy and when to sell, free to watch for himself the turn of the market, and to promptly adopt the latest invention without having to wait for the consent of a committee." Progress, therefore, was dependent not on a structural change in society but on closer cooperation between workers and employers.

In order to create a symmetry of change Toynbee argued that employers had changed their attitude toward their workers and their interests. Legislation enabled the humane employer to stand his ground against unscrupulous competition. It had helped the honest employer to safeguard the interests of his worker, both as an employee and as a consumer. However, legislation was unable to tackle fluctuations of prices and the instability of industrial conditions, problems of growing concern due to the agricultural depression and the diminishing competitiveness of English goods abroad. Having dismissed fluctuations in prices, in his first lecture, as "an evil which would not be met by any scheme which had yet been proposed," an evil relatively insignificant when compared to the great benefit of free trade, Toynbee was now forced, possibly in view of his audience's reaction, to reconsider the matter.[65]

Fluctuations were redubbed, "the greatest evil of our time." They were partly due to natural causes—changes in seasons and in weather—over which there was no control. But they were also caused by imperfect industrial organization, by production that was not regulated by a careful investigation of demand, and by the abuse of the credit system. These imperfections could be largely modified by a process already in motion: the growing cooperation between con-

sumer and producer forced by the development of distributive cooperatives. With the shift in "modern political economy" from examining economic reality from the point of view of the producer to
that of the consumer, stabilization of demand was made possible.
Once prices were stabilized fluctuations in wages would disappear
and the regulation of the hours of labor would be made possible.
Toynbee admitted that his solution had not been thoroughly worked
out but he felt confident that it was feasible. He reasoned that a careful evaluation of consumption was in the interests of both consumers
and producers. Once the problem was solved "it would be possible
for the great mass of the people to slowly rise from their present social
condition, and qualify themselves for a higher political equality and
independence."

Toynbee virtually admitted that the attractiveness of the idea of
fixing consumption through producer-consumer cooperation was
more in the principles it embodied than in its technical practicality
(which he was, at the time, unable to determine). His faith in its
feasibility was due to its compatibility with his vision of the future
industrial society. It suggested the creation of "a great community in
which there was a common spirit and a common purpose. . . . The
great duty of the time was for all classes to unite—employers, and
labourers, and students—for one common end, and to remove those
antagonisms of interest which had withstood all endeavours to promote unity of spirit. (Loud applause)."

The key to progress, whether in dealing with price fluctuations or
in wage negotiations, was class cooperation, and it was in the promotion of such cooperation that Toynbee found his initial calling to
preach political economy. Referring to himself as representative of a
neutral group—students—he saw his task as twofold. Workers and
manufacturers were to be brought together by overcoming their
mutual suspicions, and men of practice from both classes were to
join with students in seeking solutions for current problems. Toynbee
felt certain that "if these three classes would unite for a common
purpose, England might lead the nations in solving the greatest industrial problem that the world had ever seen. (Loud and prolonged
applause)."

Toynbee's idea of what he referred to as "modern political economy" was very much that of a newcomer to the subject who applied
an external criterion to a new object of intellectual interest. Modern
political economy, as far as Toynbee was concerned, was any theory

that qualified laissez-faire on scientific grounds and rejected it on moral grounds. Methodology was a secondary issue so long as the old theories, especially the wage fund theory, were rejected. Thus Toynbee had no difficulty in lauding both Cliffe Leslie's work and John Elliot Cairnes's "Political Economy and Laissez Faire,"[66] while completely overlooking their disagreements concerning the applicability of Comte's concept of a unified science of society to the study of political economy.

In early September 1880 Albert Grey, who had become interested in the political economy courses delivered by the Cambridge Extension lecturers to the Northumberland miners, sent to Toynbee copies of some letters, published in the *Newcastle Daily Chronicle,* which brought the problem into relief. At the center of the correspondence stood Patrick Lloyd Jones, a veteran Owenite who had supported in his time Christian Socialism, cooperation, and trade unionism. In 1876 he had joined the staffs of the *Newcastle Weekly* and the *Newcastle Daily Chronicle* and it was through these that he launched, during the late summer of 1880, an attack against the contents of the extension lectures in political economy. Lloyd Jones accused the lecturers of teaching orthodox doctrines in the service of the upper classes. He was quoted at an extension meeting as having stated that "instruction directed specially to the working men of the Country on Political Economy has nearly always had for its object the destruction of the people's faith in combined action in connection with their several trades, and in such teaching it is far more easy to see the schemings of a class interest than any love of knowledge for its own sake."[67]

Lloyd Jones criticized political economy on two fundamental points. He argued that there was no such thing as "new" political economy adapted to the needs of the working class and that political economy was not a science but, at best, an incomplete "fabric of postulates and dogmas, many of which oppose each other; many are in opposition to the plainest every day experience; and all of them are undergoing constant change." He challenged political economists to prove him wrong.

If there is a new science of political economy there ought to be no difficulty in saying where it differs from the old. If old dogmas have been winnowed away by the breath of new knowledge, whose, I ask, is the thought, whose the words, whose the structural arrangement of the new system? Every friend of the working man must be anxious that he should master the new thought, that he should comprehend and seek to enforce the new law; but at the same time they ought to be just as anxious that he should not continue to be enthralled by the old dogma.[68]

To the defense of political economy and the extension lectures came two local miners, John Bryson and J. D. Pringle, both of whom were active in organizing lectures through the Northumberland Miners' Association and thus were something of Grey's protégés.[69] At a meeting of the association Bryson loyally defended the contents of the lectures. He

urged that both the working classes and the masters required a knowledge of political economy. (Hear, hear.) As he had often said before, thousands of pounds had been wasted in the past, and hundreds of families thrown into misery; all of which might have been averted but for ignorance of political economy. Huge sums of money need not be wasted if employers were conciliatory towards their men, and if men had better knowledge of the trade, and of the circumstances which affected the industries in which they might be engaged. Political Economy taught these things, and instead of doing harm it could only do good.

However, Bryson and Pringle were no match for Lloyd Jones. He stated that he was not opposed to extension lectures as such but rather questioned their contents; he continued to maintain that there was no discernible coherent and consistent body of economic doctrines. As an example he cited the differences between the early and the late J. S. Mill regarding the wage fund theory.[70]

Underlying the exchange seemed to be the aftermath of a previous debate concerning the suggestion that, due to a drop in the price of coal, the miners should organize in order to limit its production, thereby artificially raising its price. As might be expected, W. M. Moorsom, the extension lecturer, advocating free trade and free competition, rejected the suggestion, as did some of his miner students. Lloyd Jones had supported it. The issue reemerged in Pringle's letter,[71] and was harshly dealt with by Lloyd Jones who stated, "What we require is harmony between the two forces [supply and demand] if we can get it, and this is what we should trouble our heads about just now and not the overweening pretensions of political economists, and the half wild suggestions of working men bewildered by their sufferings."[72]

Grey rightly felt that Lloyd Jones's attacks constituted a significant threat to the popularity and reputation of the extension lectures, which Grey was eager to promote. The answers of Pringle and Bryson as representatives of the working classes lacked force and a detailed answer by an extension lecturer might lack credibility. He therefore sent Toynbee copies of the exchange containing Lloyd Jones's challenge which, he felt certain, Toynbee could not ignore. In response he received a detailed account of Toynbee's concept of modern political economy, a version of which was soon published in the *Newcastle Daily Chronicle*.[73]

Toynbee argued that Lloyd Jones misunderstood the nature of modern political economy and had, in fact, attacked the old discredited doctrines. He repeated the substance as well as some of the phrases of his Bradford lectures, including his claim that the "bitter controversy between economists and human beings has ended in the conversion of economists," and reiterated that his views were representative of modern economics best exemplified, in his view, by the Marshalls' *Economics of Industry* (1879).

If Mr. Lloyd Jones would turn to this admirable little treatise he would find recognized many of the criticisms he himself has made. . . . he would find the proper distinction made between political economy as a theoretical science, and political economy as a practical science; he would find the relations of political economy to social science explained; and, above all, he would observe with pleasure that abstract political economy, the laws of which are true only under certain assumptions, used not to blind men to the facts of the industrial world, but to throw light upon them in all the confusion and entanglement of actual existence.

In modern political economy, Ricardo's theories were "rejected as intellectual imposture" and the "fatal" wage fund theory had been abandoned. He wished to assure all that "economists are no longer animated by the old narrow spirit of confident dogmatism; that through the intellectual criticisms of Mr. Cliffe Leslie, the English disciples of Comte, and the German economists of the historical school, their minds have at last been open to the justice of the moral denunciations of Ruskin and Carlyle; that they are only too eager to learn from men . . . intimately acquainted . . . not with the mere theorems of the subject but with the minutest details of industrial life and history."

As for the particular issue concerning the possible limitation of the production of coal Toynbee chose to approach the matter as if it were a question of oversupply. He could therefore argue that modern political economy was not necessarily opposed to Lloyd Jones's suggestion, assuming that it could be shown that it would improve the conditions of the miners without seriously harming the rest of society. Under such circumstances the prosperity of any one part of society was in the interest of the whole since "the whole community suffers whenever any one group of producers does not receive remuneration sufficient to enable them to live a secure and independent life"—a position regarded by Pringle, a firm free trader, as too conciliatory.[74]

At this point Grey brought W. M. Moorsom into the discussion. Moorsom was probably the first to point out to Toynbee that his views might not be entirely representative of modern theory. He disputed Toynbee's claim that all modern theorists rejected Ricardo and the old doctrines. Rather than breaking with the past Moorsom described modern theory as firmly based on it. "I have just been reading MacCulloch's [sic] essay written in 1825; he points out the limits within which Ricardo's theory of Wages and Profits is true, and outside of which it is not true. I don't think the modern school of Economists have much improved upon what he says, though they have illustrated and enforced and extended it."

Moorsom extended his criticism to Toynbee's view of the role of the economist in society. In his view political economy was merely a tool and should remain that way. It was the economist's duty to perfect it, as the astronomer did the telescope, in order to record what the layman could not see with his naked eye. "My idea is that the modern school are too much inclined to give advice to practical men, and if they do, an increase of practical knowledge is sure to show that they have been too hasty. What economists can do, and do well, is to ask practical men to look at facts from their point of view; if practical men can be persuaded to do this, they will recognise that the Economists' point of view is the true one, and they will draw the practical conclusions for themselves far better than men of the study can draw them."[75]

Toynbee, to whom Moorsom's letter was forwarded by Grey, was forced to admit that differences did exist. The rejection of the old doctrines and the role of the economist in society were fundamental components of his view of the nature of the study of economics. Although in private as well as in some later lectures he was to modify slightly his condemnation of Ricardo his position remained basically unchanged. On both issues he differed with Marshall whose work he had proclaimed as representative of the new school. Hence he was forced to admit that his views may not represent an actual consensus. In his reply to Grey he accepted that he and Moorsom

differ mainly in this—that whilst he thinks it wise for economists to restrict themselves to an exploration of the abstract laws of economics with occasional applications (I think he would include this) of these laws to the elucidation of actual facts, I am convinced that . . . an economist . . . must apply a gospel of life to the dealings of men with the facts of wealth,—and this . . . function of the economist I call his use of political economy as a practical science. Now I am aware that I differ from other economists on this point—from Marshall himself even, who though he distinguishes between an art or practical science and a science proper, would say it was not the business of Political Economy to frame rules— that that must be left to those who are masters of the *Art of Life*. But here I disagree with him, and my disagreement is based on an examination of the actual influence of the old Political Economy upon practice. I maintain that had the economists had this gospel of life the misconceptions most fatal to Political Economy would never have existed, and economists themselves would have been saved from more fatal mistakes.[76]

The old economists and their followers then were wrong because their teachings were devoid of a "gospel of life," an external philosophy that would have guided their work. Such a gospel was, therefore, necessary in order to counter the effect of their mistakes and to prevent their recurrence. Toynbee continued his letter, which, he stressed, was not for publication, with an explanation of his view of Ricardo:

When I spoke of Ricardo's Political Economy as an imposture I used language liable to be misunderstood, but I used it advisedly, because though Ricardo never intended it, his Political Economy as a system became by the force of circumstances a sort of complete philosophy of industrial and commercial life. It was not, as every economist knows, so much owing to particular theories that Ricardo's system did mischief (though particular theories were productive of much harm) as to its general attitude towards social questions, and its half unconscious pretension to be a complete explanation of economic facts as they are found to exist. For Ricardo I have the highest admiration; indeed I think he stands above all economists in point of sheer power of abstract reasoning, (I have never been able to find a flaw in his actual reasonings, the error is always in his premises), but I consider that it was just this extraordinary power that made his influence so fatal.

Through erroneous interpretation and false application Ricardo's work became synonymous with all that Toynbee regarded as false and dangerous in political economy. His name became identified with the old school and was thus used in Toynbee's criticisms of the orthodox doctrines.

Unlike Moorsom, Toynbee argued that the new school was fundamentally different from the old. "The corrections as to actual theories are of great, and the change in the general attitude of the science is of fundamental, importance." This view was based largely on his own selective impressions rather than on the views of other contemporary economists. Toynbee was aware of the danger of his disagreements with Moorsom undermining his appeal to the working class to reconsider its attitude toward political economy. He therefore insisted that, although real, the differences did not affect his main argument concerning the working class. In his view, "my reference to Marshall's book, which Moorsom, I think, accepts as a good exposition of the subject will prove that the difference cannot be deep enough to separate us altogether in our estimate of the science."[77]

This was more than mere wishful thinking for, despite the acknowledged differences, Toynbee was still confident that a new school corresponding to his previous characterization was in the process of being formed. He felt that he could prove his point conclusively by producing "an accurate survey of the changes Political Economy has undergone since Adam Smith, to state as clearly as I can the position it at present occupies, and to point out, as far as it is possible, the work that lies before it in the future. Perhaps when I have finished and printed this we shall find that we [Toynbee and Moorsom] agree?" Toynbee had probably referred to an unfinished essay he had begun in 1879. Although his work on it was somewhat erratic he continued to regard the project as important despite recurring diversions. Fragments of it as well as part of an uncompleted essay on the same subject entitled, "Ricardo and the Old Political Economy," have survived.

One of the fragments contains a detailed exposition of Toynbee's gospel of life, regarded by him as the essential premise for all economic inquiries. It is in part a generalization from his own experience aimed at providing political economy with a moral focus.

There is no one who has not at some moment of his life been appalled by a vision of human misery; suggested perhaps by a visit to a workhouse or a sweating den or by the mean and squalid interior of a labourer's house; with most the vision fades rapidly and is forgotten[;] with some it lingers on but gives . . . to nothing more than occasional outbursts of fierce invective; with a few it is an inspiration for work, a test by which every religious faith and every political creed is tried if by chance they may bring relief to the world. These last men are many of them foolish, some of them mad but their folly and their madness confound the wisdom of the wise. One or two of them discover in their wild explorations great truths, truths which sober and industrious men of the world in time appropriate and adapt to the use of the human race. This has been the history of most social reformers and the fate of most dreamers of utopias. The awakening vision of hunger and want has not been the same in every age, nor has it been equally terrible, that wh[ich] haunts us is not more than a century old and is the offspring of a vast revolution in men's views as of satisfying wants and of obtaining wealth. The destruction of the simple and primitive ways of life wh[ich] prevailed up to the middle of the last century tho' it did not create pauperism or degradation, gave often a new and terrible appearance, with the steam engine and the factory came haggard faces and pestilential streets and courts, with the accumulation of vast fortunes came more numerous droves of broken and destitute labourers. It was in this period, a period when misery assumed a[n] . . . irresistible form that man began to dream more hopefully than ever of the disappearance of poverty and the removal of injustice.[78]

Toynbee wished to place the modern school within a tradition of social reform. Historically the same tradition included many of the socialists with whose fervor Toynbee sympathized despite his criticism of their analysis of the reasons for poverty and its cures. Ricardo's work was definitely placed outside of it. Hence, modern theory was to be described as originating from a tradition other than orthodox political economy.

In his letter on the matter to Grey, Toynbee reassured him that he would "certainly take care to do full justice to the old economists." By "full justice" he seems to have intended to demonstrate the way in which their theories were expressions of the traditions and circumstances of their age. In his unfinished essay Toynbee identified two distinct traditions. The first one was the methodological tradition within which Ricardo formulated his theories and due to the popularity of which his theories gained their wide acceptance. Toynbee regarded Ricardo as the product of the school of deductive and abstract reasoning dominated by Bentham, James Mill, and John Austin. Ricardo had developed his theories within a tradition that unconsciously led him to fall "into the habit of regarding laws, which were true only of that society which he had created in his study for purposes of analysis, as applicable to the complex society really existing around him."[79]

The entirely hypothetical theory formed by Ricardo had been eagerly seized upon by a confused and bewildered age as a clear-cut answer to their problems. With their eagerness to replace doubt with certainty his contemporaries accepted his logical artifice as the true picture of the real world. Thus an approach that, on the face of it was a harmless and legitimate intellectual exercise, became morally wicked. His age accepted his view of the world as consisting of "gold seeking animals, stripped of every human affection, for ever digging, weaving, spinning, watching with keen undeceived eyes each other's movements, passing incessantly and easily from place to place in search of gain, all alert, crafty, mobile,"[80] as real. It was a world that was amoral and therefore immoral.

The elimination of all human factors except greed from Ricardo's imaginary world made it uncomplicated and therefore more attractive.[81] This view of the world constituted something of a mental block to future generations of economists. Even J. S. Mill and Nassau W. Senior, who identified the presuppositions tacitly assumed by Ricardo, failed to go beyond his world and "to ascertain from actual observation of the industrial world they live in how far these assumptions were facts, and from the knowledge thus acquired to state the laws of prices, profits, wages, rent, in the actual world."[82] The whole "world had become political economists of the Ricardian persuasion. . . . Ricardo's brilliant deductions destroyed observation. A method so clear, solutions so simple, carried all before them."[83]

Ricardian theories had served to remove restrictions on economic activity. However, after 1846, the assumption that the removal of restrictions would solve every existing difficulty failed to provide adequate means to tackle the remaining problems, especially those concerning labor. "Instead of a healer of differences it became a sower of discord,"[84] mainly by indiscriminate opposition to the imposition of any restriction, including the Factory Acts. Reaction to the inability of deductive political economy to deal with the problems of labor resulted in a revival of the method of observation. "Political Economy was transformed by the working classes,"[85] hence the change in focus and method in the works of Thornton, Cairnes, and F. A. Walker.

The works of the economists of the 1870s indicated the new road on which the science would continue to travel. Deductive theory would "take its place as a needful instrument of investigation, but its conclusions will be generally recognised as hypothetical. Care will be taken to include in its premises the greatest possible number of facts, and to apply its results with the utmost scrupulousness to existing industrial and social relations. It will no longer be common error to confuse the abstract science of Economics with the real science of human life."[86] Toynbee's previously expressed indifference to the issues of methodology began to change.

Despite factual weaknesses Toynbee's argument had, so far, been reasonably straightforward and simple. The old theories ignored reality and, when confused with reality, had had a detrimental effect on society. The modern theories took account of reality, addressed themselves to real problems, and consequently provided a valuable aid to progress. However, following his exchange with Moorsom, Toynbee realized that basing his argument merely on methodological differences was insufficient. He had come to admit that the modern economists he so enthusiastically approved of, were far from united on the question of methodology. He would therefore have to demonstrate that they differed from their predecessors in their basic philosophy. Accordingly he attempted, in the essay's second part, to support his argument concerning the development of economics from a different angle.

Toynbee now argued that the work of the old economists had been permeated with two basic philosophical assumptions that could be first identified in Adam Smith. "Two conceptions are woven into every argument of the *Wealth of Nations*—the belief in the supreme value of individual liberty, and the conviction that Man's self love is God's providence, that the individual is pursuing his own interest in promoting the welfare of all."[87] Therefore, although Ricardo may be considered the most outstanding exponent of the deductive approach, his work is based on much earlier philosophical presuppositions.

Toynbee's apparent intention was to develop a relatively simple argument. Having first demonstrated the extent to which the old philosophy dominated old economics, he would base its rejection on its position regarding labor, contrasting it with a modern approach to labor, thereby producing an argument symmetrical with its methodological counterpart. Toynbee maintained that "Adam Smith believed in the natural economic equality of men. That being so, it only needed legal equality of rights and all would go well."[88] When extended to industrial relations it resulted in the defense of the "free competition of unequal industrial units," the competition of capital and labor. Thus, in the name of liberty, economists since Adam Smith have opposed any attempt to redress by means of legislation the inequality in wage bargaining and labor conditions, including the Factory Acts and the abolition of the combination laws. Consequently they have provided "the greatest impulse to socialistic speculation in England,"[89] while exposing their science to popular condemnation.

In lieu of this philosophy Toynbee presented his own views which, he believed, were representative of the modern school and its approach to labor.

The influence of a recognition of the economic inequality of men on our estimate of competition is immense. Not admitting with the socialist, the natural right of all men to an equal share in the benefits of civilization, not proposing with the socialist, to stamp out competition, and substitute a community of goods, we yet plead for the right of all to equal opportunities of development, according to their nature. . . . The old economists thought competition good in itself. The socialists think it an evil in itself. We think it neither good nor evil, but seek to analyse it, and ascertain when it produces good and when it produces bad results. . . . We accept competition as one means, a force to be used, not to be blindly worshipped; but assert religion and morality to be the necessary conditions of attaining human welfare.[90]

So far the two arguments followed symmetrical courses, but when they were combined Toynbee ran into new difficulties. He had claimed that the old economists' faith in their philosophy and their confidence in their science had led them to regard the laws of economics as possessing the validity of laws of nature. They had entered into an alliance with the capitalists, whose interests were justified by their theories, against the laborers. Soon they found themselves attacked, by philosophers, moralists, and even statesmen, for supporting individualism and thereby threatening all forms of domestic, political, and national association. The only true alternative to this philosophy was, in Toynbee's view, his gospel of life: "Morality must be united with economics as a practical science."[91] Neutrality, that is, the absence of a moral philosophy, was impossible in an age that demanded practical solutions to its pressing problems. Yet that was precisely the position maintained by many contemporary economists. Although critical of laissez-faire and the old philosophy many of them advocated the purge of economics from all philosophical bias rather than the replacement of one philosophy with another. It is therefore not surprising that, having reached this point in his argument, being unable to offer a factual description of a modern school that would contrast with the old one on the lines he had indicated, Toynbee abandoned the unfinished essay. He did not revise his views on the nature and aims of the study of economics but he was forced to admit that most economists had not gone quite so far as he had in reshaping the science. If the trust of the working class were to be regained it was best to emphasize agreement among contemporary economists rather than discord, especially since he could present the rejection of laissez-faire as uniting most modern economists.

In his next public address at Bradford on 31 January 1881, Toynbee dropped his claim of representing modern political economy. Instead he emphasized the advantages of addressing his subject, "Industry and Democracy," from the point of view of a student. In giving his version of the scientists's impartiality Toynbee stated:

The student will not—at any rate at first—be suspected of class prejudice or political prejudice. . . . But there is a stronger point still in favour of the student: he is not only free from prejudice, he is able to take those wide, connected views of things which are often to the political and practical man impossible. They live in the world, immersed in its cares, distracted by its cries—are in the arena carrying out the struggle. The student lives retired, watches the world from afar, and discerns many things unnoticed by those who are too often borne along in the tumult they seek to guide. From his watch-tower he looks before and after, pursues with diligent eye the preceding past, and with anxious expectation forecasts the future.[92]

Toynbee did not adopt Marshall's scientific neutrality argument. Having described the advantages of the student over politicians, who were becoming "less and less leaders and teachers, and more and more the instruments of the people," he proceeded by arguing in favor of "the necessity for the intervention in political and social affairs of a new order of men, who may indeed be enrolled as members of this party or that, but who shall not suffer party connections or personal aims to hamper them in the elucidation of the questions which it is the function of politicians to settle. Is it quite impossible to conceive of such men?—of men who shall be as students impartial, as citizens passionate?"[93] Such men, Toynbee doubtlessly believed, constituted the "Regeneration of Humanity" Society.

The relative lack of enthusiasm within the society for church reform did not indicate its members' loss of commitment to its initial aims. During the early months of 1880 Oxford Liberals and Tories were busy preparing for the general elections scheduled for April. Campaigning in Oxford and neighboring constituencies reflected the new spirit of political commitment among undergraduates of both camps. The Liberal *Oxford Chronicle*, noting this new feature in local electioneering commented, "Our readers will have observed from the reports in these columns that several undergraduates of the University, distinguished members of the Union Debating Society, have been pressed into the service of both political parties. This is a new feature in our election struggles."[94] Specifically the *Chronicle* named Mr. Ready of Wadham College, president of the Oxford union, who campaigned for the Tories, and E. T. Cook of New College, president of the Palmerston Club, who spoke on the behalf of the Liberals in some of the town's wards and neighboring villages.[95]

One of the main targets of Oxford Liberals and the subject of repeated attacks in the *Chronicle* was Randolph Churchill, member for Woodstock. Since Oxford City was considered relatively safe for Sir William V. Harcourt, much of the effort of the young Liberal campaigners concentrated on the outlying villages and towns. Cook campaigned in Kidlington, Osney, and Woodstock, and B. R. Wise of Queen's College, treasurer of the Palmerston Club and with Cook one of the younger recruits to Toynbee's society, in Osney.[96] Toward the end of March Toynbee and Cook took part in a large Liberal rally in Woodstock that was more against Churchill than in support of the local Liberal candidate, William Hall. Rather than deal with local issues Toynbee and Cook chose to speak on national party politics. According to the *Chronicle,* "Mr. Toynbee entered into an exposition of the difference between Liberal and Conservative principles, and said that the Liberals, in giving to the people equal rights, and in trying to remove all class distinctions and to break down the barriers which separated the different classes of the community, endeavoured to unite the people, while the Conservatives, by privilege and class distinction, were doing that which tended to bring about an entirely opposite state of things. (Applause)."[97]

At Kidlington, Cook came somewhat closer to addressing the immediate problems of rural Oxfordshire, but, like Toynbee, he chose a national angle. Cook blamed the Tory government's foreign policy for the agricultural depression, a convenient argument in a campaign in which foreign affairs overshadowed social policy. He argued that the constant anticipation of war fostered by the Tories unsettled trade and deterred capital from investing in land as much as war itself. In addition, the atmosphere of uncertainty had held back the capital investment required for land improvement. The way out of the agricultural depression was not through the reversal of the policy of free trade but in the creation of a favorable environment for capital investment in land.

Toynbee's speech seems to have made little impression one way or another. Cook, on the other hand, struck closer to home to the extent that his speech provoked a scathing response from Churchill. Churchill ridiculed Cook's effort to teach Kidlington's farmers their business, an attempt he described as trying to teach their grandmothers to suck eggs.[98] Churchill won the seat by 512 votes to 452 compared to 569 to 165 in 1874 when he ran against George C. Brodrick (elected early in 1881 Warden of Merton College). Harcourt won his Oxford City seat with a 112-vote majority and was soon given a seat in the cabinet as secretary of state for the Home Office.[99] Consequently his Tory rival, Alexander W. Hall, issued a writ for a by-election, invoking the seldom-used Queen Anne statute concerning the seat of an MP who joined a cabinet.[100]

Another consequence of the campaign was action taken by the proctors to bar undergraduates from taking an active part in local politics. It was argued that, while their interest in such matters could not be objected to, it was not the reason for their being at Oxford.[101] Early in May 1880 the vice chancellor and proctors issued a notice reminding all bachelors of arts and undergraduate members of the university that it was unlawful for them to interfere in any way in the election of members of Parliament for the City of Oxford. However, it was pointed out that this did not apply to those who were on the city's register of voters, nor did it seem to apply to elections to the City Council.

Harcourt lost the May by-election to Hall by fifty-four votes.[102] This, according to the *Chronicle,* was accomplished with the active help of Tory undergraduates, some of whom canvassed their trades-men using their custom for leverage, and all of whom ignored the vice chancellor's notice.[103] They had joined ranks with a number of clergymen incensed by Gladstone's appointment of Lord Ripon, a Roman Catholic, to the Governor-Generalship of India. Rather than accept this setback, as the local Liberal Association seemed in-clined to do,[104] T. H. Green and five other Liberals (including G. Rolleston, Linacre Professor of Physiology) signed in June 1880 a petition filed in the Court of Common Pleas complaining against the legality of the return of Hall "on the ground of bribery, treating, intimidation, personation and the employment of an excessive num-ber of voters as clerks and messengers" in his brewery.[105] Hall was eventually deprived of his seat and the city was disenfranchised for seven years. A commission of inquiry revealed widespread corrup-tion and illegal practices on both sides; hence the reluctance of the local Liberal Association to support the petition.

The commission's report, published in April 1881, did not confine itself to national politics but also shed some light on city elections. It found that "[National] Politics have for a considerable period largely influenced the municipal elections for the different wards, and al-though the expenditure at these elections has been far below that incurred at the parliamentary elections, it is certain that money has frequently been expended in the municipal contests in ways which . . . would not bear the light. On the other hand, some of these elections have been carried on without any excessive or corrupt expenditure."[106] It was the expressed view of John Culcutt, Con-servative councilman for Oxford's North Ward (corepresented by T. H. Green), that "so far as he knew, there never was in Oxford a municipal contest which was conducted without corruption. Money is spent in the same way as at a parliamentary election, but on a smaller scale." Although the *Chronicle* dismissed Culcutt's al-legations as absurd, it admitted that it was only in the case of the North Ward that it could be maintained that perhaps "to some slight extent money may have been spent to influence votes."[107]

5. The Industrial Revolution

During the first months of 1881 Toynbee addressed audiences in Newcastle-upon-Tyne, Chelsea, Bradford, and Bolton on "Industry and Democracy."[1] Up to and including "Industry and Democracy," Toynbee could hardly have been considered a historian. Having abandoned his essay on the history of economic theories he was yet to embark upon a coherent and comprehensive research program. His public addresses were mainly commentary on current affairs in which references to various recent works and developments were supplemented by some research. The research, on the whole, appears to have consisted mainly of facts collected at random, and used in order to substantiate Toynbee's interpretation of recent trends. "Industry and Democracy" could be described as an attempt to use Henry Crompton's *Industrial Conciliation* (1876) as proof of some of Toynbee's arguments concerning the nature of progress. At the same time it may be argued that Crompton's work provided Toynbee with the conceptual outline of his Industrial Revolution lectures as well as some of their basic terminology and concepts.

It is not clear when Toynbee came across Crompton's *Industrial Conciliation*.[2] Some of Crompton's statements closely resemble the positions Toynbee adopted in his earlier addresses, most notably Crompton's view on the nature of the study of current social phenomena. He argued that moral and economic laws could not be separated while the use of both must be undertaken with caution.

"Not only must the economical and moral be combined, but they must be rightly combined, or error and failure will surely follow."[3] The method that would ensure the right combination was practically identical with Toynbee's methodological position. "Business facts and economical facts have to be determined irrespective of other considerations. But the moment we step from dealing intellectually with facts to applying them practically to conduct, our economical conclusions must be combined with social and moral considerations."[4] It is not unlikely that, as with other books that had a strong influence on him, Toynbee picked out of Crompton's work different things at different times. In reading it he may very well have applied his old reading method of going through it "pretty fast at first," thereby gaining a general notion of its contents and then returning to it, possibly at a later date, for a more careful examination of Crompton's evidence and views.[5] It seems reasonable to assume that Crompton's Comtist and organic view of social progress, added to Cliffe Leslie's similar position,[6] may have been responsible for some of Toynbee's earlier notions concerning the nature of modern political economy.

In stating the Comtist view of the study of society Crompton argued that industrial developments should be studied in relation to their wider social context. "The industrial movement is not separate or distinct from the other parts of the human progress. Industry is but one aspect of social life, and cannot be separated from other aspects, intellectual, moral or political."[7] This, Crompton argued, was true not only of current social phenomena. If one was to understand the course of progress the same approach must be given a historical perspective that would empirically reveal the evolutionary laws of industrial and social progress.[8] This was not suggested as a purely hypothetical approach. Crompton felt confident that in the matter of industrial conciliation he possessed a historical understanding of its development and its place in the general course of progress. "We may well look back to the beginning of this long struggle by labour to achieve freedom, and compare the condition of the working classes in the past to that of the workmen in the best modern employment, where each man's freedom is assured, and the fullest respect paid to the worth and dignity of labour. Such a contrast is no less than that between the slave and the citizen. The independence of the working classes does not constitute the industrial progress, but it is a prime factor in that progress."[9]

Crompton found that there had taken place "a great intellectual and moral progress among employers and employed."[10] This progress had resulted in a substantial diminution in the intensity and recklessness of industrial disputes and it, in turn, was a direct result of industrial changes. The challenge for the future was to continue the process: "The constant tendency throughout the long past, dating from the period when slavery or serfdom was the mode of industrial rule, has been for employers and employed to become more distinct, more different, and more unlike. . . . The past has been remarkable for the increase of actual force—the force of combined numbers on the one hand, of concentrated wealth on the other. The problem of the future is therefore a double one: that of combining the two and regulating their action."[11]

Improved mobility of labor, greater organization of workers and of employers, increasing imbalance in the distribution of wealth, and greater equality in wage negotiations were the distinguishing features of industrial change. They all found their expression in the operation of boards of conciliation whose success provided the clue for the shape of things to come both materially and morally. Toynbee adopted Crompton's argument, extracted it from his detailed discussion of the operation of boards of conciliation, and developed it into the theme of an address concerning the nature of industrial progress.

In retrospect the most significant addition Toynbee made to Crompton's argument was his introduction of the term, "industrial revolution," to describe the nature of the changes in English society wrought by industrialization. The conjunction of revolution and industry was not exclusively Toynbee's invention. It had been used in France as early as 1806 in order to describe technological changes in the woollen industry.[12] The phrase originated in a comparison with the French Revolution and while it is most unlikely that Toynbee was aware of its early usage its relation to the French Revolution is of considerable significance.

At the time, the term "revolution" whenever used by historians had predominantly political connotations. Macaulay in the introduction to his *History* had referred to "the revolutions which have taken place in dress, furniture, repasts, and public amusements,"[13] but *the* Revolution was the Glorious Revolution—a political event denoting a new stage in the linear course of progress rather than the completion of a cycle as the term was used in the seventeenth century (e.g., in describing the Restoration of 1660). During the nineteenth century, the term had been mainly used by historians to describe the

French Revolution and the events of 1848 which were typified as political events. In a three-part article published in 1870 J. R. Seeley described what he called, "The English Revolution of the Nineteenth Century," as the change in public opinion that had forced the abolition of monopoly.[14] The legislative process had begun with Wellington's ministry conceding to the demand for Catholic emancipation in order to avoid a civil war. Despite this somewhat dramatic interpretation Seeley, not unlike Macaulay, equated revolution with reform. Accordingly, Seeley also described the English revolution of the nineteenth century as "the third Reformation," a stage in a process of "perpetual change and unintermitted improvement." The revolution was "limited in its range, leaving entirely untouched the foundations and framework of the Constitution." The process was perpetuated by the growing power of public opinion. Its "absolute sovereignty" had transformed the process of legislation: "Laws now are like commodities; the supply of them is regulated by demand."

In Seeley's view the nineteenth century had been witnessing a radical change in England's political structure. Political power was gradually being appropriated by public opinion. He did not explain how public opinion identified the public's interests or how it had come to realize the power it held over government, but he readily admitted that the course of future reform depended on the education of public opinion. In his view the most obvious reforms already had been accomplished. More advanced reform required a measure of political awareness that could be developed through political education. In terms of current politics Seeley implied that the political future of England lay with the Liberals. They were to become "a vast reforming party," embodying the public's growing consciousness of its interests and powers. Liberalism and reform had effected a major conceptual change. It had "made us change our conception of a state as an unchanging thing, which has only to be watched and protected from the impact of foreign bodies for a conception of it as a growing and developing thing perpetually shifting, advancing, and putting forth new organs, and requiring therefore to be studied with method, to be helped and directed in its changes with boldness and expertness, and capable of being indefinitely developed and improved by genius." Seeley, however, did not provide an account of the historical process that had wrought this change.

In describing some of the features of this new English revolution Seeley referred to the undoing of economic monopoly: the abolition of the East India Company, the introduction of free trade, and the abrogation of state intervention in economic matters. This economic aspect of the revolution consisted mainly of the state's abdication of its right to apply its authority, and in particular its taxing power, in order to favor particular industries.

The identification of free trade and free competition with material progress, described as an "industrial revolution," had appeared in the works of some English economists. J. S. Mill, in describing the benefits of international trade, explained how it might affect a society in "an early stage of industrial advancement."

A people may be in a quiescent, indolent, uncultivated state, with all their tastes either fully satisfied or entirely undeveloped, and they may fail to put forth the whole of their productive energies for want of any sufficient objects of desire. The opening of a foreign trade, by making them acquainted with new objects, or tempting them by the easier acquisition of things which they had not previously thought attainable, sometimes work a complete industrial revolution [in later editions, replaced by "a sort of industrial revolution"] in a country whose resources were previously undeveloped for want of energy and ambition in the people.[15]

The term was used in a much more concrete way in order to describe a specific phase in English economic development by William Stanley Jevons in *The Coal Question*. Jevons referred to the second half of the eighteenth century as "a period of commercial revolution," a term he professes to have taken from M. N. Brivionne's *De l'Industrie en Belgique* (1839).[16] Later in the book he refers to the same period as having witnessed an "industrial revolution."[17] Whatever the term, the characteristics of these "revolutions" were identical in detail.

In the second half of the last century our population, previously stationary, began to grow at a growing rate. When we consider that at this period the engine was coming into use, that Arkwright's cotton machinery was invented, that the smelting of iron with coal was immensely increasing the abundance of valuable metal we cannot hesitate to connect these events as cause and effect. It was a period of commercial revolution. It was then we began that development of our inventions and our coal resources which is still going on. . . . Instead of learners we became teachers; instead of exporters of raw materials we became importers; instead of importers of manufactured articles we became exporters. What we had exported we began by degrees to import; and what we had imported we began to export.[18]

Both Mill and Jevons linked the period of rapid industrialization with free trade.[19] There is also an indication in Mill that trade may provide the initial impetus for industrialization. Another characteristic is the mechanization of industry. The reference to the technological changes of the late eighteenth century as revolutionary in nature seems to have been a relatively common association.[20] A somewhat obscure work, *The Silent Revolution: or the Future Effects of Steam and Electricity upon the Condition of Mankind* (1852) by M. A. Garvey, a London barrister, suggested a causal connection between technological innovations and the effectiveness of a laissez-faire policy. Garvey argued that the "free concourse of individual minds is the origin and mainspring of all social improvements."[21]

England had, since Henry VIII, been undergoing a gradual process by which communications between individuals had been made more free as well as technically easier. But it was the use of steam for locomotion and electricity for communication (by telegraph) that was found to transform not only England but the world. Freedom of trade and of association could now, thanks to the technological innovations, realize its full beneficial potential. Internally, "it will in time destroy the exclusiveness of classes, parties, and professions."[22] Externally, the "natural resources of all lands will be developed by a universal system of communication, and important additions made to social happiness."[23] Free trade would result in a "blending of the interests of mankind" and a "multiplied relations and dependencies," heralding a final end to war and the reign of universal peace and happiness.

A more significant link between the economic and political connotations of the word revolution when used to describe recent English history was provided by the socialists. The term had been used by J. A. Blanqui in *Histoire de l'economie politique* (1837), with an emphasis on technological innovations. It was repeated by Marx in *Das Kapital* with similar connotations.[24] Friedrich Engels, in the introduction to *The Condition of the Working Class in England* (1845), wrote, "The history of the proletariat in England begins with the second half of the last century, with the invention of the steam-engine and of machinery for working cotton. These inventions gave rise, as is well known, to an industrial revolution, a revolution which altered the whole civil society."[25] At the same time, Engels pointed out that beyond the obvious link between contemporary social and industrial conditions and the technological inventions of the previous century, "we have not, here and now, to deal with the history of this revolution, nor with its vast importance for the present and the future. Such a delineation must be reserved for a future, more comprehensive work."

It was clear that Engels did not mean to confine the term to technological change. The industrial revolution transformed society and could therefore be compared in its effects to other revolutions. "The industrial revolution is of the same importance for England as the political revolution for France and philosophical revolution for Germany; and the difference between England in 1760 and in 1844 is at least as great as that between France under the ancien régime and during the revolution of July."[26] Engels did not actually equate the industrial revolution with a political revolution. He argued, as would Marx, that it had created the conditions for a political revolution through the creation of the proletariat. Industrialization made the realization of capitalism technically possible with the result that, within the foreseeable future, class conflicts would "break out into a Revolution in comparison with which the French Revolution, and the year 1794, will prove to have been child's play."[27]

By 1880 the term industrial revolution had already gained some currency as a characterization of the period of radical structural change in the English economy that had occurred during the second half of the eighteenth century. Mill and Jevons had associated the process with two related developments: the ascent of the policy of free trade and technological innovations (which were also part of the socialists' image of the industrial change). It is not clear whether they could be understood to imply a causal relation as well (e.g., market pressures caused by free trade stimulating the development of new machines in order to supply increasing demand that could not be provided for by traditional industry). Or, as may have been suggested by Garvey, the developments should be viewed as part of a historical process that had led to the gradual and continuous improvement of internal means of communications resulting in technological innovations that made an international policy of laissez-faire possible. In any case, it is clear that the industrial change was related to the transformation of both the English economy and English society. The transformation of society was strongly emphasized by the socialists, who linked it with an anticipated political change that would complete a process that had begun with the advent of capitalism (which in turn had replaced medieval feudalism). Although Marx could not be said to have advocated unhurried linear progress, his view of the place of industrial changes in the history of England was conceptually close to the Comtists'; it was apparent to him that radical economic and social change could not but lead to political change. The various processes could not be isolated and still retain their significance as part of a more comprehensive change.

Toynbee's innovation was in adapting the wide-angled socialist concept to the liberal concept of progress, making a liberal-historical study of the period of industrialization possible without losing the socialists' wide perspective. He did this through a modification of Macaulay's argument concerning the Glorious Revolution. Rather than describe the Revolution of 1688 as an isolated event, Macaulay argued that "the history of England is emphatically the history of progress. It is the history of a constant movement of the public mind, of a constant change in the institutions of a great society."[28] The process preceded the Glorious Revolution and has continued since. The whole of English history could be described as "the successive stages of one great revolution. . . . When examined in small separate portions, it may with more propriety be called a history of actions and reaction," but seen from the perspective of centuries one could not fail to detect the general course along which society was proceeding.[29] Thus industrialization and its consequent social and economic changes could be described in terms of "action and reaction," but if the historian succeeded in keeping in mind the general perspective he could also provide it with a meaning in terms of the overall course of English history. In following Macaulay Toynbee argued that in the same way in which the events of 1688 constituted an English revolution, the process of industrialization could be defined as a revolution.

According to Toynbee, technological change and industrialization did not prepare the ground for the great political upheaval confidently anticipated by the continental socialists. A change in the distribution of power and wealth was taking place as an integral part of what he called the industrial revolution. The revolution was underway, and it was a typically English revolution, that is, gradual and relatively peaceful rather than sudden and violent. It was to be contrasted with the French Revolution. Although both aimed at establishing democracy by replacing all previous forms of political, social, and economic order, they were fundamentally different. Hence the term revolution used to describe both events denoted their ends rather than the internal workings of the events themselves.

Finally, it is not clear whether and to what extent Toynbee had been aware of the previous usage of the term "industrial revolution," although it seems safe to assume that he knew of at least some of the earlier citations. He had studied J. S. Mill's work in considerable detail and he referred a number of times to Jevons's *The Coal Question*. He did not refer in his lectures to Engels, but he seems to have read at least parts of Marx's *Das Kapital* in its French translation. Apparently it was generally assumed that he was at least conscious of Marx's use of the term. C. R. Fay tells us, "Ask an Oxford student who is being viva'd in Modern Greats, 'Who invented the term Industrial Revolution?' and he will reply smartly, 'Arnold Toynbee, who got it from Marx.' "[30]

Toynbee may have aimed in his address at the diffusion of the term revolution as used by radical socialists by constantly using revolution to describe industrial change—thirteen times in the address's final form. He did not dwell upon the misery of the new industrial proletariat, although he fully acknowledged its existence. In the address his main target was not the revolutionary socialists who, like himself, hoped for a change in the distribution of power and wealth, but the revisionists and the romantics represented by Carlyle who called for a return to the old order of things. Although critical of the results of industrialization, they could not be bunched with revolutionary socialists such as Engels and Marx. Engels had argued that the pre-industrial English agricultural laborer had lived comfortably in a state of "silent vegetation." History was not reversible and nostalgia was not factually justified. In Toynbee's view the socialists may have misunderstood the nature and course of English progress, but they, at least, did not wish to set the clock back.

Toynbee identified a revolution in three areas: agriculture, cotton, and iron. He developed his argument from a brief description of their state at around 1760. His primary sources were Adam Smith's *Wealth of Nations*, which he had studied for his degree, and some eighteenth- and early nineteenth-century accounts of rural life, such as William Cobbett's. He described pre-industrial England as a simple economic system with limited internal and external trade, enjoying relative stability. Widespread depressions of trade and overproduction were unheard of. At its core the system was based on a close mutual dependence of laborers and employers, often working side by side under identical conditions. Consequently, the class differences between employers and employed were often virtually unnoticeable. Mobility of labor was practically unknown. Industry was regulated by custom, for example, through guilds, and by laws such as the Poor Law and combination laws. In describing these laws Toynbee adopted Lujo Brentano's interpretation. The laws were the legal manifestation of the concentration of political and economic power in the hands of a small class. "Except as a member of a mob, the labourer had not a shred of political influence. The power of making laws was concentrated in the hands of the land-owners, the great merchant princes, and a small knot of capitalist-manufacturers who wielded that power."[31] Political power and economic power were linked. Progress therefore would mean a change in the distribution of both, a change that could be demonstrated by a change in industrial relations between employer and worker, and in the legislature through a redefinition of the ends of legislation and the class interests it was to promote.

According to Toynbee, the new industrial age had been heralded by *The Wealth of Nations* and the steam engine, a combination of free-trade principles and the new technology. The principles of the new order were "first, an assertion of the right of the workman to legal equality and independence; second, an assertion that industrial freedom is essential to the material prosperity of the people."[32] But, as he had argued in his unfinished essay on Ricardo, legal equality did not necessarily entail actual equality in wage negotiations. The English economy enjoyed for over a period of seventy years swift and continuous expansion, but with change came new kinds of hardships. The expansion of internal and external trade resulted in occasional trade depressions caused by overproduction. The old bonds between employers and workers were severed, and, although more wealth was being produced, its distribution became increasingly uneven. Toynbee attributed this inequality in distribution to three major causes: retrogressive laws (like the old Poor Law and the Corn Laws), the physically exhausting conditions produced by the new industrial technology, and the redundancy of skills inevitable in periods of technological transition. These he contrasted with Carlyle's reasons for the people's sufferings: the want of permanency in employment and the reduction of all social relations to a cash basis. Carlyle's solution was the return to the older form of industrial organization which guaranteed permanency of employment and which was based on a paternalistic relationship between employer and worker (an ideal defined by the radicals as Toryism).

Toynbee argued that the refutation of Carlyle was not merely a theoretical matter. In his view the problems of industrialization were being resolved by popular pressure for democratization, the advent of public opinion Seeley had identified as the prime mover of the new English revolution. Admittedly the process had been delayed by the repercussions of the French Revolution, but nevertheless since then many of the factors that perpetuated the unequal distribution of wealth had been removed. The Corn Laws, the old Poor Law, and the Combination Laws had been repealed, the workers had been awarded the franchise and had been allowed to form trade unions. "The workman had at last reached the summit of the long ascent from the position of a serf, and stood by the side of his master as the full citizen of a free state."[33]

A new state of equality was being accomplished by a process in which society moved further away from the old state of equality of conditions advocated by Carlyle. With industrialization workers and employers grew increasingly apart. Since political democracy was powerless to directly affect industrial conditions, workers were forced to unionize. By association and action through representation the last remnants of the old personal ties between employer and worker were eradicated. Action through trade unions, in which class interests replaced individual interests, and corporate action superseded individual action, was in itself a sign of progress. Toynbee could therefore argue that the breakup of the old employer-worker ties was necessary in order to enable the eventual reunification of society on a basis of a new equality. The gulf between employer and worker resulted, at first, in class hatred. But the organization of workers in unions introduced equality into wage negotiations thereby rebridging the gulf. Conciliation boards, in which the compatibility of class interests was recognized, were made possible and class struggle was reduced to "business bargains."[34] The old system was never to return, and the misery inevitable in a period of transition was gradually being mitigated. There would follow a new unity. "If history teaches us that separation is necessary, it also teaches us that permanent separation is impossible. The law of progress is that men separate— but they separate in order to unite. The old union vanishes, but a new union springs up in its place. The old union founded on the dependence of the workman disappears—a new union arises based on the workman's independence. . . . workman and employer parted as protector and dependent to unite as equal citizens of a free state."[35]

As elsewhere Toynbee constructed his argument so as to culminate in a moral conclusion. He applied to morals the same historical rules that applied to other aspects of human activity. Change in society entailed a change in its morals. The new age therefore required "moral ideas appropriate not to the feudal, but to the citizen stage,"[36] which would help society to overcome class antagonism. The new moral creed was the gospel of duty, but, rather than present it as his own belief or attribute it to T. H. Green's philosophy, Toynbee chose to ascribe it to Mazzini, "the true teacher of our age." Mazzini's criticism of Carlyle offered a convenient contrast in an address that dealt mainly with the refutation of Carlyle.

An English translation of Mazzini's essays, *On the Duties of Man,* had been published in 1875 and had enjoyed a certain vogue. Although Toynbee read him after having formed most of his social and philosophical views, he nevertheless found the experience of encountering very similar views expressed in a relatively simple and straightforward language extremely gratifying. In one of the versions of "Industry and Democracy," he proclaimed *The Duties of Man* as "the greatest book written in this century of man's relations to man."[37]

However, Mazzini cannot be described as a major influence on Toynbee comparable, say, to T. H. Green. The main message Toynbee attributed to Mazzini was that now that the people had been given rights it was appropriate to discuss their duties. He did not choose to elaborate on Mazzini's views beyond this statement, perhaps indicating that his use of Mazzini as an authority may well have been a matter of convenience. Mazzini was certainly more accessible than Green to the general public.

Toynbee concluded his address by returning to Crompton's main theme. Conciliation as an expression of economic and moral change would become a fixed feature of industrial society. The future would most likely witness the boards of conciliation developing into "permanent councils of employers and workmen, which,—thrusting into the background, but not superseding Trades' Unions and Masters' Associations—for these must long remain as weapons in case of a last appeal to force, should in the light of the principles of social and industrial science deal with those great problems of the fluctuations of wages, of over production and the regulation of trade, which workmen and employers together alone can settle."[38] Thus boards of conciliation came to replace trade unions in Toynbee's vision of the future of industrial society by providing a solution to economic fluctuations by means of regulation through class cooperation. Further, Toynbee did not confine his vision to the national community. In a variant of the Manchester school's internationalism, with the possible intention of presenting a symmetrical alternative to socialism, he argued that the future of industrial society would witness an international equality of culture. "We are participators in the life of mankind and joint-heirs of the world's inheritance."[39]

Toynbee found his audience's reaction to his address extremely encouraging. After the Newcastle-upon-Tyne engagement he wrote to Grey, "Everything at Newcastle was delightful. My host was delightful—my audience delightful, and I got the sweetest praise I ever had in my life, for working men got up and said I understood them and their position, and what could I want more? . . . I shall endeavour with all my might to keep true to the ideal with which I have tried to begin—devotion to God's service."[40] After delivering the same address at Bradford a member of the audience expressed his hope that "Mr. Toynbee would come amongst us oftener."[41] He again wrote to Grey, "The enthusiasm was quite moving, and I believe both employers and workmen were convinced of the justice of my claim to speak with impartiality."[42]

Exhilarated by the response to his message Toynbee asked Grey's help to arrange more meetings in other towns. Convinced of the vital importance of his "gospel," Toynbee offered to cover his own expenses wherever financial considerations might preclude an engagement. He felt that his readiness to forego remuneration would help to place his motives above any suspicion, thereby contributing to his credibility as an objective observer.

Toynbee's various addresses on economic and social subjects were all set within the same moral framework, and all led to similar conclusions concerning the moral aspects of future industrial society. In the letter in which he asked for Grey's help in organizing lectures in areas in which he felt they were most needed (specifically Lancashire), he stated that "in distant years when I have matured my thoughts I shall speak on religion—the subject I care for more than any other." By then religion and church reform were becoming for Toynbee two distinctly different matters. The CRU was preoccupied with the chances of various legislative measures. Toynbee, on the other hand, was becoming increasingly certain that they were on the wrong track, a conviction that may have been strengthened by the response to his lectures.

During the spring of 1881 the CRU had been preparing for a new effort to present its case at the forthcoming Church Congress at Newcastle, with the hope of overcoming some of the internal resistance to reform. Toynbee, who was one of the CRU's prospective speakers, decided after some deliberation to withdraw from CRU activity on the national, as opposed to the local, level. In a letter to Barnett he disclosed some of his misgivings.

The next time I speak on Religion I mean to make perfectly clear my negative position—disbelief in Divinity of Christ, in miracles, in the supernatural, in the ordinary idea of God. I don't see how I can say these things in your presence without doing harm to your cause. . . . This is my opinion, you perhaps think that it is unnecessary to dwell on the negative side at all, and that it is possible to say all that ought to be said without producing the wrong impression. I can't agree,—I have come to very decided conclusions on this point. Personally even if the occasion were a fit one for saying what I thought I should prefer to wait for yet a little while. . . . We both agree that a religious change is necessary; we differ perhaps as to how and in what manner of persons it can be brought about.[43]

The likely reaction to Toynbee's views within the CRU might be gauged from a letter by W. H. Fremantle to Grey, in which he was informed that "Davies has a keen sense of danger that religious men may cease to respect us and our aims if we seem to hold less to Christian dogmas."[44]

Toynbee clearly realized the likely repercussions of a public statement of his views. In explaining his decision not to address the Church Congress he wrote to Grey:

I feel more and more that the political part of the Movement must fall into your hands and those of other practical politicians, whilst I must devote myself to the religious side. The two aspects of the question will probably get separated pretty quickly, and I have no doubt that it will be best for both causes if their advocates act in independence. . . . It will be no small advantage to me in carrying out my work in the future, to be able to start entirely free of any such connections as is implied in the position of a regular actor in the proceedings of a Congress. . . . And in addition to this, whilst still holding my original opinions as to the Reform of the Church, I feel less and less in harmony with the beliefs of even the most advanced adherents of the Church in its present state, and therefore more and more unwilling to identify myself with them on religious questions, though still willing to act with them from the political side.[45]

Following the Congress he wrote again to Grey:

I'm not sure that I shouldn't have done more harm than good if I had come. It seems to me that you have organised the society admirably as a body with definite practical aims, and that vague and injudicious people like myself should only damage you at a meeting of this kind. . . . what I can do . . . is try and appeal to people on the religious side. I don't feel that I have any aptitude for expounding and enforcing the views of our society from the political side, and the side of religious organisation. If I had carried out my original idea and spoken at Newcastle I should probably have alienated all your supporters there. The whole thing presents itself to me in a very radical light (religious and political) and I am sure that the majority of your adherents would not agree with me.[46]

Toynbee had not been imagining things. Many if not most of the veteran reform campaigners felt that they should concentrate their efforts on legislative action. Questions of general religious doctrine only confused the issue and impeded their prospects of influencing public opinion. In a letter to Phelps concerning the organization of a CRU meeting at Oriel, Grey stated that he was "strongly opposed to our mixing up questions of organisation reform with questions of Doctrine." He was against "hampering our movement in favour of Church Organisation Reform, with questions so vague and alarming as those relating to the Doctrinal basis of the National Church." He came to believe that as a matter of policy "at all public meetings of the Church Reform Union we should confine ourselves to emphasizing the fact that the Rights of the People in the Nat[ional] Church are witheld from them, [and] that the interests of the country require that their rights should be restored to them."[47]

If Toynbee still had any doubts about the unease his views created within the CRU or about the manner in which he should work for church reform, these were dispelled in a meeting he and Gell had with George Joachim Goschen, then MP for Ripon. Goschen, who had been cautiously supporting Grey's legislative efforts on behalf of the CRU, managed to reassure Gell and Toynbee *"sine dubio that he has the cause of the Union at heart."*[48] However, the meeting began with Goschen "expressing his nervousness as to our implied theological attitude. Toynbee's views (as reported to him) had frightened him." Toynbee came away from the meeting determined to prevent his further damaging the CRU. In a letter to Grey he wrote,

I am more convinced than ever, after our conversation with Goschen, that the extreme left had better place the conduct of the movement in the hands of the Parliamentary section of the society, and either withdraw from all active participation in the Church Reform Union, or devote what energies they can give to a faithful advocacy of the programme of reorganization with a view to bring the Church into closer relation with the mass of the people.

The extreme party would then be free to say what they think right without fear of compromising the responsible leaders of the movement, and the responsible leaders of the movement would be no longer embarrassed by the opinions of men who can do nothing but harm to the cause—as interpreted by you and the parliamentary section. And it is my deliberate opinion, reached after much reflection, that this separation is the wisest thing for both groups. What I hoped for from the movement will I believe still come, but it will come as a result not of one agitation but two—and these agitations will necessarily be directed by different sets of persons who whilst I believe, having the same ultimate aim, will work on different lines for a different immediate purpose.[49]

Toynbee's decision was not accompanied by a crisis of faith. On the contrary, in the afterglow of the reception given to his "Industry and Democracy" address he felt more confident than ever that change, whether economic or moral, could be best accomplished through a direct appeal to the people.

Toynbee did not lose interest in the CRU. During the autumn of 1881, after Gell had obtained a job with the publishing firm of Cassell and Galpin, he showed some concern over the choice of a replacement as secretary of the CRU.[50] He also took some part in organizing a CRU conference at Merton College, held on 7 December 1881.[51] However, he was determined to pursue his own course of action with the hope of being able eventually to combine the social and the religious messages. In a letter to Seeley he explained in some detail his view of the ideal relation between the two aspects of future progress as expressed in his own work: "I do really believe in the existence of personal religion as distinct from social religion; . . . By social religion I mean a passionate devotion to our fellow man, to the higher interests of civilization; by personal religion I mean the effect of such a devotion, [and] of other pursuits, [and] of our general conceptions as to the world we live in, on the inner life. . . . The ideal I have had before me has been the close union of these two aspects of religion."[52] Hence his declaration to Grey of his intention in his future work "to undo that part of Bradlaugh's work which has been badly done, and to carry on and complete in ways not foreseen by him that part of his work which has been well done."[53]

Despite Toynbee's confidence in his choice of direction and in the substance of his message, he managed to remain critical of the academic aspect of his argument. Having adopted a Comtian view of the scope of economic inquiries,[54] as his references to the "law of progress" seem to indicate, he became concerned with the scope and depth of his own inquiries. Following his lectures in the north he set out to prepare a version of "Industry and Democracy" for publication but soon found its scholarly and literary standard unsatisfactory. Uncertain of how he should proceed he turned to Seeley for advice.

As a speech it was successful, but I am afraid that when read through it is not very effective. In fact it seems to me wanting in literary skill, pretentious and rhetorical; and I am inclined to put it aside altogether instead of printing it as I at one time thought of doing. My only object in printing it would have been to further the cause on which you have so much insisted—the cause of non-partisan politics. It seemed to me that it might perhaps suggest to other men of my age the adoption of a similar course. But I don't feel satisfied with the address now I have written it out.[55]

Whatever Seeley's advice, Toynbee decided not to publish "Industry and Democracy." Instead he concentrated on two areas in which he felt his work to have been unsatisfactory. With the help of some of the members of his society he began to develop a more comprehensive and detailed position on various prospective reforms. At the same time he began work on a more elaborate historical survey of the course of progress since industrialization following the general lines laid down in "Industry and Democracy." By the autumn of 1881 Toynbee was planning a new round of popular lectures. He had in mind two possible topics: radical social policy and free trade, the latter still a relatively controversial issue.[56] However, Toynbee was inclined to believe that the fair trade agitation had been slackening. Furthermore, he confessed to Grey, "I myself am rather weary of exposing Protectionist fallacies and passing panegyrics on Free Trade."[57] His weariness of the subject may have contained an element of disenchantment with free trade as a sufficient or even appropriate solution to the problems he had begun to study.[58] He decided therefore to concentrate on a presentation of radical-liberal social policy as an alternative to socialism, a choice of which Grey approved.

In describing his decision to Grey, Toynbee admitted the complexity of the task. A refutation of Carlyle and the "golden age" theory was significantly different from offering the working class a comprehensive alternative to socialism that would also be acceptable to the rest of society. It was not sufficient to profess faith in the continuity of progress or to confine one's observations to the significance of current trends. Since Toynbee believed in a prevailing harmony of interests that transcended class differences, in his own scientific objectivity and in the power of common sense, a comprehensive and generally acceptable reform program did not seem impossible. The need to deal with what he regarded as the apparent contradictory nature of the solutions offered by each class is evident in his letter to Grey. Toynbee wrote to reassure Grey that his advocacy of radical social reform through limited state action, which he believed was an approach acceptable to the working class, did not indicate his abandonment of middle-class liberal principles.

Don't imagine that I am likely to deal with the subject in such a way as to demoralize my hearers by vain hopes of a millenium to be attained by means of state help. The main argument of my address will be an attempt to show in very strong relief the absolute necessity of self-help and independence. I shall try to explain in detail the huge difference between the limited state help advocated by radicals and the unbounded tasks which the socialists propose of individual self-reliance. It is just that misconception which I wish to guard against. I intend to show what radical principles are *not* by a review of the old Poor Law and the ideas on which it was based.[59]

Favorable popular response was essential. Without it much of Toynbee's work would have been pointless. A failure to communicate with a large audience of all classes might indicate that either the working class was not responsive to the commonsense approach or that the gulf between the classes had become unbridgeable. This might be interpreted as the result of the wrong choice of means. But, since the choice of means—the creation of popular support for reform to precede a legislative initiative—was an essential part of Toynbee's concept of progress, his failure to influence workers to act in harmony with their middle-class neighbors and vice versa would indicate the failure of the principle. Thus addressing sympathetic northern crowds provided Toynbee with a vital reassurance. After one such meeting, which was followed by an encouraging talk with R. Spence-Watson, who had organized his lecture at Newcastle, Toynbee wrote to him, "The conversation I had with you gave me more hope than ever of the political future. South of the Trent . . . political pessimists swarm and I shall try whenever they are too much for me to escape North and renew my hope."[60]

Toynbee opened his address, "Are Radicals Socialists?," in Newcastle with some further comments on the "student" theme.[61] He acknowledged his lack of political experience and his ignorance of the intricacies of politics. Nevertheless he felt confident that "however deficient in many respects he may be, a student who is not devoid of the interest and passion of a citizen, ought to be able to contribute something towards the solution of such a question as I propose."[62] In the past Toynbee had presented the student as an unbiased bystander whose observations could be regarded as an objective account of reality. This position was now discarded. Toynbee intended to discuss party policy and, in view of his political commitment, the claim of objectivity could, at best, have only a very limited application.

"Are Radicals Socialists?" constituted an attempt to take a clear stand on the question of the principles of the Liberal party. His intention was to defend radicalism from its socialist critics by offering a clear statement of its principles. Beyond a clear commitment to the Liberal party his statement constituted also a commitment to one of the main camps within the party, a camp intent on inducing the party to adopt a clear radical program of reform.[63] Toynbee felt that the party's present state—a coalition of various camps each representing a limited interest—was harmful. "A great party which is uncertain as to its principles ceases to be a party, and becomes an aggregate of factions without vigour or coherence."[64] In his view radicalism was the core of liberalism. His intention was to present a clear statement of the original radical creed and the creeds that it opposed and to consider the possible modification of the original radicalism in view of circumstances, mainly the Irish Land Bill of 1881.

Toynbee dated the original radical creed from the 1840s. It could be reduced to three principles: justice, liberty, and self-help. Justice and liberty were to be guaranteed by the extension of suffrage to all classes. Self-help was to be promoted by the removal of all restrictions on trade. All forms of state intervention were regarded by the radicals with abhorrence, whereas their faith in the people's ability to help themselves was unshakable.

Toynbee discerned two classes of "old" radicals: the middle-class radicals who identified the Corn Laws as the root of all the evils from which society had been suffering and the working-class radicals, or Chartists, who considered the Corn Laws as merely one facet of a corrupt system that could only be abolished through democracy. The Chartists did not aim at anything beyond a democracy for, although they hoped to shake the middle classes from their complacency, they had no intention of depriving any class of its share in the government of the nation.

The original Chartists—Lovett, Heatherington, and Watson—all of whom had repudiated the use of violence, had been replaced by Feargus O'Conner and his followers who openly advocated the use of force. They, in turn, collaborated with the Tory socialists, although the latter disclaimed the association. The Tory socialists, or Tory Chartists, which included J. R. Stephens and Richard Oastler, insisted on the preservation of the old constitution. But, although they denied the people's right for a share in political power, they emphasized the duty of the holders of power to protect the poor and the weak. The poor had a right to a share in the nation's wealth regardless of any individual's merit or lack of it, a doctrine considered by Toynbee to have been "most pernicious."[65] The Tory socialists were the defenders of the old Poor Law which offered indiscriminate relief "and had completely demoralised the people," an institution that, in Toynbee's view, encouraged vice and idleness while discouraging honesty and thrift. Yet the same group, following the same principles, supported the Ten Hours Bill. It was, therefore,

ridiculous to argue, as the land nationalists did, that England's
workers had been consistently repressed by a conspiracy of the
aristocracy consisting mainly of landowners. Whenever the aristocracy's interests were not directly concerned, it had attempted "in a
rough and blind sort of way, to do justice to the people." Hence,
although it had been responsible for much suffering and injustice,
the Factory Acts passed by the aristocracy helped to avert a
revolution.[66]

Toynbee's main concern was to distinguish among the various
types of socialism. A demonstration of the multiplicity of socialist
creeds enabled him to contrast what he would label false and harmful socialism with true and salutary socialism. Proving that no single
group had a monopoly on socialism would serve to establish his claim
on the term. He aimed to show that radical liberalism embodied the
true socialist tradition. This was accomplished by never actually defining "socialism" beyond the vaguely implied assumption that it
could be applied to any policy concerned with the improvement of
the conditions of the poor. He therefore felt quite free to employ
the term at will; his eventual claim on the title lacked no credibility
among his contemporaries.[67] In discussing Stephens, Oastler, and
company, he wrote, "These men were sometimes called Tory Chartists, but they ought to have been called Tory Socialists for their
doctrine was Socialism in the most unmistakable form."[68] Hence
Toynbee accepted that a Tory policy of the state ensuring the welfare of the poor without allowing them a share in political power
was socialism. Elsewhere he referred to Owen as "the first great
English Socialist" and, accordingly, to the policy that "meant not
that the poor had a claim on the wealth of the rich, but voluntary
association with common property and equal division of wealth" as
socialism.

Toynbee concluded his historical survey by presenting the main
improvements in the conditions of the working class since the 1840s
as the work of the middle class, or philosophical radicals, including
Joseph Hume, Mill, Bright, and Cobden, who had acted in good
faith on behalf of the Chartists. They had pledged to help obtain
the vote for the working class in return for its help in repealing the
Corn Laws. And, although the Chartists seemed beaten at the time,
it may be said that much of the Charter had been accomplished.
The repeal of the Corn Laws and the constitution of free trade restored material progress. The repeal of the paper duties and the

stamp duty on newspapers allowed for the spread of knowledge among the lower classes. Once suffrage had been secured, trade unions were legalized and the conspiracy laws repealed. Through the endeavors of middle-class radicalism the relations between workers and employers had been completely transformed and were now closer to equality than ever before. It could therefore be argued that the middle-class radicals could be trusted to carry out the rest of the Charter that, according to Toynbee, entailed the assimilation of borough and county franchise, free trade in land, reform—and perhaps even the abolition—of the House of Lords, and, finally, universal suffrage.

From his historical survey Toynbee turned to consider current trends. First there was the question of those commonly known as socialists. Toynbee chose to rename them German socialists, thereby enabling him to distinguish them from English socialists. He regarded the socialist argument concerning the inevitability of a revolution as an essential component of their creed.[69] The German socialists argued that under the existing system a worker could not hope to raise his standard of living above the level of bare subsistence. Therefore, despite some diffusion of political power the inability of the workers to effect the distribution of wealth would inevitably lead them to revolt.

Toynbee's answer to the German socialists was a variation of his revolution argument. He maintained that, historically, slow and continuous progress had always modified conditions that had seemed to lead to imminent revolutions. The imbalance in the distribution of wealth had been considerably rectified through working-class self-help, evident from the amount of capital invested in savings banks, friendly societies, and cooperatives. If workingmen could save it obviously meant that they earned more than bare subsistence. The worker had trade unions that put him on equal footing with his employer when it came to wage negotiations. The state provided protection for the worker in the form of the new Poor Law and the Factory Acts. The changes that the German socialists thought could only be accomplished by a revolution had been gradually accomplished in England by continuous, peaceful progress.

Having dealt with the various socialist creeds Toynbee turned to the question of the application of socialism to contemporary radicalism. In the absence of an official or otherwise Liberal party program of reform Toynbee's argument was mainly a generalization based on the Irish Land Bill. Toynbee argued that "the Act marks not only an epoch in the history of Ireland, but also in the history of Democracy. It means—I say it advisedly—that the Radical party has committed itself to a Socialist programme." The radicals had admitted the cardinal principle of true socialism: "that between men who are unequal in material wealth there can be no freedom of contract."[70] Hence contemporary radicalism combined the best of the old radicalism with the principle of applying state intervention wherever individual rights were in conflict with the interests of the community and whenever members of the community required help to help themselves. As Toynbee had tried to explain to Grey, they had not completely abandoned all the traditional principles of liberalism.

We have not abandoned our old belief in liberty, justice, and self help but we say that under certain conditions the people cannot help themselves, and that then they should be helped by the State representing directly the whole people. In giving this State help, we make three conditions: first, the matter must be one of primary social importance; next, it must be proved to be practicable; thirdly, the State interference must not diminish self-reliance. . . . To a reluctant admission of the necessity for state action, we join a burning belief in duty, and a deep spiritual ideal of life, . . . we do not hesitate to unite the advocacy of social reform with an appeal to the various classes who compose society to perform those duties without which all social reform must be merely delusive.[71]

Toynbee had, in effect, questioned the old liberal taboo on state intervention while offering a more catholic approach to the choice of means in order to redress material inequality. In his address he elaborated on one application of the principles of new radicalism: the search for a solution to the problem of dwellings for the poor. It had been generally assumed by the older liberals that the main obstacle preventing an adequate solution was the unnaturally high cost of land caused by an artificially limited supply. T. H. Green, in an address to the Oxford West Ward Liberal Association in February 1881, advocated the intervention of the state in freeing the land market by allowing the sale and division of large estates "on the simple recognised principle that no man's land was his own for purposes incompatible with the public convenience."[72] Despite Green's caution in suggesting the application of the principle its bearing on the status of private property was quite radical. Toynbee on the other hand seems to have had fewer reservations about its application. He suggested the reform of local government to effect the redistribution of the burden of local taxation, the enforcement of sanitary laws and the Building Acts, and better representation of workmen on all local boards as well as on town councils. Private housing should be supplemented by municipal or state action by awarding governments the power to purchase land and to let it below market value in order to reduce the cost of constructing and letting decent dwellings for workers. Toynbee's suggestions went beyond lifting the restrictions on the free sale of land advocated by Green; by extending the application of Green's principle of intervention he actually advocated government action in controlling the land market to the advantage of one sector within the community. Toynbee argued that the urgency and importance of the problem justified the means which, in any event, were already being partly applied (although most local governments preferred control through extensions of the sanitary laws rather than by challenging the rights of property).[73] Bad housing constituted among other things a serious moral problem (an opinion supported by John Simon, London's first officer of health), hence sustained action was vital. By providing decent housing, "a higher standard of comfort would be reached, and improved habits of living established among the people; a great diminution in pauperism, drunkenness and crime would inevitably follow."[74]

Throughout the address Toynbee strove to sustain the duality of his appeal. His criticism of socialist creeds was directed both against Tory socialism—a middle- and upper-class movement advocating a return to paternalism—and against German socialism which, it was assumed, appealed to the working class. The symmetry was accomplished by the liberal use Toynbee made of the term socialism. He did not entirely condemn either creed but rather tried to demonstrate how the new radicalism embodied their best features. New radicalism was presented as a creed transcending class ideologies in that it incorporated the best in various class creeds while rejecting their fallacies. He appealed to the capitalist to use his wealth for the benefit of the community as a whole, to help secure the worker's material security, and he appealed to the worker to use the benefits of material progress to "reform his own social and domestic life. . . . Material prosperity, without faith in God and love to our fellowmen, is as little use to man as earth to plants without the sun."[75]

Toynbee ended his address with one of his few references to the empire. The growth of England's overseas commitments and responsibilities meant an increased responsibility of each citizen. Ensuring the material progress of the working-class man was vital

in order that he may have the intelligence and the will to administer the great trust which fate has committed to his charge; for it is not only his own home and his own country that he has to govern, but a vast empire—a duty unparalleled in the annals of democracy. We demand it, I say, in order that he, a citizen of this inclement island, washed by the dark northern seas, may learn to rule righteously the dim multitudes of peasants who toil under the fierce light of tropical suns, in the distant continent of India.[76]

Although not quite a "little Englander," Toynbee had, until now, displayed little interest in imperial matters. As tutor to the Indian Civil Service candidates he could hardly ignore the empire, but his main concern was the solution of England's social problems. He regarded the empire as a trust committed to England's care by fate. He seemed to ignore "Greater Britain" as well as the controversy over England's foreign policy in Africa. The question of England's Indian policy was reduced to the ways in which the best government could be secured for the empire.

Toynbee's academic duties for the year 1881–82 were extended to include lecturing to Balliol students reading modern history. College lecturers were generally considered crammers whose task was to prepare their students for the specific papers set in the finals. In modern history these included optional papers on economic history and on economic theory (based mainly on Adam Smith). Toynbee tried to combine the subjects of the two papers in a series of lectures that would also represent his own research interests. Having abandoned his attempt to deal separately with economic theory and bearing in mind the lessons he believed should be derived from the history of social and economic conditions, Toynbee attempted a combination. The result was an incomplete course of lectures that was to provide a survey of English economic and social history since 1760.[77] The subject covered by the course was to be divided into three periods, with the essential characteristics of each period expressed in the work of its most representative economist. The periods were: England on the eve of the industrial revolution (the description of which was to include an outline of *The Wealth of Nations*), England in the midst of the industrial revolution (reflected in the work of Malthus), and England and its problems since the Napoleonic Wars (as seen by Ricardo). Thus Adam Smith, Malthus, and Ricardo were used more as primary sources providing valuable evidence for the study of their respective periods than as theorists whose work warranted a nonhistorical study. It was Toynbee's professed intention to demonstrate that "economic laws and precepts are relative."[78]

Toynbee hoped to teach his students the right method of economic and social investigation by demonstrating the value of the right combination of deductive theory and historical research. He would thus establish the relativism of theory while helping the student of history to deal with economic phenomena. In addition the study of "modern" political economy would provide his students with an important mental discipline: "the habits of mind acquired from it are even more valuable than the knowledge of principles which it gives especially to students of facts, who might otherwise be overwhelmed by the mass of their materials."[79] His methodological comments in the introductory lecture were largely an adaptation of J. S. Mill's position, as stated in the essay, "On Method."[80] The application of theory was determined by the actual existence of the premises on which it was based. He argued in the defense of deductive theory that it was its misuse that had rendered it a subject of criticism. Much of the criticism was due "to a neglect on the part of those employing it to examine closely their assumptions and to bring their conclusions to the test of fact; to arguments based on premises which are not only not verified but absolutely untrue (as in the wage fund theory); and generally to a failure to combine induction with deduction."[81] Although Toynbee argued that Cliffe Leslie had gone too far in his condemnation of theory, and that theory as such was not necessarily wrong, having adopted the relativistic view of the development of theory it was naturally relegated to a secondary position in his historical survey. On its own it was a pure science, formal in structure, and of little general interest. Only when used in conjunction with historical and factual research could it furnish "a body of rules and maxims to guide conduct."[82]

By awarding applicability top priority in the economist's work Toynbee had somewhat reversed the emphasis in Mill's argument.[83] Mill declared the a priori method to be the only means of discovering truth in the moral (i.e., social) sciences, whereas the a posteriori method helped to verify its findings. By concentrating on applicability Toynbee chose to emphasize Mill's observation that without a command of the facts the deductive theorist "must rest contented to take no share in practical politics; to have no opinion, or to hold it with extreme modesty, on the application which should be made of his doctrines to existing circumstances." More a social investigator than a deductive economist, Toynbee, perhaps unknowingly, modeled himself on Mill's "speculative politician" who "must make a large allowance for the disturbing influence of unforeseen causes, and must carefully watch the result of every experiment, in order that any residuum of facts which his principles did not lead him to expect and do not enable him to explain, may become the subject of a fresh analysis, and furnish the occasion for a consequent enlargement or correction of his general views."

Toynbee had clearly been converted to the historical approach, to the study of social and economic development as the most appropriate methodology for the analysis of current problems. In this he represented a strong trend in English historiography that was becoming almost commonplace among a young generation of scholars.[84] For example, E. T. Cook, at a lecture on "The Fruits of Fifty Years of Liberal Legislation" to the East Ward Liberal Association delivered in March 1881, stated that "the truly wise man . . . was he who looked before and after—who studied the history of the past in order to find guidance for the future."[85] Shortly after, in a lecture to the Oxford Co-operative Society on the Irish Land Laws, William R. Anson, Warden of All Souls, stated that "he proposed to deal with the subject historically, partly in order to ascertain if possible the mode in which the present difficulties arose, and partly because the historical study of political difficulties was always useful as conducing to a calmer judgement of present events."[86] Thus, within his immediate intellectual environment, Toynbee was not out on a limb when he stated in his introductory lecture:

It would be well if, in studying the past, we could always bear in mind the problems of the present, and go to that past to seek large views of what is of lasting importance to the human race. . . . If I could persuade some of those present to study Economic History, to follow out the impulse originally given by Malthus to the study of the history of the mass of the people, I should be indeed glad. . . . You must pursue facts for their own sake, but penetrate with a vivid sense of the problems of your own time. . . . pay special attention to the history of the social problems which are agitating the world now, for you may be sure that they are problems not of temporary but of lasting importance.[87]

In the course of the lecture Toynbee demonstrated his meaning. The politics of 1881 had been dominated by debates concerning the Irish Land Bill and the possible application of its principles to English conditions. Toynbee argued that in this particular instance without "the aid of the Historical Method it would be impossible . . . to understand why one half of the land in the United Kingdom is owned by 2152 persons." It might be said that the whole course was permeated by Toynbee's commitment to various current problems to the extent that they increasingly dominated his lectures. In a prefatory note to the 1908 edition of the *Industrial Revolution* Charlotte Toynbee, his wife, pointed out that "in the later lectures of the course he aimed at giving his hearers a general idea of the development of industry, and of economic speculation, in the period with which he was dealing. The time at his disposal only allowed of this being done in outline, hence the sketchiness of these later lectures."[88] This is not entirely accurate since the confusion of the last lectures is more likely attributable to Toynbee's growing preoccupation with certain current problems and his persistent attempts to fit them into his narrative.

With the exception of certain laws, such as the law of diminishing returns, Toynbee rejected in his introductory lecture the universality of most economic laws. Yet his relativism was qualified since, having accepted the Comtian view of the study of society, Toynbee allowed for the existence of universal laws of social evolution such as the "law of progress" mentioned in some of his previous addresses. Such laws were derived from a comparative analysis of the various stages of development in different societies. One such law, based on the German Mark theory and propounded by Henry Maine and Emile de Laveleye, pronounced the tendency of societies to pass, as they progress, from collective to individual ownership. Another law, known as Maine's Law, established that the movement of all progressive societies was from status to contract.[89] Both of these laws were at the heart of the land reform controversy. Thus, for instance, it was argued that the attempts to lift all restrictions on the sale of land went against Maine's Law and that the return to collective ownership, thereby replacing contract with status, was fundamentally retrogressive.[90] On the other hand, the supporters of reform used the German Mark theory as a precedent on the basis of which they demanded a restitution of the people's ancient rights on land. Toynbee, who accepted in principle the validity of such laws, found it necessary to revise Maine's Law so that it would conform with the land reforms he supported and justified on ideological grounds in "Are Radicals Socialists?" "It is true that there is a movement from status to contract; yet if we look closely we find that the State has over and over again had to interfere to restrict the power of individuals in which this movement results. The real course of development has been first from status to contract, then from contract to a new kind of status determined by the law,—or, in other words, from unregulated to regulated contract."[91] It seems safe to assume that this reformulated universal law followed, rather than preceded, Toynbee's commitment to state restriction of private ownership of land.

Despite the resolute and final tone with which Toynbee stated his position on methodology he did not remain entirely consistent. While discussing in a later lecture the defects of Ricardo's deductive reasoning he appears to have reconsidered his position regarding the balance between theory and facts, bringing it closer to Mill's.

The historical method . . . is impotent of itself to give us a law of progress, because so many of the facts on which it relies are, in Economics, concealed from us. By the historical method we mean the actual observation of the course of economic history, and the deduction [induction?] from it of laws of economic progress; and this method, while most useful in checking the results of deduction is, by itself, full of danger from its tendency to set up imperfect generalisations.[92]

Hence, rather than use deduction as an aid in historical research, history is to be used in order to confirm the conclusions of deductive theory. As elsewhere this change in position is not a result of an isolated mental effort confined to the problems of method. It seems more like an attempt to furnish his previous comments on Maine's Law with a methodological explanation. Having first attempted to modify the law, Toynbee now dismissed it as failing to take account of the constantly changing nature of society: "in predicting the actual course of industrial progress, we must not be content to say that because there has been a movement in a certain direction in the past—for example, one from status to contract—it will therefore continue in the future."[93]

Toynbee went on to suggest a methodology that might be named "functional relativism": "Every single institution of society is brought to the test of utility and general national well-being hence, private property in land, if it fails under this test, will not continue. . . .

We must always apply the test. Does it fit with the urgent present requirements of human nature?"[94] In the context of his discussion of Ricardo's theory of rent this new argument of discontinuity of trends served a specific purpose. It allowed Toynbee to argue that, although rent had risen during the period 1790–1830, it was likely that in the near future the trend would reverse itself and that rent would steadily drop, thereby rendering land nationalization pointless. Furthermore, by linking rent to wages in an inverse proportion he could then argue that the anticipated drop in rent would result in a corresponding increase in wages despite it not having been the trend in the past.[95] It seems that Toynbee's methodological inconsistency was due to the importance he attached to various nonmethodological considerations.

The course contained a number of similar inconsistencies, some internal, some in relation to previous statements. The ninth lecture, on "The Growth of Pauperism," opens with the statement, "Malthus tells us that his book was suggested by Godwin's *Inquiry,* but it was really prompted by the rapid growth of pauperism which Malthus saw around him."[96] However, in the beginning of the next lecture, "Malthus and the Law of Population," the change of subject seems to have changed the facts, hence Malthus when writing his *Essay* "was not thinking directly of the Poor Law, but of Godwin."[97] In his address in 1880 Toynbee dismissed cooperative production as an inevitable failure. However, in the course's last lecture, on the future of the working classes, he argued that its lack of success had been due to faults in the character of the workers and to their lack of education. It was therefore to be expected that, as their character and education improved, the difficulties that had prevented cooperative production from succeeding would vanish.[98] Two paragraphs later the statement is qualified by the observation that, although there was every prospect of "productive co-operation making great progress in the future," it was unlikely to prove in the near future an important contributor to working-class progress.

Some of the inconsistencies may be attributed to the initial absence of an authoritative version of the course, especially of the later lectures. However, some of them appear to be genuine and are to some extent characteristic of Toynbee's work. His peculiar intellectual development and the intensity of his ideological commitments seem to have combined in precluding the single-mindedness required of purely academic work; he found himself unable to concentrate on one subject. His scholarly work formed an integral part of a developing "gospel" and, although his faith in progress and in its moral outcome was unshakable, like Mill's speculative politician, he constantly found it necessary to interpret and to deal with current events. The more difficult the interpretation of developments according to his gospel, the more urgent was the pull to deal with them. Driven by the need to demonstrate the comprehensiveness of his vision each new factor had to be digested, each new theory had to be either incorporated or challenged. Problems could not be left unresolved or challenges unanswered. Each new work with some bearing on his subject required attention.[99] The result was chronic digression. Projects were begun and discontinued, arguments abandoned or contradicted, and previously expressed positions conveniently forgotten when they seemed inconsistent with the gospel. His position on methodology, in one context presented as a matter of principle, is abandoned in a different context because the main argument—at the time of immediate relevance—seemed to contradict it. In one instance, forecasting the future of cooperative production on the basis of its record of failure served to stress class interdependence. In a different context, preparing a paper for the Co-operative Congress of 1882, the perspective changed and the future of cooperative production was considered irrespective of its past.

Lectures 2–6 were well within the outline Toynbee had sketched in the introduction. They contained a survey of social and economic conditions in England in 1760 leading, in the seventh lecture, to a discussion of *The Wealth of Nations* as a reflection of those conditions. They were based on detailed research and relied heavily on contemporary accounts, including work by Defoe and Arthur Young, and Eden's *State of the Poor,* as well as on various eighteenth-century pamphlets. Each lecture dealt with a sector that eventually underwent radical change. These included population, with an emphasis on the ratio between its distribution in rural and in urban areas; agriculture, including a demonstration of the connection between the increase in enclosures and the improvements in agriculture; and manufacture and trade, including the rise of the woolen trade in 1760 and the relative position of the iron trade. In addition, Toynbee furnished short surveys of the cotton, hardware, hosiery, and linen trades as well as of the relatively backward state of industrial technology. Toynbee gave two main reasons for England's relative prosperity in the eighteenth century: the waterways, which offered a convenient alternative to land transport, and the absence of internal custom barriers.[100] Although it was possible to detect the beginnings of a factory system most of the production was done domestically; each trade had its center in a provincial town with an additional exchange outlet in fairs to which products were brought by traveling merchants.

Toynbee rejected the golden-age view of pre-industrial England. Many of the evils that continental socialists such as Sismondi and Lassalle had attributed to industrialization were already evident, especially in the export manufactures. "Already there were complaints of the competition of men who pushed themselves into the market to take advantage of high prices; already we hear of the fluctuations of trade and irregularity of employment. The old simple conditions of production and exchange were on the eve of disappearance before the all-corroding force of foreign trade."[101] Similarly he questioned in his last lecture the romantic image of pre-industrial employer-worker relations which he himself had previously tended to accept. "The relations between masters and workmen were then extremely close, but this close relationship had its bad side. There was often great brutality and gross vice. The workman was at his employer's mercy."[102]

The continuity of the survey of England in 1760 was disrupted by lecture 5, "The Decay of the Yeomanry," apparently part of an unfinished article. The reasons for its inclusion in the published version of the course are not clear since it is at best digressive. Yet its substance is consistent with some later digressions so that it is not entirely out of place, although it should be classified with the later lectures. It opens with an attack on individualism and Spencer's Social Darwinism as applied to the issue of the Irish Land Bill, and it constitutes a step in the reversal of Toynbee's position concerning the continuity and regularity of historical processes. Social Darwinism was used to counter demands for radical changes in the existing system. By adopting and developing "functional relativism" Toynbee was able to reject the blind acceptance of the linear continuity of institutions. Since all institutions should be examined historically on the basis of their initial and eventual purpose it was possible that some existing institution might prove to have originated in injustice toward certain classes; that injustice is perpetuated by the institution's survival. Radical change, although technically disturbing continuity, would in such a case rectify a fault in the system rather than contribute to its destruction.[103]

Having examined the land issue in great detail Toynbee abandoned any attempt to produce a universal law of progress applicable to land ownership. Instead he evolved a somewhat confused argument in an effort to reconcile his notion of progress with evidence of historical injustice. He argued at the outset that the concentration of land in England in the hands of a small number of landowners and the disappearance of the yeomanry had in fact contributed to the overall progress of the community. The process had been the result of the "existence of the system of political government which has made us a free people."[104] In turn it had helped to preserve the system as well as contributing significantly to the material progress of the country. Nevertheless the actual process of enclosure, which had dealt a severe blow to the small freeholder, "was done by the strong at the expense of the weak. The change from common to individual ownership, which was economically advantageous, was carried out in an iniquitous manner, and thereby became socially harmful."[105] Social injustice and material progress appeared to be historically compatible.

At first Toynbee attributed the disappearance of the yeomanry mainly to social and political reasons rather than to economic ones. The two main factors that, after the Glorious Revolution, made the ownership of land desirable were the social and political power that came with land ownership and its enormous social prestige, which appealed greatly to the newly rising commercial class. The alliance of the landed gentry and the new wealth resulted in the concentration of land in fewer hands supported by protective legislation passed in parliaments controlled by the representatives of the landowners. The accompanying economic factors, although relatively unimportant, "served to accelerate the change."[106] They included the greater efficiency of the larger farms, the gradual decay of domestic industries which had provided the small farmer with a source of supplementary income, and "owing to the consolidation of farms and industry," the gradual disappearance of small towns and villages and with them the small farmer's market. However, in his previous lecture Toynbee had argued that the pre-industrial conditions of production and exchange had been gradually transformed by the effect of foreign trade, a relatively independent economic factor. When applied to the case of the yeomanry it meant that not only were the economic factors indicated independent of the political and social conditions he had described but that they also surpassed them in importance. Consequently, having first dismissed the economic factors as relatively unimportant, two paragraphs later Toynbee summarized his argument by qualifying his conclusions. "It is probable that the yeoman would in any case have partly disappeared, owing to the inevitable working of economic causes. But these alone would not have led to their disappearance on so large a scale. It was the political conditions of the age, the overwhelming importance of land, which made it impossible for the yeoman to keep his grip upon the soil."[107] So the social injustice described had only quickened and intensified a probably inevitable process. Nevertheless, social injustice had been shown to be a prerequisite of progress.

The next lecture, "The Conditions of the Wage-Earners," resumed the survey of conditions in 1760. Toynbee found that during the mid-eighteenth century the English agricultural laborer enjoyed a distinct improvement in his material conditions due to the rate of economic growth having outpaced the slower rate of population increase. It was the best period the agricultural laborers of southern England have ever enjoyed. During the following century the relative conditions of laborers south and north of the Trent were reversed. In explaining the 1760 prosperity, Toynbee tried at first to demonstrate the application of theory in historical research. "Arguing on the deductive method, we should conjecture a large demand for or a small supply of labour, and, in fact we find both these influences in operation."[108] This he soon qualified when he observed that "there were many local variations of wages which are far less easy to bring under the ordinary rules of Political Economy." These deviations from theory could only be understood if one realized that "men do not always act in accordance with their pecuniary interest." This occurred either through choice, compulsion, or ignorance. Furthermore, the mobility of labor, which is a presupposition of the theory of wages, was largely a fiction.

As for industrial wage earners Toynbee maintained that, despite the widening gulf between workers and employers, their conditions had undergone during the past century a distinct improvement. This was especially true of the artisans. However, the comparison of their conditions with that of their ancestors was not a simple matter. Industrialization had created many new classes of workers and, although wages have, on the whole, increased, the artisan has suffered from the loss of some of the advantages of life in the country and of the relative stability of the pre-industrial economy. There had been a time when the "distribution of wealth was, indeed in all respects more equal,"[109] and the conditions of employer and employed, whether in agriculture or in manufacture, were similar, if not identical—an echo of the golden-age view of pre-industrialization that, in his last lecture, Toynbee would try to qualify.

Toynbee's survey of pre-industrial England was concluded in lecture 7 with an examination of Adam Smith and the mercantile system. The structure of his argument was based on the assumption that each economic theory expressed specific social and economic conditions. A radical change in "the methods and organisation of production" coincided with a correlated "change no less radical in men's economic principles, and in the attitude of the State to individual enterprise."[110] England of 1760 had, in essence, retained the medieval system that had originally been based on the notion that the state as a religious entity was responsible for the eternal welfare of its citizens. Nothing of any consequence was left either to chance or to the operation of self-interest. Yet, despite the system's archaism England had enjoyed a relative prosperity. Adam Smith had identified the freedom of internal trade as its cause and sought to extend that freedom to the movement of labor and to the operation of capital. Toynbee questioned the validity of Adam Smith's assumption concerning the actual operation of the legal restriction (e.g., the old Poor Law) on the mobility of labor. It seemed to him that Smith's bitter attack on corporations as restrictive factors was based on the particular experience of Watt being refused a license to set up his trade in Glasgow. Toynbee argued that it was doubtful whether the restrictions were actually as stringent as Smith made them out to be. There were free towns, such as Birmingham and Manchester, and even in the incorporated towns the system seems to have been reasonably flexible. "We may probably conclude that nonfreemen were often unmolested."[111]

The same, Toynbee felt, was true of Smith's portrayal of the regulation of wages "as part of a general system of oppression of the poor by the rich."[112] Toynbee contended that this was not strictly accurate. In many instances the regulation of wages was operated in defense of the workers' interests. The system was often approved of by the workers themselves, and its operation was not much different than that of the much-lauded boards of arbitration. Toynbee appears to have had an instinctive objection to the description of pre-industrial England as a battlefield of class interests in which the weak were taken full advantage of by the powerful within a system morally unjust and economically unsound. At the same time he rejected the golden-age image, hence his somewhat confused and not entirely consistent narrative.

Toynbee, with a side glance toward state enterprise, proceeded to dispute Adam Smith's treatment of the restrictions on foreign trade. Smith's argument that the directors of corporate trading companies, dealing with the capital of others, were bound to become negligent, was an example of unjustified a priori generalization based on an inaccurate psychological observation. He also rejected the inductive argument that as a rule joint stock companies could not succeed unless they were monopolies, as demonstrated by the internal competition in banking. Joint stock companies have over the years proved in many instances to be economically superior in spite of the fact that at the time of their establishment it was erroneously assumed that public and private interests were antagonistic.[113] Smith's mistake was in basing a universal law on the rejection of both an erroneous principle and independently successful means.

Rather than discuss the earlier forms of mercantilism and their alleged concentration on securing England's store of precious metals, Toynbee concentrated on what he defined as "modern protection," the policy aimed at protecting native industries, historically best exemplified by the Navigation Acts. As in the discussion of the trade companies it may be safely assumed that Toynbee had in mind the current question of fair trade. Toynbee admitted that as a solution to certain immediate problems protection had offered a viable and relatively successful policy. In this he followed both Adam Smith and J. S. Mill. However, when it came to the actual details of his argument some of Toynbee's faults as a scholar emerged. He stated that, as a result of the Navigation Acts, "the price of freights were raised, because English ships cost more to build and man than Dutch ships, and thus the total amount of our trade was diminished."[114] As one of his references he cited *The Wealth of Nations,* in which Adam Smith had argued that the acts resulted in a diminution in England's European trade while its colonial trade was increasing at a rate that more than compensated for the continental losses. The statement had been questioned by J. R. McCulloch in his edition of

The Wealth of Nations who claimed that "all the branches of our foreign trade have been gradually increasing during the last hundred years," a claim borne out by modern scholarship.

Toynbee's inaccuracy of itself is of little consequence, but it does demonstrate how his preconceptions influenced his actual research. He had already accepted that most historical economic policies aimed at solving immediate problems were generally successful in the short run. At the same time the lack of political flexibility in adapting existing policies to changing circumstances was detrimental to progress. As a free trader, Toynbee could not very well argue that, beyond the solution of certain immediate problems of the mid–seventeenth century, protection had proved successful in the long run as well. His final verdict was: "Protection involves this great disadvantage, that, once given, it is difficult to withdraw, and thus in the end more harm is done than good. English industries would not have advanced so rapidly without Protection, but the system, once established, led to perpetual wrangling on the part of rival industries, and sacrificed India and the colonies to our great manufactures."[115] Such a verdict could not coincide with an acceptance of McCulloch's factual observation; therefore, it was completely overlooked as was the inaccuracy of his *Wealth of Nations* reference.

Toynbee continued his criticism of Adam Smith by questioning his reducing the politics of protection to a simple case of the clever and sophisticated merchants tricking the landed gentry into believing that protection represented the public's interest. Toynbee pointed out that by then strong family and business ties had already been established between the gentry and the merchants. Their interests were far from being incompatible and in any event the gentry had extracted a bounty on the export of corn in return for its support of protection. Protection had served the interests of more than one small and selfish class. Yet it was not a true national policy in that it reflected the relative power of various economic and commercial pressure groups such as the woolen trade and the tanners who enjoyed political support. It tended therefore to come at the expense of other sectors. It reduced the Irish and the colonial policies to simple calculations of immediate economic profit preferring exploitation to development, the results of which could be seen in the American Declaration of Independence (and, by a simple extension of his argument, in the Irish troubles).

In summing up Adam Smith's work Toynbee chose to emphasize

its defects rather than its merits. "Many people on first reading the *Wealth of Nations* are disappointed. They come to it expecting lucid arguments, the clear exposition of universal laws; they find much tedious and confused reasoning and a mass of facts of only temporary interest. . . . he was only groping his way and we cannot expect to meet with neat arrangement and scientific precision of treatment in his book."[116] In conclusion Toynbee stated, "Original people always are confused because they are feeling their way," an epitaph that might well be used to describe Toynbee himself.

Toynbee's summary of Adam Smith's faults closely resemble Walter Bagehot's verdict in his essay, "Adam Smith and our Modern Economy."[117] Bagehot argued that, although "a great mental effort in its day," Smith's work had been "altogether superseded and surpassed now." He had written "in an extinct world and one of the objects always before him was to destroy now extinct superstitions."[118] Toynbee had read Bagehot with considerable care as is evident from his references to the various essays in Bagehot's *Economic Studies*.[119] Both judged the "old" economists from a contemporary angle. However, Bagehot set out to prove his thesis concerning the current value of Adam Smith's work by demonstrating its inadequacy to deal satisfactorily with some of the specific questions of modern economics. Toynbee, on a similar tack, concentrated on the inadequacies of the more general policies and philosophical implications of *The Wealth of Nations*. While Bagehot intended to prove the decisive superiority of modern theory, Toynbee wished to expose the fallacies of Smith's social philosophy, which had furnished the foundation of the doctrine of laissez-faire.[120]

Toynbee did not reject outright all of Smith's recommended policies. He had accepted some of his praise of protection and continued by approving his "cosmopolitanism," which he considered a precursor of Cobden's internationalism. He lauded Smith's advocacy of free competition as leading to optimal division of labor, thereby ensuring the ability of each individual to acquire his wants at a minimum cost. But, Toynbee argued, the principle of free competition had its limits, a fact not recognized by Adam Smith or provided for in his philosophy. It was false to assume that, whatever the circumstances, "it is the interest of the producer to supply the wants of the consumer in the best possible manner, that it is in the interest of the producer to manufacture honest wares,"[121] as was demonstrated by the need for the Adulteration Act. Adam Smith also did not foresee that free internal trade might result in natural monopolies that could be broken only by free international trade. Finally, he did not realize that "in the distribution of wealth there must necessarily be a permanent antagonism of interests."[122]

In this last point Toynbee clearly rejected the likelihood of a natural harmony in distribution, as well as the natural harmony between individual interests and the public good. His position on the matter seems to have originated in negative observations concerning the results of the operation of laissez-faire policies. "A period as disastrous and as terrible as any through which a nation ever passed; disastrous and terrible because side by side with a great increase of wealth was seen an enormous increase of pauperism; and production on a vast scale, the result of free competition, led to a rapid alienation of classes and to the degradation of a large body of producers."[123] Toynbee once again admitted, although now in a wider context, that, historically, material progress, made possible by the adoption of the policy of laissez-faire, has caused extensive misery. Redress of the imbalance in the distribution of the fruits of progress could not be left to the operation of free competition. There were partial solutions, such as the boards of conciliation, that helped to reduce class friction but could not be expected to overcome it entirely. Only multifaceted corporate action based on an accurate understanding by all classes of the problem could set into motion a process that would lead to a more just distribution. In this respect the conversion of Oxford undergraduates, the country's future leaders, was as important as that of the working class. Oxford had become a sphere of agitation as important as industrial centers.

Having accepted the common association of industrialization with free trade, Toynbee opened with it in the eighth lecture, his first on the actual course of the industrial revolution. The creed of free competition had produced economic science as well as its antithesis, socialism.[124] Following the outline of the course, but wishing to underline the relevance of his survey, Toynbee added another to the three economists representative of the three main stages of industrialization: J. S. Mill, who expressed the nature of the fourth stage, the present. Toynbee argued, in what appears to be an extension of "Are Radicals Socialists?" that Mill introduced into economic science the question of "how wealth *ought* to be distributed." Under the influence of the socialists' criticism of classical economics, Mill's *Principles of Political Economy* "though a restatement of Ricardo's system, . . . contained the admission that the distribution of wealth is the result of 'particular social arrangements,' and it recognised that competition alone is not a satisfactory basis of society."[125]

Toynbee continued this digression from his narrative by restating his concept of "modern" economics, which complemented "modern" radicalism. Free competition, accepted unquestioningly by Ricardo and even by Mill, was an unsatisfactory guide to social policy, giving rise to some grievous fallacies. The most recent, borrowed from Darwinism, was the contention that all forms of competition were variations of the struggle for survival failing to distinguish between the fight for existence and competition "for a particular kind of existence." The latter most commonly decided an individual's occupation and was limited by the finite ability of each individual to perform certain jobs. It was a misapplication of Darwinism to argue that competition, being a particular case of the struggle for existence, was a law of nature that must not be tampered with. "To that I answer," Toynbee stated, "that the whole meaning of civilisation is interference with this brute struggle. We intend to modify the violence of the fight, and to prevent the weak being trampled under foot."[126]

Toynbee was still troubled by the link between progress through free competition and misery. There was also the question of the compatibility of his suggestions for state-controlled competition and his observations concerning the direct contribution of free competition to material progress. He tried to resolve the apparent inconsistency by differentiating between competition in production and competition in distribution. While the former had been entirely beneficial to the community the latter could be identified as the cause of most of the accompanying evils associated with progress. Under free competition in distribution, "the stronger side will dictate its own terms; and as a matter of fact, in the early days of competition the capitalists used all their power to oppress the labourers, and drove down wages to starvation point. This kind of competition has to be checked; there is no historical instance of its having lasted long without being modified either by combination or legislation, or both."[127] Here was the historical justification for trade unions and factory legislation. Competition as such was neither good nor evil. It was a force that must be studied if it were to be controlled. Toynbee believed that in this, modern economists had adopted a position significantly different from the old economists. During the heyday of industrialization "it came to be believed in as a gospel, and, the idea of necessity being superadded, economic laws deduced from the assumption of universal unrestricted competition were converted into practical precepts, from which it was regarded as little short of immoral to depart."[128] Again, Toynbee's identification of two types of competition, which seemed to serve the immediate purposes of his argument, were not entirely consistent with his previous defense of control over competition in production as practiced by the Adulteration Act.

Having added another stage to the industrial revolution, thereby bringing its findings up to the present, Toynbee returned to his narrative. His intention was to construct a narrative that would be symmetrical to his survey of England in 1760. He characterized the industrial revolution by the rapid absolute growth of population, the relative and absolute decline of rural population, the shift in the center of population density from the midlands to the north, and the change in the relative size of the populations of England and Ireland.

These changes, which were primarily examined through their effect on the rural population, were the results of an "agrarian revolution" in the course of which the common field system was abolished, common and waste lands were enclosed, and small farms were incorporated into large ones. Enclosures resulted in a diminution of the number of farmers and farm laborers, many of whom were driven to seek employment in the towns. As indicated in lecture 5, a great advance in agricultural productivity was coupled with a severe deterioration in the conditions of the rural laborer.

In manufactures the main feature of the revolution was the change from domestic to factory production. This was the result of the great mechanical inventions in the cotton and iron industries and of the rapid and extensive development of the canal system, which increased trade opportunities and both forced and helped the process of industrial concentration. Among the results of these changes Toynbee noted the growing dependence of the work force in the developing industries and "the regular recurrence of periods of over production and of depression," this last a feature peculiar to large-scale production for distant markets.

A revolution in production entailed a revolution in the distribution of wealth. In agriculture the result was an enormous rise in rent which "represented a great social revolution, a change in the balance of political power and in the relative position of classes."[129] The farmer who held onto the land prospered and adopted the habits and manner of the upper classes. The agricultural laborer, on the other hand, lost his common land rights, his wages fell, and he was the first to suffer from the rising prices. The gulf between him and the farmer, with whom he had previously lived and worked in close intimacy, widened into alienation.

"Exactly analogous phenomena" occurred in industry. The new wealth accumulated in the hands of a relatively small number of capitalist employers by then entirely isolated from the life and working conditions of their numerous workers. The old bond between employer and worker disappeared, replaced by the "cash nexus." Consequently both sides organized in combinations in order to defend their now antagonistic interests. By now Toynbee had partly abandoned his previous argument concerning the relative improvement in the lot of the industrial worker. Instead he extended his observation concerning the link between progress and rural misery to industry. The new industrial working class suffered in some industries from a fall of wages, and on the whole from a deterioration in conditions of work, from a rise in prices, and from fluctuations of trade. "The effects of the Industrial Revolution prove," Toynbee concluded, "that free competition may produce wealth without producing well being,"[130] a conclusion that, if "may" is replaced with "does," is identical to Henry George's point of departure.

In his introductory outline Toynbee had stated that the second part of the course would deal with Malthus's work on the causes of poverty and the explanation of the distribution of wealth. Having ended lecture 8 with the social effect of industrialization, a discussion of pauperism and Malthus's attempt to deal with it was a logical choice for the subject of the next lecture. However, lecture 9 consisted mainly of an independent discourse on pauperism and the various English Poor Laws.[131] Research into the Poor Laws was most likely motivated by Toynbee's determination to apply himself to his duties as a Poor Law Guardian (since April 1881) in a scientific manner. Accordingly, he described his point of departure as combining the examination of Malthus's influence on the new English Poor Law and the current (i.e., his own) realization that what was required in poor law administration "is not the repression of the instincts of benevolence, but their organisation. To make benevolence scientific is the great problem of the present age. . . . now we see that not only thought but historical study is also neces-

sary. Both to understand the nature of pauperism and to discover its
effectual remedies, we must investigate its earlier history."¹³² Toynbee added a note of caution, emphasizing the essentiality of the
relativistic perspective. "We should take to heart two warnings: first,
not to interpret medieval statutes by modern ideas; and secondly, not
to assume that the causes of pauperism have always been the
same."¹³³

Toynbee's immediate concern was rural outdoor relief, on which
he had adopted the Charity Organization Society's position. He had
already commented on some of the causes of modern pauperism and
he repeated them following a survey of the history of poor law
legislation. However, he now chose to extenuate the decisiveness of
his previous observations. Misery was not a necessary outcome of
progress. Agricultural pauperism might have been avoided or at
least mitigated had enclosures been compensated for by providing
farm laborers with private plots. As for high prices, their effect was
mainly felt in the midlands and the south, whereas in the north industrialization had saved the agricultural laborer from pauperism. A
solution might have been higher wages in the rural areas, but the
farmers, rather than assume responsibility for their workers, were
content to relinquish it to "the justices and county gentlemen." The
result was "the principle which radically vitiated the old Poor Law
. . . an unconditional right on the part of the poor to an indefinite
share in the national wealth. . . . the right was granted in such a
way [i.e., the Speenhamland system] as to keep them in dependence
and diminish their self-respect."¹³⁴ This policy of "bribing the people
into passiveness," which Toynbee had previously attributed to the
Tory socialists, had been further strengthened during the Napoleonic
Wars in order to ensure a healthy and large manpower reserve.

Having finally stopped short of Henry George's maxim, as applied
to rural conditions, Toynbee could now argue that, strictly speaking,
rural poverty was perpetuated not by economic conditions but by the
policy of unconditional outdoor relief. Rectifying what amounted to
a historical mistake was the task of the legislator, whose duty it was
to discover "how to combine political and material freedom."¹³⁵ Having ensured the course of material progress, the main challenge facing
the current generation was how to guarantee that progress produced
both wealth and well-being.

In lecture 10, Toynbee returned to his narrative and to Malthus.
As in his criticism of Adam Smith his use of Bagehot's essays is evi-

dent.[136] Like Bagehot he described Malthus's primary motivation as
the exposure of utopias, especially Godwin's communism.[137] On this
particular issue Malthus had since been proven wrong by the experience of the communist societies in America, in which absence of
private property did not result in a disappearance of moral restraint.
The validity of Malthus's general theory was based on two premises:
the law of population (which stipulates that population, if left un-
checked, will double itself every twenty-five years) and the law of
diminishing returns (which Toynbee had already accepted as one
of the universally valid laws of economics).[138] Malthus's weakness
therefore lay in the questionable validity of his first premise.

Toynbee prefaced his own criticism of Malthus by citing with
approval some of his previous critics, namely T. Doubleday, Herbert
Spencer, H. C. Carey, F. A. Walker, Bagehot, and Cliffe Leslie.
However, in keeping with the nature of his previous digressions, he
chose to single out for special, although brief, consideration Henry
George's attack on Malthus in Progress and Poverty.[139] Toynbee had
clearly been impressed by George's book. In a letter to his sister
Grace, dated 29 August 1881, which contained a reading list of works
by American economists he wrote, "Perhaps the most interesting of
all the American writers is Henry George (a workman by origin),
whose recently published work on Poverty and Progress [sic], though
extravagant and crude, is full of ingenuity and power."[140]

His sympathy toward Henry George is clearly evident from his
commentary on George's criticism of Malthus. His own main criticism of George is of the latter's rejection of the law of diminishing
returns. Toynbee argued that there were specific instances of peasant
proprietors' communities (e.g., in France, Norway, and Switzerland)
in which it was indisputable that poverty was the result of the
working of the law of diminishing returns, rather than of social injustice, that is, of Malthus's first premise, overpopulation. Facts, then,
contradicted George's total rejection of the possibility of Malthus's
law of population ever being in actual operation. Toynbee approved
of George's objections to the false analogy between man and the
animal world and, more significant, he partly accepted George's main
argument by readmitting that "a large portion of pauperism and
misery is really attributable to bad government and injustice."

Toynbee's own treatment of Malthus commenced with the establishment of the relevant context of Malthus's work: a rapid rate of
population growth. A proper evaluation of the value of his work

required a comparison between Malthus's explanation of demographic changes and the explanations furnished by current analysis. Malthus's explanation of the growth in rural population was based on his criticism of the maladministration of the Poor Laws. This, Toynbee argued, was only part of a wider phenomenon: the change in rural social habits caused by the agricultural revolution. A similar cause explained the parallel trend in urban population growth. Having dealt with Malthus's analysis there remained the question of his prescribed remedies: abolition of the old Poor Law and moral restraint. These Toynbee compared with what in his view were the actual reasons for the changes in demographic trends. He confidently stated that the Poor Law reform of 1834 was "perhaps the most beneficient Act of Parliament which has been passed since the Reform Bill."[141] Its effect has been "very remarkable," although "the Poor Laws are by no means perfect and great reforms are still needed."[142] Another successful remedy, which "Malthus despised," has been emigration, greatly aided by steam navigation. Improved navigation has not only eased the pressure of labor through emigration of labor surplus, but has also improved the workers' conditions through the import of cheap food paid for with industrial produce. As for the moral restraint, its effect, as analyzed by W. S. Jevons, has been only marginal among the working class but more significant among artisans and the middle class.

Finally Toynbee turned to consider artificial checks—clearly another digression since it was neither suggested by Malthus nor had it been historically adopted in England. The discussion seems to have been stimulated by Henri J. L. Baudrillart, *Les populations agricoles de la France; La Normandie* (1880), the subject of some notes in the Toynbee papers.[143] Baudrillart's work dealt with the depopulation of the rural district of Eure through the use of artificial checks, resulting in considerable material prosperity. Toynbee's fervent condemnation of artificial restraints was motivated mainly by moral revulsion. His sense of outrage is discernible in his extensively underlined notes which contain an outraged passage concerning celibacy and the avoidance of parenthood by married couples.

A *diminution of births* as the result of *celibacy* has to be *condemned* on *moral grounds*—it is known that *criminality* is *tripled* among *celibates*. It seems that those who *in marriage do not accept its responsibilities fall within the same law;* they are more idle, more given to intemperance and to libertinage, more exposed in fact to not find in marriage those restraints against crime and disorder which it is supposed usually to exercise (emphasis Toynbee's).

These were understandable sentiments for a son of a large Victorian family, but curiously out of context coming from a twenty-nine-year-old married, but childless, Oxford don.

Toynbee explained the adoption of artificial restraint as motivated by selfish materialism and therefore fundamentally immoral. It effected a rise in the rate of criminality in the region, he felt, and in the long run was contrary to economic reasoning. Such an attitude, in addition to being immoral, was self-defeating.

Man with all his faculties and the dormant productive forces he holds within him, has come to the point of *stultifying himself* before the idea of *material possessions*. Such a way of looking at human life ends at destroying all *confidence in the future*; it would succeed at last in killing all creative energy.

The rule of material selfishness was also reflected in family relations,—it is not less tender than formerly, children are indeed oftener *spoilt*—the instinct prevails and reigns, but it is associated with little idea of duty—the peasant has *one fixed idea* with recall to his children, *to leave them wealth,* thinking much less of bequeathing them virtues. What had obviously diminished is the *respect* of children for their parents (emphasis Toynbee's).

Toynbee seemed to associate the decline of family morals with an increase in crime. In Baudrillart's work he found evidence of a disproportionate rise in the Eure of the rate of murders, assassinations, infanticides, petty thefts, poaching, and intemperance.

Toynbee drew two conclusions. The first, which he elaborated in both his notes and in his tenth lecture, identified moral with lasting material progress. An artificially stationary population was both materially unhealthy and immoral. It eliminated the struggle for existence, which provides an essential stimulus to progress. It was preferable to raise a normal-sized family whose children, having been brought up in a wholesome moral environment, will become conscientious citizens contributing to the community by their individual endeavors. He had previously argued that emigration contributed to progress by reducing the supply of labor, thereby raising wages. He now added that the proper attitude for the "breeding" classes to adopt was that "a man in the superior artisan or middle classes has only to consider *when* he will have sufficient means to rear an average number of children; that is, he need only regulate the time of marriage, and the willing emigration of some of his children when grown up, does, in his case, meet the difficulty. He need not consider whether there is room in the world for more, for there *is* room."[144] Morality and practicality were always linked. Morality was not only the true acid test of any reform scheme, it also preceded all other considerations. "To reach the true solution we must tenaciously hold to a high ideal of spiritual life. . . . The true remedies . . . imply a growth towards that purer and higher condition of society for which alone we care to strive."[145] If a solution was immoral it was also of necessity detrimental to true progress.

A second conclusion suggested in the lecture is a development of the somewhat stilted reasoning of the first conclusion. In the first part of his analysis of Malthus, Toynbee based his criticism of the law of population on historical evidence that demonstrated that the actual rate of population growth in England was far below that predicted by Malthus as well as below the rate of increase of food production and of capital. Toynbee did not define what he considered as a normal rate of population growth in a healthy society. Having stated categorically that there was room in the world, he added that in the interests of civilization it was desirable that a nation with a great history and great qualities should also grow in size.[146] Stopping short of setting a limit on such growth and not indicating at what point the universal law of diminishing returns would begin to effect the ratio between population growth and food production, placed Toynbee in agreement with Henry George. George had argued that no predetermined limits could be set on the possible growth of population without it overreaching its means of subsistence. Both appear to have accepted that the normal growth of population was naturally regulated in accordance with the nation's needs, state of progress, and future prospects.[147]

Malthus also furnished the point of departure for the subject of lecture 11: the wage fund theory, of which Toynbee found the fullest statement in J. S. Mill's 1869 review of Thornton's *On Labour*. The theory was the product of the special circumstances that had prevailed during the period 1795–1815, during which, while population was increasing at a greater rate than the means of subsistence, increased money wages could not purchase larger quantities of food. Malthus assumed that at any given point in time the amount of food available was fixed. Having mistakenly identified food with capital he proceeded to develop the theory that at any given moment the amount of capital available for wages was fixed.[148] A later restatement of the theory identified wage capital with the various items that constituted the worker's means of subsistence (the total amount of which at any given moment was considered fixed). Therefore, the rate of wages at any given moment was determined by the size of the fund of items available and the number of workers. Since its formulation the law had been pronounced both historically and analytically false. Its premises were erroneous whether applied to an individual employer or to the capital of the community as a whole. With Mill's acceptance of the variability of the standard of comfort, the concept of wages tending toward a fixed minimum was discarded. Finally since "Lassalle and the Socialists" had based their theories on the wage fund theory in its Ricardian formulation, their premises were as invalid as those of the "old" economists.[149]

Yet the critics of the wage fund theory did not produce an adequate alternative either to Ricardian doctrine or to George's theory of wages, both of which suggested extremist solutions that appealed to those dissatisfied with present conditions.[150] Toynbee therefore chose to digress once again by offering the outline of a theory of wages, much of which is contained in his 1880 address on the subject (repeated in February 1882 at Firth College, Sheffield). Wages, according to Toynbee, were determined by the total amount of produce and by the deal the worker was able to make with his employer. The latter factor partly depended on the ratio between the number of laborers seeking employment and the amount of capital seeking investment. Beyond the rudiments of a wage theory, Toynbee reintroduced an issue he had dealt with in 1880: the reasons for the differences in wages among America, England, and Europe. On the difference between American and English wages he basically reiterated his previous explanation: better machinery and the beneficial effect of American internal free competition (which might eventually be canceled out by American protection policy).[151] As for the differences between European and English wages, Toynbee added a political factor: "our political institutions, being favourable to liberty, have developed individual energy and industry in a degree unknown in any other country."[152] The relatively superior efficiency of the English worker explained why his wages were relatively higher than wages on the continent despite the inaccessibility of free land (which had served to explain high American wages). In a

Lamarckian vein, Toynbee argued that greater efficiency was the result of a historically stable work force that had formed "castes" of workers in certain employments in which "inherited aptitudes" were passed from one generation to the other. Efficiency had been described as one of the variables determining the rate of wages, hence its explanatory importance, but wages were also determined by competition in the labor market. It was therefore necessary to add to the causes of higher American wages "the great competition for employment in the over-stocked labour-market of this country."[153]

Toynbee next turned to the question of the upper limits of wage settlements. In an elaboration of his 1880 view he observed that the limit was determined by two major factors: whenever "any further rise will drive the employer out of the trade, or when the increased price of the commodity will check the demand."[154] Toynbee may have sensed the rising militancy of the emerging new unionism since he concluded his digression on wage theory with a short comment on the possible effect of a general strike, a concept that had remained virtually dormant within the labor movement since its Chartist days. Toynbee enumerated some possible long-term consequences of such a strike on wages. It might result in a drop in employers' remuneration thereby effecting a decrease in the number of employers, a diminution in the demand for labor, and, finally, a drop in wages. It might result in a drop in the rate of interest, thereby checking the accumulation of wealth and diminishing the demand for labor. On the other hand, the rise in wages achieved by the strike might prove permanent and the remuneration of the employers might still provide sufficient profit and therefore the rate of the accumulation of capital might remain unchanged. Finally, higher wages might result in a higher efficiency which would prevent a fall in profits. In any event it was "impossible to decide on *a priori* grounds which of these results would actually take place."[155]

The structure of lecture 11 became further convoluted when Toynbee tried to combine his theory of wages with his discussion of Malthus. Having already explained why Malthus's theory had been applicable to conditions between 1795 and 1815, he now restated the problem to fit his discussion on wages. Toynbee now restated the Malthus theory as the reason that had caused a fall in wages while rent had doubled and interest nearly doubled between 1790 and 1820,[156] a condition that, in his view, disproved George's theory concerning the relation between the growth of rent and the growth of interest. His answer offered an elaboration on his previously stated main reason: bad harvests caused a limited supply of food that could not keep up with the increase in population. To the harvests he added as additional factors high taxation, an increase in the national debt that withdrew money from industry, bad coinage, and the truck system. Other special circumstances that affected rural conditions were enclosures and the rise in cottage rents.

Toynbee's narrative had been a circuitous one. Rather than follow lecture 8, which outlined the general characteristics of industrialization and its consequences, with a concise description of pauperism and its reflection in Malthusian theory he had been constantly distracted. The result was a series of digressions that were of secondary value to the development of the course's main theme but were of considerable bearing on immediate issues. Toynbee's concluding remark at the end of lecture 11 brought him back to the general consequences of industrialization. "The misfortunes of the labouring classes were partly inevitable, but they were also largely the result of human injustice, of the selfish and grasping use made of a power which exceptional circumstances had placed in the hands of landowners, farmers, and capitalists."[157] Having covered all possibilities with a statement approaching a tautology, Toynbee ended the second part of the course.

In the second part, the detailed narrative evident in the first part was replaced, in terms of space and attention, by a more elaborate discussion of theory. The same is true of the third part, which dealt mainly with Ricardo. Economic change is seen through economic theory and not vice versa as in the first part. Hence, Ricardo was introduced in lecture 12 not as representative of the third stage of industrialization but as the father of the deductive method of political economy. The main issues were the soundness of his method and the validity of his theory considered from a distinctly contemporary perspective. Toynbee repeated some of his earlier statements concerning method and theory, including his general rule of collective replacing private ownership. His main theme, however, was Henry George.

For his criticism of George Toynbee chose a familiar theme. He argued that throughout Ricardo's work it was assumed with the decisiveness of a law of nature that the present constitution of society was permanent. Socialists, such as Lassalle and Marx, who have accepted this view believed that only by overthrowing the existing system could they change conditions that were otherwise unalterable. Toynbee's aim was to place George in the same category, that is, as "purely and entirely a disciple of Ricardo,"[158] despite George's statements concerning interest and wages rising and falling together. Toynbee maintained that George's main contention was that with material progress rent must rise; in this he was merely repeating Ricardo's theory that identified the owner of land as the person most likely to benefit from progress. Hence their theories of progress were in fact identical. Disproving one would be as good as disproving both.

In his attempt to confute Ricardo, which made use of a recent article by J. E. Thorold Rogers in the *Contemporary Review* (April 1880), Toynbee intended to demonstrate Ricardo's faults and to suggest modifications. Ricardo's theory of rent proved historically inaccurate. The rise in rents during the period 1790–1830, which had led Ricardo to formulate his theory, was the result of improvements in agriculture, growth of population, a series of bad harvests, and a supply of food limited by the operation of the Corn Laws. Ricardo's mistaken notion that improvements in agriculture caused a fall in rent (the subject of Rogers's criticism) was the result of the special circumstances following 1815, when "a sudden coincidence of agricultural improvements and good harvests" resulted in an "overproduction of corn."[159] Under normal circumstances, rent was determined by an increasing demand from a growing population and by the availability of land, an explanation that in Toynbee's view applied to both agricultural and urban rents.

Turning to George, Toynbee attempted to show how changing circumstances under the existing system served to diminish rent. As communications improved, the quantity of land available for agriculture was increasing, thereby reducing agricultural rents. Social changes, which were "probably imminent," would reduce the value of town (i.e., London) land, freeing it for agricultural use. Toynbee believed that the improvements in telegraphy would cause London to lose its position as the monetary center of the world. With the anticipated breakup of large rural estates (possibly forced by the state intervention advocated elsewhere), there would be fewer owners of great estates residing in London, thereby detracting from the city's appeal as a social center. London was already losing its ascendancy as a political center (presumably with the growing political importance of provincial industrial centers, a view that overlooked its position as capital of the empire). Finally, improved means of transport were likely to effect greater demographic diffusion. No institution was sacrosanct, including private ownership in land, but if society was indeed "on the eve of a certain and permanent fall in agricultural rent,"[160] George's scheme became pointless. Private property in land would of itself become a relatively insignificant institution, and it was best to allow change to take its natural course.

The issues and the solutions contained in Henry George's work gradually came to dominate Toynbee's thoughts, a process evident from the contents of the final lectures of the Industrial Revolution course. He came to regard *Progress and Poverty's* main appeal—its "ingenuity and power"—as a threat, likely to mislead the general public. At one point in the course of his lecturing he wrote, "I have known George's book for a very long time. I always thought it, while full of fallacies and crude conceptions, very remarkable for its style and vigor, and while no economist would be likely for a moment to be staggered by its theories, it is very likely to seem convincing to the general reader. I remember last year [1881?] at the Master's [Jowett], Mr. Fawcett asking me to tell him about it—he had not read it even then."[161] Fawcett's ignorance may have heightened Toynbee's sense of mission by demonstrating that few economists had realized the danger of George's popular appeal, and even fewer felt called upon to do something about it. Toynbee had already conceded that industrialization and free competition had often resulted in widespread working-class distress. He now set out to collect figures that would establish that, since the repeal of the Corn Laws in 1846 (i.e., the fourth stage of industrialization), "it is a fact that though the cost of living had undoubtedly increased, [real] wages have risen in a higher ratio."[162] Thus, after a very brief consideration of Ricardo and the third stage of industrialization Toynbee continued the course by proceeding beyond the chronological framework given in the introductory lecture. Furthermore, rather than concentrate on a historical analysis of current problems, he transferred his attention to the likelihood of the future progress of the working class. "Economists have to answer the question whether it is possible for the mass of the working classes to raise themselves under the present conditions of competition and private property,"[163] or, more specifically, how can the worker "secure his complete material independence."[164] In the face of real problems and the threat from the revolutionary left it was the economist's duty to utilize his knowledge to furnish the politician with the solutions for the problem of unequal distribution of wealth.

Suggesting practical measures and the refutation of Ricardo and George had become by now fairly standard themes in Toynbee's work. The novelty of his final lectures was in his insistence that a measure of material progress had already affected the life of the working class. Ricardo was wrong. The workers could better and have bettered their material conditions. Interest had been stationary or had fallen slightly but, with further progress, was likely to rise despite the anticipated continued rise in labor's wages. George, whose theory was based on observations made in America was similarly wrong. Interest and wages did not always rise and fall together. Since 1846 rents and wages had risen while interest had remained stationary. Furthermore, it was possible that with an increase in wealth all three would rise together; it was even possible for the capitalist's wealth to increase at a faster rate than that of the landowner.[165]

With digressions came further inconsistencies. Toynbee kept moving back and forth from one argument to another, offering different answers to the same questions differently phrased. In lecture 12, when his main concern was Henry George, he stated confidently that the problem of urban rent would solve itself. At the end of lecture 13, which appears to be infused with a sense of urgency concerning the need to provide a positive gospel rather than long-term assurances, Toynbee referred to the problem of urban land rent in different terms. He admitted that it was most likely that "the problem of the distribution of wealth is sure, in the near future, to take the form of the question, how to house the labourers of our towns."[166] It was true that a considerable measure of inequality was inherent in the prevalent system of private ownership of urban land, but in stating this George had only "restated more forcibly what Adam Smith and Mill advocated." In other words, economists had been aware of the problem, vide Toynbee's own previous suggestions on the matter of housing which emphatically did not suggest waiting for the matter to resolve itself.

Toynbee's main message to the working class was that, despite Ricardo and George's bleak predictions, they had since 1846 improved their lot. This had occurred mainly through the operation of free trade, factory legislation, and self-help. Free trade had increased the aggregate wealth and with it the demand for labor. It had steadied trade as well as wages and the price of bread. The worker was better paid and more frequently employed. The current ("the great") depression in trade was caused by the bad harvests from which some of England's clients had been suffering. It temporarily reduced demand for some English manufactures with a result of "the depression in one industry spreading to others."[167] The depression was an occasional and unavoidable consequence of free trade, temporarily affecting an otherwise stable and prosperous system. The salubrious effect of free trade had been supplemented by factory legislation which had imposed a limit on the hours of work and had improved working and living conditions (especially in the area of sanitation).

The remaining agent in the progress of the working class was self-help, which had taken the forms of trade unionism and cooperation. Trade unions had contributed to the system's stability by helping to avert social and industrial disorder. The English, unlike the continental worker, "does not look to the State or to revolutionary measures to better his position. . . . English Trades-Unions resort to a constitutional agitation which involves no danger to the State."[168] The worker's preference for self-help was evident from the success of the cooperative movement. The future of the working class would find expression in the expansion of trade union activity and in the extension of cooperation toward production.

Extreme measures of state intervention, such as advocated by George and the land nationalists, would only impede the free and beneficial operation of free trade and self-help. Free trade ensured increasingly cheaper corn and increasing real wages all over the world, thereby constantly stimulating further trade. The rate of population growth may not diminish, but there was no reason to suppose that emigration would cease to offer an outlet for surplus labor. There was also no reason to doubt that cooperation would realize its ultimate object: cooperative production.

Working-class material progress has been matched by moral progress. This was especially noticeable in working-class temperance, orderly behavior, personal appearance, dress, and a growing aversion to "immoral talk."[169] With the extension of suffrage the workers' horizons have widened and "the discussion of the newspaper is supplanting the old foul language of the workshop." Finally, by organizing in trade unions the worker has established himself as his employer's equal. Since 1860 the class antagonism brought about by the "cash nexus" has been replaced by mutual respect. Trade unions made boards of conciliation possible providing the new equality in industrial relations with an organizational expression. "The new union of employers and workmen which is springing up in this way, is based on the independence of both as citizens of a free state."[170]

Toynbee had named his fourteenth and final lecture, "The Future of the Working Class" (a possible allusion to Mill's "On the probable futurity of the labouring classes"). Not content with identifying the current trends that were transforming society toward his vision of the future, he added a discussion of some other views of the future. Toynbee described the Positivist position advocated by "Mr. Frederic Harrison and his friends" as based on their belief in "a gradual change in the moral nature of capitalists,"[171] while dismissing the potential of cooperative production and similar schemes. Toynbee did not dismiss this vision outright. It was not unlikely that in the future the prevailing passion for wealth among employers might lose its intensity. A changed public attitude toward the accumulation of wealth was likely to affect distribution. However, a moral revolution was not likely to take place within "a reasonable space of time."[172]

Toynbee had greater hopes for industrial partnership as described by Sedley Taylor.[173] Taylor regarded industrial partnership as a combination of "economic science *enlightened by the spirit of the gospel* and pointing over the heads of lower antagonisms to a higher unity, that an ultimate solution is to be looked for."[174] Toynbee felt that, although profit sharing was more realistic than the Positivist vision, its universal adoption was not likely.

As an afterthought Toynbee added to his survey "the ordinary Communist solution" in its two more important forms: voluntary associations based on common property (which could only succeed on a small scale) and the nationalization of the means of production (which was, in his view, impractical).[175] This did not preclude socialism in the form of limited state intervention. Toynbee had already adopted a sympathetic attitude toward limited state action. He repeated his observations concerning the beneficial effect of the Factory Laws, adding to them the Employers Liability Act (1880). He felt that, although "the extension of regulative interference . . . is not likely to be of much further importance," the principle would "probably attain a wide-reaching application in the readjustment of taxation which would produce great changes."[176]

As in his previous statement concerning workers' housing the subject of state intervention gave rise to Toynbee's more radical suggestions, certainly more radical than his standard support of trade unions or cooperation. In the course's final paragraph he suggested that the state through the readjustment of taxation could "supply for the people many things which they cannot supply for themselves. . . . the State might take into its hands such businesses of vital importance as railways, or the supply of gas and water," to which he added his previous suggestion of municipalities purchasing land and letting it below its market value in order to subsidize workers' dwellings. His suggestions appear to have been derived from municipal socialism, but it is significant that Toynbee made the step of applying municipal practices to national issues. He concluded with a note that reflected his vision of the society he had been hoping to help realize (e.g., through his Poor Law Guardianship), a society "founded primarily with philanthropic objects" in which various voluntary bodies, like the societies for artisan dwellings or for providing inexpensive music, would, within the municipalities, take over the care of the poor unprovided for by the strict operation of the Poor Law.

In the course of the lectures Toynbee's position of the unbiased student was transformed into that of the radical reformer. At first his message had been confined to matters on which he, as an individual, could have little, if any effect. He could not substantially aid the cause of free trade or working-class self-help except by trying to convince all classes to help to support them. His main theme had been to demonstrate the reality of progress. The many interventionist measures that he had praised, such as the Factory Acts, were historical accomplishments that did not necessitate further action beyond the odd supplementation. His approach changed while considering the issue of workers' dwellings. He came to admit that current conditions were less than satisfactory and by implication that the present grievances of the revolutionary socialists were real. A practical and effective answer would have to be offered for dealing with each grievance if the appeal of revolutionary socialism were to be checked. The natural operation of free trade and self-help could not provide those answers. Concrete intervention was required and it was his duty to help to guarantee it. Hence many of the course's digressions and inconsistencies are due to this transition in Toynbee's positions and to his reluctance, or perhaps inability, to abandon totally one while adopting another.

6. A Speculative Politician

As an Oxford Liberal and a friend of T. H. Green, Toynbee was almost inevitably drawn into public life even before he had formulated his own principles of concrete political action. Political involvement had been one of the ends of the "Regeneration of Humanity," and, while the society was to work out the principles and details of political action, it was also assumed that each individual member would seek a way of fulfilling his duty as a citizen. This attitude toward civic duty among Oxford men was not peculiar to Toynbee and his friends. The *Oxford Chronicle* of 23 April 1881 reported Toynbee's election to the Oxford Poor Law Guardians in which he joined W. A. Spooner, A. H. D. Acland, Robert Ewing, and L. R. Phelps, all of whom were elected by the heads and bursars of colleges entrusted with appointing eight out of thirty-five of the Oxford guardians.[1]

Some months earlier the Oxford Co-operative and Industrial Society's Education Committee, of which Acland was a member, announced a course of six lectures on political economy by Toynbee.[2] In addition, the committee advertised a series of single lectures to be given at the Liberal Hall by members of the university including Spooner, H. S. Holland, B. R. Wise, and Andrew C. Bradley (on Mazzini).[3] These lectures were combined with tours of Oxford colleges in which Oxford dons served as guides. Their aim was to improve relations between members of the cooperative society and the university by introducing them to its scholarship, architecture, and art treasures. In this and other forms of public activity Toynbee had joined a loosely defined group of like-minded dons and graduates whose names reappear with some regularity in the lists of supporters of various reform-oriented schemes. For many of the younger liberals civic duty was linked with political action. Thus, at the second Palmerston Club dinner, at which Acland, A. Robinson, A. Sidgwick, Milner, Toynbee, Graham Wallas, T. H. Warren, and E. T. Cook were present, it was declared that "the political situation demonstrated that the best hope of furthering the welfare of modern communities lay in the development of party discipline."[4]

In the course of 1881 Toynbee had also joined the Oxford Anti-Mendicity and Charity Organization Society, of which Percival was president, Ewing, vice chairman, and Spooner, honorary secretary. At its 1881 annual meeting it was decided that Toynbee and Sidgwick should join its general meeting.[5] Toynbee and his fellow Poor Law Guardians saw no contradiction in their serving both public and voluntary relief agencies. They regarded their activities as complementary, although it was felt by some, including Toynbee, that these two spheres of responsibility should be kept separate.[6] In describing his position on Poor Law administration, Toynbee's fellow guardian L. R. Phelps attested that Toynbee "had a strong view with regard to some of the evils that he felt were almost inseparably bound up with it, but at the same time his knowledge of its problems had led him to the belief that they were capable of no such easy solution as the abolition, at one blow, of out-door relief."[7]

Toynbee's organizational solution to charity administration called for the institutional separation of indoor from outdoor charity. The first would be administered by the Board of Guardians and would constitute its main responsibility. As for outdoor relief the main problem was of examining the individual cases of deserving poor and ensuring that each would receive relief in the manner most conducive to his welfare and, in cases of the temporarily unemployed, providing an incentive for self-help. This would require the reorganization of the voluntary charity bodies. At the 1881 annual meeting of the Oxford Anti-Mendicity and Charity Organization Society he produced his scheme for such a reorganization.

There were a few Unions who had abolished outdoor relief and in those places what had been called a pension committee had been formed, the object of which had been to give relief to deserving people. This Committee was altogether distinct from the Charity Organization Society. They did not investigate cases, but took the report of the district committee and then decided applications. He thought they might try to establish a pension committee in Oxford, which could work in connection with the C.O.S. and enable the Board of Guardians . . . slowly to get rid of outdoor relief.[8]

It was the one area of Toynbee's interests in which, perhaps because of its vogue among North Oxford dons, he was joined by his wife. In an article published in 1900 she restated his scheme, clarifying some of its details. State administration of charity was to be confined to indoor relief, treating the cases of "inevitable" poverty, the results of sickness, death, "sin and vice."[9] Boards of Guardians were deemed incapable of effectively dealing with individual cases of outdoor relief, often causing more harm than good. This was especially the case whenever the "respectable poor" were forced "to pass by scores before the board" only "to have thrown down to them miserably small and inadequate doles." Wherever self-help was possible state intervention would most likely do mischief by encouraging a demoralizing dependence. In this function it was best replaced by independently managed private funds that, if applied intelligently, would provide an outlet for philanthropic zeal and help those whose poverty was potentially remediable.

Oxford Liberals had a bad year in 1881. In the November municipal elections they had lost five out of the ten contested seats, all of which had previously been Liberal. Their losses included two of the North Ward seats, which were won by W. Simmonds, a coal merchant, and Walter Gray, Steward of Keble College.[10] Simmons and Gray beat by a considerable margin the Liberal candidates: Robert Buckell, secretary of the Liberal Hall Company and the Oxford Reform Club, who had represented the North Ward on the council since 1877, and Lowe, the outgoing mayor.[11] The North Ward with its two breweries had previously been a Tory stronghold with a firm popular base among the brewery workers residing in the ward. Earlier in 1881 Buckell, who had also been the president of the North Ward Liberal Association, admitted that "the North Ward had been the battleground of the two parties, and municipal contests had been fought there on a scale and with all the enthusiasm of parliamentary elections."[12] In other words both parties resorted to illegal practices of the type for which Buckell was cited in the committee's report on the 1880 elections.[13]

Curiously enough these practices were defended by none other than T. H. Green, Liberal representative of the North Ward, at the ward's Liberal Association's annual meeting. Green argued that it was wrong to denounce the ward's Liberal Association for employing some of the ward's poor Liberal voters. "They were employed in a *bona fide* manner. They were kept at work and their work was recorded. They were not overpaid, but they were employed in order to keep them true to their previous allegiance to the Liberal party." They had voted Liberal in the past therefore it could not be maintained that their votes were bought whereas "to have refused employment would have been simply to throw up the election."[14]

It was assumed at the time that the ward's floating vote was mainly the working-class vote. The Liberals felt certain that workers who voted for the Tories did so either through ignorance or by submitting to the temptations offered to them by the Tory-controlled breweries.[15] Accordingly, the speakers on behalf of the Liberal candidates in the 1881 elections (including Green and E. T. Cook) appealed mainly to working-class self-respect.[16] This, however, did not preclude other measures.

By 1881 both parties had recruited considerable support from within the university. Nevertheless this involvement was still something of a novelty and an attempt was made to manipulate the position of one of the Tory candidates—Gray, as steward of Keble College—to awaken some of the latent town-versus-gown animosity. A letter by Buckell, published in the Liberal *Oxford Chronicle* of 22 October 1881, headed "The Northern Lights" and signed "A Citizen," alleged that in his capacity as steward, Gray had shown his hostility toward Oxford's tradesmen by attempting to divert the college trade to "foreign sources." Gray dismissed the allegation as "groundless and untrue" and argued that in the ten years of the college's existence it had spent £500,000 of its trade in Oxford.[17] Although the *Chronicle* did eventually admit that it was the college's practice to trade mainly with Oxford tradesmen,[18] it nevertheless blamed the Liberal defeat in the North Ward on "the college authorities and the High Church party joined with the publicans," an alliance dubbed "Bible and Beer."[19]

At the next annual dinner of the North Ward Liberal Association, held in January 1882, Green confirmed that "it was a time of great trial and difficulty to their Association . . . a time of great anxiety both for Liberal politics generally and in particular for the Liberal cause in Oxford."[20] He professed dissatisfaction with the "slackening of energy" that had overcome the Liberals in Parliament and in the constituencies despite, or possibly because of, the great effort to pass Gladstone's new Irish Land Bill. An improvement in trade and the rising cost of parliamentary campaigning had combined to create a house membership consisting mainly of wealthy men indifferent to the "interest of the struggling and suffering classes of society." The solution within the constituencies called for the reorganization of the local party machine on a more voluntary basis. Let volunteers replace salaried party workers, thereby creating a cheaper and more committed organization. The next step would be to use the new party machine to elect parliamentary candidates who, with the help of the party, would not have to depend on private or external means to finance their campaigns. Such candidates would be elected for their "disinterestedness, high mindedness, and the strength of character which they could thoroughly trust." They would have to possess a true understanding of the complex problems of modern society as well as "the strength of character" to devote himself to their solution. "They wanted a man whom they could trust to work in the peoples' cause, because in his heart he loved it." A new organization and the right candidate would win back the working-class vote and lead the Oxford Liberals to victory.

Green did not elaborate on a definite program for legislation. He had stated repeatedly his unshakable faith in Gladstone and his admiration for his second Irish Land Bill. He stuck to the old Liberal principle: "the removal of all obstructions which the law could remove to the free self-development of our English citizens," but he also admitted that the problems of society were becoming increasingly complicated. Later the same year, and shortly before his death, when he did comment on government policy, it was only to restate his support of Irish reforms to which he added a careful reference to the House of Lords, which in principle should be abolished unless it ceased to constitute a "club of great landowners."[21] He insisted on the need for social legislation while deriding the Tories as "the party of vested interests and naturally afraid of legislation." But he did not elaborate on what the details of such legislation should be.

Green's sudden death on the morning of 26 March 1882 came to Toynbee as a considerable shock. He had just returned from an enjoyable lecture tour in the north, where the audiences had been most appreciative, and was to lecture again at Leicester on 28 March. On the day of Green's death he wrote to his sister Gertrude, "I am sick and miserable to-day, for Green, the Professor of Moral Philosophy, whose lay sermons you have read and whom I loved deeply (more than I knew), died suddenly this morning. How broken one feels after a blow like this! . . . I've got to speak at Leicester on Tuesday. I wish I were a thousand miles away."[22]

Toynbee did not cancel the Leicester engagement, but it nevertheless took him some time to overcome his despondency. Rather than return to Oxford he spent some days at his mother-in-law's in Wimbledon from whence he wrote to L. R. Phelps, "I don't care very much what goes on in Oxford now Green is gone. The place will be utterly different and I almost dread going back there. I shall value the few friends like yourself I have there all the more now. It is not a place to live in without friends whom one can sympathize with and lean upon. But I have no right to complain more than anyone else. All those who came under his influence must feel the same."[23] He returned to Oxford about a week later.

In the course of his lecture at Leicester it was first indicated that in some respects Toynbee might be considered as Green's successor in realizing his political and social ideals. Green had previously delivered at Leicester his "Freedom of Contract" address and was therefore not unknown to Toynbee's audience.[24] The chairman at Toynbee's lecture—the president of the Leicester Liberal Association—expressed in his introduction the sense of loss he felt by Green's death. Toynbee answered that "If he, as [Green's] pupil, following in his footsteps and endeavouring to attempt a political survey [in "Are Radicals Socialists?"], could catch some of the spirit which he infused into all his pupils, and could communicate some of that spirit to them, he should not upbraid the fortune which forced him to speak to them at a time when the sense of his loss was so fresh upon him."

The theme was repeated when, following the lecture, a vote of thanks was proposed. The vice president of the Leicester Liberal Association declared that

they were exceedingly obliged to Mr. Toynbee for leaving his quiet life at Oxford and coming face to face with the living multitudes in the great towns, following so well in the steps of his revered teacher their late friend Professor Green. It was a sign of hope for the future that Oxford should send some of its most promising sons to lecture to the people in their great town. They saw . . . a fine specimen of the young Oxford of today, they saw also, he believed, a very fine specimen of what Oxford would be to-morrow.

The seconder added that he found himself strengthened "by the very pleasing fact which had been brought before them that evening, that the mantle of the eminent lecturer who had passed away had fallen upon his pupil, the principle speaker of that evening. (Cheers)."

Political conditions in Oxford seem to have contributed to Toynbee's being groomed as Green's political heir and perhaps even the personification of Green's ideal candidate. In addition to the North Ward's newly elected Tory representatives the ward was represented by two Liberal councilmen (elected in 1878) who were up for re-election in the autumn of 1882. Green's death vacated one of these seats. Buckell was nominated but he lost the by-elections held on 13 April 1882 to the Conservative candidate, E. Turner, an iron-monger of Little Clarendon Street.[25] The *Oxford Chronicle* considered this new Liberal defeat as nothing less than a "public calamity." It alleged that the "whole organization of the Church, combining the influence of the Clergymen, the Visiting Ladies, and the Guilds' was brought to bear against Buckell"—a Dissenter. Repeating Green's prescription after the previous defeat, the *Chronicle* argued that victory in the November elections could be achieved by reorganization of party machinery and by the better education of the public.

A move in the direction of furnishing a better political education for the electorate was made in the opening of the Oxford Junior Reform Club, on 9 August 1882, at the Liberal Hall.[26] It was announced that the club's aim was to educate the younger members of the community, in the belief that "the dissemination of political knowledge will form the surest foundation for the strength and permanence of the Liberal cause." The opening was celebrated by a luncheon addressed by Toynbee and J. E. Thorold Rogers. It was obvious from Toynbee's address that local politics were gradually entering his plans. He explained that local politics were not intrinsically different from national politics so that, although his main interest lay in national politics, the unity of issues and principles justified an involvement on the municipal level. "He knew there were some people who said that municipal elections ought not be made an arena of party conflict, but he thought their opinion was entirely wrong.

(Hear, hear.) Large political questions drew out capable men, and if they confined these elections to the narrow issue of municipal politics they would not get the same stamp of men to come forward. (Hear, hear.)"

Toynbee's gradual drift into municipal politics was further facilitated by the continued difficulties of the Liberal party machine as well as the growing confidence of the North Ward Conservatives. The latter had recruited J. C. Wilson, a lecturer in Jurisprudence at Exeter College, and J. W. Hoste, a commoner of Magdalen College, to address a North Ward Conservative meeting.[27] The ward's three Conservative councilmen confidently predicted that the days of the corporation's old Liberal clique were numbered.[28] In addition, the prodenominational members of the school board succeeded in blocking the election of Buckell as Green's successor on the board, thereby keeping the balance between pro- and antidenominational at five to three in their favor. The move was interpreted by the Oxford Chronicle as aimed specifically against Buckell. Buckell himself referred half-jokingly to his position as that of "a played out politician."[29] Rather than face another defeat, Buckell accepted an invitation to become a candidate for the safe West Ward thereby vacating the candidacy of the North Ward for the forthcoming November election.[30]

The Conservatives were quick to discern the signs of panic in the Liberal camp.[31] They discovered that Buckell had been changing the registration of voters eligible to vote in more than one ward to the South and West wards in order to secure some of the remaining Liberal seats. The move was interpreted as a practical abandonment of the North and Central wards to the Conservatives. Sensing a general swing in their favor, the Conservatives now declared that, despite their belief that "the Council should be common ground unaffected by politics," they were forced by the Liberals to introduce into the campaign issues of national politics. With justified confidence they anticipated a repetition of their victories in the parliamentary by-elections and the municipal elections.

While Buckell had been forced to abandon his North Ward candidacy it seemed reasonable to assume that the Liberals might still be able to hold onto their last surviving seat in the ward if a candidate could be found who could reproduce Green's appeal. Toynbee was persuaded to stand,[32] the nature of his candidacy made clear by his advertisement published in the Oxford Chronicle:

It is only after very great hesitation that I have accepted the invitation of a large number of the Burgesses of the North Ward to become a candidate for the Representation of the Ward in the Town Council.

My only claim to your confidence is the fact that I was the friend and pupil of your late Representative, Professor Green, whose principles I should, with however inferior powers, endeavour to uphold. These principles I understand to be—purity of administration, the advancement of education, and the promotion, in a spirit of justice, of the welfare of all classes of the Citizens.[33]

The Conservatives dismissed him as "a university spark who had little recommendation but a gift of the gab."[34]

Toynbee was officially introduced to the North Ward Liberal Association at a meeting held on 19 October at Jericho House with Buckell presiding.[35] A considerable representation of university Liberals was noted, including L. R. Phelps, H. F. Pelham (Exeter College), A. Sidgwick, and F. C. Conybeare (University College). It was made clear by Buckell's introduction that the Liberals hoped that Toynbee's candidacy would appeal mainly to two classes: university members resident in North Oxford and artisans. Much was made, by Toynbee's cocandidate, G. W. Cooper, of Toynbee's lectures to working-class audiences. Green's memory was invoked, and it was asserted that Toynbee's understanding and sympathy with the working class would combine ideally with Cooper's experience as a local party man.

In his first address to his constituency Toynbee tried to combine his various academic and ideological positions with his limited experience as a Poor Law Guardian to offer a platform of sorts. Most of his current interests were represented, including some of the subjects of his last Industrial Revolution lectures. His main theme was the need for greater working-class participation in all forms of local government. Only thus could Oxford's two communities become one. He believed that the main obstacle in the way of meaningful change was working-class apathy, the result of misconceptions concerning the nature of progress and its past and future effect on their material conditions. They were unaware of the extent to which they had benefited from the Liberal economic policy of free trade, a process he was eager to present to them as a scientific fact.

He had taken the trouble to make enquiries whereever he went about wages and the cost of living in order to see whether these statements were

true that the working men had gained nothing by their national policy
. . . of free trade and economy. (Applause.) . . . he was convinced
from enquiries he made in the factories in Lancashire and Yorkshire and
about the coal-pits in Northumberland, and in various agricultural counties—enquiries not confined to one trade but extending to almost every
occupation—that a considerable rise in money wages had taken place. . . .
He ascertained, in fact, that the income of both labourer and artisan had
increased more than their expenditure, while the improvement, he admitted, was not as great as they should desire.

His main contention was that much could be done to raise their
condition to a more satisfactory level through working-class participation in local government. In a flight of rhetoric he declared, "It was
almost of more importance to them to deal firmly with local affairs,
to insist on pure government in their towns, than it was to insist on
right principles of national government." However, he must have
caught himself as toward the end he reaffirmed his previous position
that "the principles by which they obtained a just administration
. . . and just laws for the nation were the same principles by which
they could obtain just and pure administration in City affairs."

The working class's immediate interest in local administration was
largely confined to the rates. Toynbee found that in the instance of
house rents, the amount of which was largely determined by the
rates, a laborer spent as much as one-fourth of his income on housing, an artisan, one-sixth, and a member of the middle class, one-
eighth or one-tenth. Therefore, "low rates were more important to
the working man than to the middle class." At the same time it was
within the interests of the working class to invest in an efficient
administration that would enforce sanitary laws, even at the expense
of relatively high rates. Either way the working class had a direct
interest in local government. Toynbee claimed to have made "enquiries about the rents and condition of workmen's dwellings in
several towns." His findings were that substandard conditions were
due mainly to landlord avarice and inefficient enforcement of legislation, such as the 1875 Public Health Act. Efficient enforcement
would not necessarily preclude reasonable landlord profits, but it was
largely up to the working class to exert pressure in order to ensure
such enforcement.

Another sphere of public life in which greater working-class representation was desirable was Poor Law administration. Abolition of

outdoor relief would lower rates as well as establish a moral principle. "It was obviously unjust that the honest and industrious working man should pay rates to keep the thriftless and drunken in ease and comfort. (Loud cheers.)" As for the deserving poor, Toynbee claimed a measure of success for his alternative approach to outdoor relief: "Whenever a case came before the Guardians about which they had any doubt, it was referred for investigation for a week, and a committee of ladies and gentlemen looked into the question, and if a widow of a labourer who had done his best to save, and had died before he could leave sufficient support for his wife, they determined to give a pension and find her work if possible, so that the respectable might be severed from the disreputable. (Applause.)"

In support of his main thesis Toynbee argued that, since the reform of 1867, the emergence of working-class electoral power had generated considerable "working class legislation" such as the repeal of the conspiracy laws (1875) and Forster's Elementary Education Act. Toynbee declared his resolution to extend the process to local government, thereby setting himself up both as Green's heir and as the people's tribune. He stressed his determination to pursue a political career in the interests of the people of Oxford. He would endeavor to help make Oxford into "a place where students and citizens laboured together for the public good." Thus he seems to have hoped to impress his constituents with the seriousness of his commitment as well as the selflessness of his motives.

It appears to have been felt that Toynbee was handicapped by the university's negative image among the town residents. Two of the other speakers, Pelham and Sidgwick, both of whom were members of the university, were at pains to impress upon the audience Toynbee's complete sincerity in his wish to represent the interests of the whole community. Pelham emphasized the unity of interests between university and town, which had been further strengthened with the development of North Oxford, and the growing involvement of resident members of the university in local affairs. University members were eager to place their education and intelligence at the disposal of the community and their offer of friendship should therefore at least be given a fair trial. Sidgwick wished to dispel any suspicion local Liberals may have had of university Liberals. The university had various types of Liberals, some of whom were distrusted by the local party. These included the Whigs ("rather a defunct specimen"), "the Liberal jingo, and the independent Liberal who was not to be depended upon." Toynbee was none of these and could therefore be completely trusted by his fellow town Liberals.

Following the announcement of his candidacy Toynbee became the main target of the North Ward Conservatives, whereas his fellow candidate, Cooper, was generally dismissed as of little consequence. Toynbee was attacked on various accounts. At a meeting of the Conservative Oxford Workingman's Association held in the North Ward on 20 October Toynbee's address to the Liberal Association was described as "a tremendous long effusion." His ignorance of local matters was ridiculed, and his claim to represent the working class was dismissed as spurious: "the way to get working men there [the City Council] was not to put bursars of colleges in it."[36] In an echo of the previous campaign it was also alleged on several occasions that as his college's bursar Toynbee had discriminated against Oxford tradesmen. Also, according to one account, he had expressed his support of the cooperative movement by preferring to deal with the local cooperative store at the expense of other local shops, an entirely groundless charge.[37] Another line of attack aimed at further discrediting him with the same class of voters (i.e., small tradesmen) presented Toynbee as the landlord's enemy. Accordingly, the Conservatives predicted that Toynbee would soon discover that "unfortunately small house proprietors in Oxford had strong representatives in the Council, and if he attempted to buy them all out he would exhaust his own and his friends' money, and even the funds of Balliol College itself."[38]

A potentially more damaging criticism referred to Toynbee's record as a Poor Law Guardian. There had been a case on which he had voted against dispensing outdoor relief to the wife of a drunkard who, having broken a rib, was laid up in hospital. Rather than ignore the matter Toynbee was driven to publish a letter (dated 26 October 1882) in the Oxford Chronicle in which he restated his position on charity administration, including his appeal to working-class moral indignation at indiscriminate outdoor relief. While he admitted that in that specific case he had indeed been inclined to refuse relief he had also initiated further investigations with the result that outdoor relief was eventually approved with Toynbee's support. Although he conceded that the results of a close examination of the case had led him to change his mind, he justified his initial position on the grounds that "every one knows that the most difficult cases with which the Guardians have to deal are those in which there is danger either of punishing the deserving with the undeserv-ing, or of encouraging drunken men to leave their wives to be sup-ported by other people. My own opinion is that often what appears the hardest decision proves the kindest in the end."[39]

The issue was also raised in Toynbee's second major campaign speech on 24 October in which he reiterated that the workhouse was a solution applicable only to the undeserving poor. As a mat-ter of principle no respectable poor should be sent to the workhouse. Each deserving case, its merits having been established by an inde-pendent voluntary body, should be allowed an adequate allowance that should be paid "out of the pockets of rich people who were willing to give," rather than out of the rates.[40] His faith in his scheme for an independent pension committee clearly remained un-shaken. He repeated it at a meeting, following the elections, of the Oxford Anti-Mendicity and the cos, adding to it evidence on the op-eration of a similar system at Bradfield (Berkshire) where the Guardians "had practically abolished outdoor relief, except in the case of aged labourers." As for widows "who he [Toynbee] thought were the most difficult people to deal with, the guardians invariably asked the widow how many children she had. Supposing she had three, two were taken, and one was left for her to support herself."[41] He even thought that a pension committee would be welcomed by the philanthropists on whose contributions it would depend for its operations. "The private committee was merely doing them a service by preventing them [from] wasting their money; and . . . they were giving them an opportunity of exercising that personal sym-pathy and care the absence of which was one of the chief con-demnations of out door relief."[42]

Aside from the Conservative criticisms, some genuine and some spurious, Toynbee's political rivals observed with some acuteness that, bearing in mind Green's relations with the local party machine, Toynbee's election might prove more harmful to the Liberals than to the Conservatives. Two of the Tory councillors, Gray and Evettes, argued that, while they agreed with Toynbee on certain issues and thought that he might make a good councillor if he stuck to his views, the local Liberals would find him difficult to control. In one instance he was described as "one of those independent radicals whom the Caucus men now dominant in the Town Council would be very sorry to see there."[43] Specifically on the matter of housing improvement it was noted that Toynbee's views were in opposition to the interests of his fellow candidate, Cooper, who, according to the Tory press, was the largest owner of small house property in Oxford. In this sense the Tories were in agreement with Jowett who in his memoir of Toynbee wrote, "He was not a party politician at all."[44]

In his second campaign speech Toynbee repeated the theme of his first speech: working-class political involvement. He admitted that he was in no position to discuss the municipal issues that were being debated by the various candidates. Invoking Green's example he chose instead to concentrate on the general principles that applied to both national and local politics. Technically he aimed at impressing his listeners with the factual basis of his argument concerning the actual improvement in the conditions of artisans and laborers. He produced various figures to support his views and quoted at least one source of information he had used in the Industrial Revolution lectures.[45] In a possible echo of Marxist dialectics he argued that workers' discontent did not disprove his figures concerning their actual welfare. With material progress came higher expectations and a sense of discontent which manifested itself in a "higher ideal of life."

Toynbee's speech attempted the dual appeal intended in "Are Radicals Socialists?" It contained some arguments that were expected to assuage middle-class fears of working-class radicalism as well as other arguments aimed at converting the working class to his broad liberalism. In addressing the middle class he stated that while he did not credit the working class with recondite political wisdom, it could not be seriously maintained that education and intelligence guaranteed acute political judgment. This he thought was evident from the opposition to the abolition of the corn laws when both Lord Derby and the agricultural laborers insisted that a lower price of corn would lower wages.

On the national level Toynbee expressed support for extending the franchise to the agricultural laborer. Only by sharing political power "the educated few might know by the pressure of the wants and wishes of the many what it was the workmen and labourers required." The most effective and, in the final analysis the safest, school for the political education of the working class was practical experience. Shifting his argument back to his appeal to the workers he argued that "if they would co-operate with educated people, with merchants, and tradesmen, and University men, they would learn more and more to assert their independence, to wipe away the reproach of corruption and resist the influence of wealthy brewers. (Applause.)"

Toynbee was accompanied at the meeting by L. R. Phelps and one of his Balliol students, Kenworthy Brown.[46] In support of a resolution endorsing Toynbee's and Cooper's candidacy, Phelps returned to the theme of the university's involvement in local politics. He pointed out that the university's isolation had ended in 1854 when it and the colleges were made to pay rates on their property. Consequently they have sought "to bear the public burdens which properly fell on them." The development of North Oxford deepened the university's local involvement, and it was only due to the peculiarities of the 1867 Reform Act that college residents were precluded from taking part in the town's political life. It was his belief that "there was at this moment throughout the University as warm a feeling in the interest of all classes, high and low, in the city as any body of men could find," a sentiment that he hoped would be represented by Toynbee in the council.

Finally, a letter from Charlotte Green, T. H. Green's widow, was read in support of Toynbee's candidacy. While she expressed regret that Buckell would not represent the ward she attested to Toynbee's being "exceptionally well qualified for the office, and I know [he] will walk worthily in the steps of him who previously held [the seat]." Thus Toynbee's position as Green's recognized political heir was given the final stamp of approval.

Toynbee's campaign was rounded off, with a mere suggestion of unease. An editorial in the *Chronicle*, expressing the official view of the local party machine, presented Toynbee's status as a newcomer to municipal politics as something of a virtue; it proved Liberal willingness to infuse local politics with new blood. It was argued that as the bursar of a not too wealthy college, "utmost skill and economy" and the qualities of "a good man of business" were required of him, all of which were certain to prove of value in the council's work.[47] It was added, somewhat feebly, that his appointment to the bursarship was made by Jowett himself who was renowned for his shrewd knowledge of character and his keen practical sense, an argument that was inevitably ridiculed by the Tory press.[48]

The elections resulted in another Liberal setback. They had lost two additional seats in the council, including their last one in the North Ward, and their majority was reduced to a parity. The North

Ward poll was: Turner (c): 1,051, F. Hall (c): 993, Cooper (L): 958, and Toynbee (L): 946.[49] Buckell, on the other hand, was elected to a safe West Ward seat and was appointed sheriff. The Liberals blamed their defeat in the North Ward on the massive support the Conservatives enjoyed among the 467 women voters (their estimate was three-quarters) and the urgent need to overhaul the local party organization on more popular and representative lines. As for Toynbee's candidacy it was felt that his main handicap had been his relative anonymity which could not have been aided by his refusal, a la Mill, to canvass a single voter.[50] Considering the number of votes he did succeed in attracting in a campaign of a mere fortnight, it was felt that his chances would greatly improve when he "comes forward again next year."

It is clear that Toynbee was determined to remain politically active. Shortly after the elections he was elected member of the Local Board of Health on the quota appointed by heads and bursars of colleges and halls,[51] and on 21 November he addressed a meeting of the North Ward Liberal Association at which he pledged to continue his political work in the ward.[52] According to a report in the Conservative *Oxford Times*, "the scene at the meeting was remarkable for its utter despair and despondency, which was visible on the faces of all present"—a probable exaggeration, although the atmosphere must have been far from jubilant.[53] The meeting's main purpose was to examine the causes of the Liberal defeat and possible remedies. It was generally agreed that the existing organization could not cope effectively with the ward's growing electorate. Hence a considerable effort would be required to "embrace the whole of the Ward with their canvassing workers." Another reason suggested was reduced party expenditure. The issue as stated by the chairman, T. W. Mallam, one of the ward's Liberal agents, was whether an election could be won without money and without personal canvassing. Mallam himself felt that the party had been justified in reducing the outlay of election funds, but he tactfully ignored the question of canvassing.

In the meeting's central address Toynbee admitted that he may have been wrong to avoid personal canvassing, a view that seems to have been generally shared by the ward's Liberals. On the other hand his insistence on basing local policies on the principles of the national party was accepted by local party leaders despite some grumbling about political and party feelings swamping "everything gentlemanly and honourable in debate," with the result that experienced and dedicated councilmen were being turned out of office. As in his previous speeches, Toynbee dedicated most of his address to the application of general principles to immediate issues, an approach that was now officially endorsed. Buckell, who appears to have been the local party leader closest to Toynbee, declared that their best prospects lay in studying the principles of Liberalism and in educating the population in their light so that they might judge "which set of principles, which policy was to govern the city of Oxford in the future."

In his address Toynbee returned to the recurring theme of his political speeches: workers' political involvement and the great promise of democracy. He commenced by describing the great anticipated benefits of working-class political representation: an effective airing of their grievances and views contributing toward the community's unity. He ended by confirming his faith in democracy as the nation's great purifier. But in between, as had often happened in his lectures, he discussed almost at random an assortment of various current issues, new ideas, and some results of recent investigations, producing a confused dissertation on the various applications of liberalism. On the national level he mentioned the need for a reform of the House of Lords to give it a more representative character and the further extension of suffrage which, despite various real and imaginary dangers, was the only means by which "the wrongs and sufferings which the people endured" could be redressed. He discussed the need to reform the systems of local and national taxation. He restated the principle of confining state intervention as a legitimate resort to cases in which voluntary association was ineffective. He defended the Liberal record on the 1880 Liability Act (which had been criticized by the trade unions)[54] as "simply an alteration of the law which enabled workmen to obtain justice," rather than a deviation from the principle of nonintervention. On the other hand the same did not apply to attempts to guarantee minimum wages through legislation. In his view "it was quite impossible for the State to do very much by direct interference to improve the condition of the workmen. He did not suppose that a single workman would believe that if the State tomorrow passed a law that every workman in the country should get 30s. per week, that such a thing would take place." Hence boards of conciliation were not contrary to the principle of minimal interference since their authority lay in enforcing laws and regulations ensuring basic working conditions. They were merely another means of helping the workers to help themselves and should therefore be strengthened by further legislation.

He next turned to a resolution of Birmingham's Council of Trades Unionists calling for the abolition of the clause by which workmen who received medical relief from local charity authorities were disenfranchised. Such a resolution was "antagonistic to the fundamental principle of the Liberal party" concerning self-help through voluntary action, and could only have been passed by workmen who "probably had not thought out the question in great detail." He had collected figures from Leicester and Oxford that proved the viability of providing medical dispensaries to which the worker could subscribe by paying a weekly sum that constituted a mere fraction of his income. Such a solution was consistent with the principle of reducing workers' dependence on public relief while consequently reducing local rates to which working-class contribution in relation to its income was disproportionately high. In his view, "without being deprived of their political rights, and without having their sense of political independence wounded . . . it was not too much to ask them to release themselves from the demand of medical relief from the parish."

As for municipal policies Toynbee introduced the question of centralization of local government. All local bodies entrusted with municipal affairs should be amalgamated into "one great municipal body." He also admitted to having reviewed his stand on housing. To his surprise (and, considering Cooper's position as landlord, possible relief) he found that as a rule the state of Oxford working-class dwellings was satisfactory.[55] Apparently, Toynbee had added the subject of housing to his projected historical survey of progress, enabling him to produce the results of some preliminary research into the causes of the improvement in housing in the course of the last two decades. Briefly, these were: higher wages, the growth of building societies that enabled working men to control the building standard of their own houses, sanitary legislation, and, in Oxford, albeit to a relatively limited extent, the operation of the Cottage Improvement Society (which had undertaken to treat some of the worst housing cases in Oxford). The cause of better housing could be further advanced by a municipal committee whose membership included working-class representatives.

Beyond these assorted issues Toynbee attempted to state his version of the main characteristics of liberalism on the basis of which he intended to conduct his future campaigning in Oxford. These included the often-stressed principles of workers' political participation and the extended application of democratic principles. However, the focus remained the ideal of social unity. In his view the main feature of the Liberal party was its national character. It "was not the party of the workmen; it was not the party of the middle class, nor the party of the capitalists, but it was a party who drew its support from every section of the people." The party should support just working-class claims, especially in view of the danger that they might be opposed by pressures the workers could not hope to resist on their own. By influencing public opinion the Liberals could actively support the working class in instances where state intervention was likely to result in more harm than good. It was essential that the workers be made to realize that the strict observance of the principle of nonintervention did not preclude active and effective help in redressing their grievances and in obtaining justice. Through the "expression of righteous indignation brought to bear against the 'interest' that stands in the way of social reform," Oxford Liberals could actively help to reduce the power of publicans, the power of the church, and the power of the rich. Toynbee seems to have succeeded in reducing his liberalism to a relatively simple formula that was acceptable to the local party machine both as a platform for future action and as the focus for the political education of the citizens of Oxford.

7. Education of the Citizen

Toynbee was drawn into active support of the cooperative movement in general and the Oxford Co-operative Society in particular by A. H. D. Acland, then student of Christ Church and secretary of the Oxford extension lectures. Acland had become an active promoter of adult education within the framework of the local cooperative society (founded in 1872) as early as 1878. On 11 March 1878 the Co-operative District Committee recommended that each society set aside an educational fund of 1.25 percent of its net annual profits.[1] It was Acland's initial ambition to channel the fund into financing adult classes and lectures rather than spending it on the usual reading rooms, social meetings, and newspaper subscriptions.[2] In 1880 he succeeded in organizing a series of lectures to the Oxford Co-operative Society given by members of the university, following which the society formed an educational committee that was to ensure that the educational work would continue.[3]

As the first secretary of the newly founded (16 June 1878) Oxford Standing Committee of Delegates of Local Examinations, Acland possessed a concept of adult education significantly different from the one developed by the more experienced Cambridge extension movement. The ideal of adult education as perceived at Cambridge was to introduce all classes of English society to science as taught at Cambridge. Accordingly, Cambridge extension courses followed as closely as possible the contents and length of one term of university work. It combined lectures with classes and weekly essays and culminated with a final examination and an honors list. Thus by attending a sufficient number of courses anyone could attain a close proximation of a Cambridge education. Acland, on the other hand, regarded the adherence to the framework of a university term's work as relatively inconsequential. His main concern was to reach, by all means available, as large a portion of the working class as possible, with an ideological rather than a purely scientific message. In an essay published in 1885, which summed up his views on the matter, he wrote:

What is then involved in trying to educate the young men and women of the working classes, especially in the matters which concern their lives as citizens? . . . There are many subjects of an educational kind, all of which may interest men and women according to the bend of their minds and their earlier training, which might each in their way be lead-ing in the right direction, and encouraging people to lead more useful, thoughtful, capable, less selfish lives in their position as citizens. We do not, however, consider such subjects as foreign languages, science, or the important question of technical education. For our young adults, oppor-tunities for scientific study, and for the study of those technical subjects which may make more skillful workmen and better wage-earners, will assuredly be afforded more and more as education improves in this coun-try. We are rather thinking of these more general topics of social and economical interest which touch the lives of all who want to live useful and capable lives as any ordinary citizen in town or country.[4]

During the early 1880s the cooperative movement's potential for self-help still occupied a dominant position in the standard liberal vision of the future of the working class. Whatever the disagreements among liberals concerning the desirable limits of government inter-vention it was generally assumed that it must assist self-help rather than replace it. Cooperation not only produced beneficial effects by encouraging thrift and by improving working-class material condi-tions, but the act of joining a cooperative society in itself was an indi-cation of progress in that it expressed the principle of self-ameliora-tion through conscious corporate action. It is therefore not surprising that Acland sought to realize his concept of adult education through the cooperative movement rather than follow Cambridge in creating an independent network of extension committees. In Acland's view, cooperation constituted "a platform, a basis, a foundation upon which any number of hopeful movements and any amount of hopeful progress may be raised."[5] He hoped to use his association with the local society in order to launch a scheme of national cooperative education. Having gained some experience in cooperative affairs as well as the trust of the local society he succeeded in inducing the annual congress to agree on Oxford as its meeting place for 1882. It was hoped that with the strengthening of the ties between the movement and the university the national educational scheme could be launched in which the university would provide the teachers and the movement would provide the organization.

Senior and junior members of the university were recruited to help with the entertainment of the cooperative delegates, thereby contributing to the atmosphere of trust and goodwill on which the acceptance of Acland's scheme depended. Members of the reception committee included Toynbee, Percival, W. R. Anson, H. S. Holland, A. T. Lyttelton (Holland and Lyttelton were to become members of the *Lux Mundi* group), L. R. Phelps, R. L. Nettleship, H. F. Pelham, A. L. Smith, T. H. Warren, A. Robinson, and D. G. Ritchie. Most of the actual entertainment of the delegates was left to the more junior members including F. C. Conybeare, Bolton King, M. E. Sadler, John St. Loe Strachey, and others. In the event, the offer of entertainment by undergraduates and young dons proved exceptionally popular among the delegates. Apparently there was some doubt as to whether the delegates, at the end of the conference's first day, would not feel too tired and rather than accept the invitations of hospitality choose to "stump back home." But, as Acland related the next morning, "though we put on ten [additional] undergraduates, we exhausted all the undergraduates before we came to the end of the delegates. I am thankful to say that two of our [senior] members threw themselves as well as they could into the breach with some others, and carried off the remaining 40 or 50 to Balliol College, where supper was provided for them in familistere style in about a quarter of an hour."[6]

The success of the entertainment was further augmented by the nostalgia of some of the movement's middle-class leaders, typified by Thomas Hughes's recollections of his days at Oriel. At a luncheon in Christ Church Hall organized by the reception committee and held on the congress's first day, E. V. Neale, another Oriel graduate, suggested that the tie between the university and the movement should be given a more permanent expression.

The University had come forward to meet the working man. Why should not the working man on his side go to the University? The co-operative societies wanted to know what to do with their surplus capital. Let them devote some of it to found a Hall in the University. . . . It would serve to ennoble labour when they could point to a Master of Arts of the University of Oxford working as a foreman in a great co-operative establishment. . . . He believed it would do much to inaugurate a new phase of co-operation between the industry of the country and its chief centres of thought and teaching. In time the Working Men's Hall might grow into a Working Man's College, which . . . would promote economical education . . . it might be called Hughes College.[7]

The idea was welcomed by the next speaker, A. Greenwood, and, although it did not quite tally with the scheme he had in mind, Acland neither rejected it nor did he think it unrealistic. Such a hall might be started with a number of scholarships and exhibitions and possibly a rented house for accommodation, all of which could be financed by cooperative central funds. Acland believed that, as a national university, it was Oxford's mission to contribute toward the bridging of the growing gulf between the classes. In this respect Oxford's contribution might be of greater significance than that of the growing local colleges.

If a young man is brought up simply in those surroundings in which he has already lived, the teaching and guidance he gets, however good, will not give him the same width of view and the same breadth of mind which he will get if he comes here and knocks up against all kinds of different people; the sons of country gentlemen, the sons of clergymen; the sons of all sorts of persons who have not perhaps come within his ken. I believe that two or three years of life in Oxford will make him a wider, broader, and better man.[8]

This firm belief in the university's national mission and in its peculiar power to fulfill it was to permeate the Oxford extension movement; the result was occasional clashes with other extension organizations and the new local colleges who resented Oxford's territorial "encroachments." As for Neale's idea, although it was raised again in his preface to the published proceedings it went no further than the founding of the Hughes Scholarship at Oriel College. It was not until the foundation of Ruskin Hall (in 1899) that the dream of an Oxford workingman's hall was realized, although not by the co-operative movement.

The ground for the reception of the education scheme was further prepared by various entries in the official *Guide to the Co-operative Congress*. The work done by members of the university in aid of cooperative education was described in the entry for the Oxford Co-operative Society,[9] and in the report of the secretary of the Southern Section.[10] Another undertaking mentioned was the Guild of Co-operators (one of whose members was Toynbee's brother, H. V. Toynbee), formed at the suggestion of the Southern Section of the Co-operative Union with the purpose of publicizing cooperative ideology and assisting in cooperative work.[11] The guild had founded a circulating library of 450 volumes arranged in boxes of thirty volumes each which were lent out to societies for three-month periods. The books included "works of history, imagination, science, travels, and social and political questions." It was further suggested that once or twice a year written and oral examinations should be held under the guild's auspices at one or more centers. Cooperators might be examined on their proficiency in various practical skills, such as bookkeeping, commercial geography, or weights and measures of various countries; they could be awarded certificates of competency for doing well. At the same time a parallel venture might offer courses in "historical and economic subjects" making use of the lending libraries and offering annual voluntary examinations. It was stated "that in the case of both these plans, the Guild should lead the way and carry them out on a small scale as an experiment."

The main presentation of the Oxford scheme was made by Toynbee in his paper, "The Education of Co-operators," read during the afternoon session on Tuesday, 30 May, in the Town Hall.[12] In it Toynbee represented the movement as the forerunner of the future industrial society, a goal the movement had long since quietly abandoned. Most modern associations aimed at satisfying some of the wants or fulfilling some of the needs of men in modern society. The cooperative movement alone united the principle of association with a moral ideal in a manner approaching that of the medieval guilds. There was in existence a multitude of modern associations, many of which were "the direct creation of that State interference against which many co-operators entertain a generous prejudice,"[13] in that they were created in order to protect their members' rights as defined by modern legislation. In this limited respect legislation "has strengthened, and not weakened the sense of moral responsibility and habits of voluntary co-operation." But they all, including trade unions, had limited practical objectives whereas cooperators possessed an ideal of the regeneration of the social system: "to put an end to competition and the division of men into capitalists and labourers."[14]

Likewise various organizations have assumed responsibility for modern society's various educational needs. State-supported elementary education—public schools and high schools—provided for "intermediate education," university colleges for higher education, the churches for religious education, and technical schools, whether set up by employers or by the state, provided for technical education. It was now up to the members of the cooperative movement to undertake the education of the citizen in accordance with the movement's national role and its ideals. It was their duty to enlighten each member of the community to "the relation in which he stands to other individual citizens, and to the community as a whole."[15]

That it was the cooperators' responsibility to undertake such a task was argued on the basis of Toynbee's interpretation of the nature and significance of modern cooperation, an interpretation not necessarily shared by the delegates present. In his view, the movement had recast Owen's original ideal of "self-complete communities" based on "equal association and the pursuit of a moral life" to encompass the whole English nation. By breaking up the ancient close-knit social units, industrialization had left society divided and structureless. Hence "the problem for us is not to re-create union at the cost of national life, but to reconcile the union of individuals with national life; not to produce union at the cost of independence, but to reconcile union with independence."[16]

Although the individual had been virtually reduced to a machine by industrialization, he had also been raised by a "law of political development" from the position of serf to that of citizen, sharing in the government of the state. It was a new status that required the training that the "education of the citizen" would provide. Toynbee did not explain why technically it was only the cooperative movement and not, say, the state, that could undertake the responsibility for providing a comprehensive, nonpartisan political education on a national scale. The outline of his scheme had nothing to do with cooperation. It might, therefore, be supposed that it had been developed independently of his interest in cooperation and could therefore seek realization elsewhere (e.g., in the work of the Oxford Junior Liberal Club).

Toynbee's scheme was based on three principal subjects, one of which—sanitary education—was mainly technical, aimed at strengthening working-class ability to enforce the sanitation laws. The other two subjects—political and industrial education—were to incorporate three approaches: an analysis of the present systems and their operations, a historical survey of their development, and a history of relevant theories and reform programs, political and social. To the subject of political education Toynbee added England's foreign and imperial relations, and to the subject of industrial education he added a history of its social aspects, that is, of the material condition of the working class.[17] Each subject's point of departure seems identical with that of all of Toynbee's inquiries: present conditions and their history, combining the history of ideas and the history of social, economic, and political institutions. Here as elsewhere he stated that a true understanding of the present based on an analysis of the past provided a vital guide to future action—in this instance, instructing the citizen "what are his duties to his fellow-men, and in what way union with them is possible."

Except for the general outline of subjects Toynbee's scheme lacked any specific details. Instead he chose to deal with possible objections. On the subject of political education he felt, like many liberal radicals (noticeably those active in the Social and Political Education League), that much of the traditional liberal creed had become inadequate. Political education need not be partisan. Toynbee felt confident that, due to the inherent harmony in society, once all members of the community managed to comprehend their true interests their political conclusions must coincide: "men's deepest interests are not the peculiar possessions of factions and parties, but the rightful inheritance of every citizen."[18] No shortage of able and willing teachers was anticipated. "In the ranks of co-operators themselves, and in the Universities, there are . . . persons who have studied political and social questions with all the keenness of partisans, but without their prejudice. The fact that these men will often, of course, have reached definite practical conclusions will not destroy their influence as scientific teachers."[19] On the question of organization, Toynbee suggested that they might follow Professor J. L. Stuart's recommendation, made on behalf of the Cambridge extension, to appoint regional lecturers responsible for teaching in each district's various cooperative centers.[20]

Despite the scheme's general conceptual content Toynbee was not entirely insensitive to the peculiar problem of convincing the delegates of its desirability and feasibility. He admitted that its main obstacle was the "difficulty of persuading workmen to listen to anything which does not concern pleasure or profit. . . . workmen are less eager now about political and social questions, because they are more prosperous, and this is the danger co-operators have to meet— the danger that material comfort may diminish spiritual energy."[21] He hoped that the delegates would realize that, despite the obvious difficulties, the effort must be made and that with the combination of an ideal and a realistic plan it could succeed.

As it happened Toynbee aimed too high. The next speaker on the subject of education, Benjamin Jones, at the time the honorary secretary of the Southern Section, came closer to the mark. He reduced the movement's aims to a much lower, and more comprehensible, level: the reinvestment of profits in cooperative production. Their objective was to bypass the evils of the existing economic system, and this could be done if "they accumulate capital to make them independent masters; become sufficiently well educated in co-operative principles to enable them to successfully combine for self employment, and to acquire a knowledge of sundry economic truths closely concerning their prosperity."[22] By the latter Jones meant the orthodox doctrines, including the "iron law" of wages, which he accepted as a valid description of the normal course of labor-capital relations regarding wages.[23] The only way of avoiding its effects, even in such matters as the future inclusion of cooperative dividends in wages, was for cooperators to become self-employed. Thus the future of cooperation was reduced to a question of profit reinvestment as well as given a distinct introspective, if not selfish, character.

Toynbee had left the care of technical education to the state and employers. Jones on the other hand thought that cooperative stores should undertake the technical training of their members and their sons, thereby contributing to the efficiency of distributive cooperation as well as to its future extension into production. In the same way in which the banks trained their employees to become better bankers, cooperatives should aim at training better cooperators. "If our members are to go on step by step, from a simple effort at shopkeeping, to the higher and more difficult stages, there must be education in co-operation, and education of a methodical and comprehensive kind." Jones called for the establishment in each store of classes, financed by the store's education fund and aimed mainly at the youth, catching them just after leaving school. The societies would furnish all the facilities and cover all the expenses. The classes would be held free of charge and the teachers, who would be recruited from within the societies themselves, would teach gratuitously. There would be examinations for various levels of proficiency and prizes for excellence. Through education, cooperators would not only realize the need for further investment in cooperative production but also be able to successfully undertake new ventures.

The obvious efforts of the reception committee and Acland's reassuring statements regarding the admiration with which university members held the cooperative movement helped to allay suspicions of condescension. Toynbee's paper was received, therefore, politely, but, as might have been expected, it was largely ignored. A typical reaction of the delegates who commented on the question of education was made by a Sheffield representative who kindly noted, "Both papers were excellent, and that of Mr. Jones was practical."[24] They all seem to have been preoccupied by the problems of their own societies and the question of investment in education at the expense of their members' dividends. As the discussion began to drift toward the question of cooperators' participation in externally organized science classes, and with the chairman displaying signs of impatience with the prolonged debate, Acland rose to rescue the university's involvement in cooperative education. Using his official status of delegate he stated his agreement with Jones that the best teachers of cooperative principles were likely to be found within the societies. However, there would still be a problem of textbooks. He suggested that Toynbee "and other friends" might form a small committee that, operating under the auspices of the Central Board, would produce short pamphlets, leaflets, and syllabi "on political economy and kindred topics" to be used by cooperative teachers.

As the discussion began to drift again, Acland's suggestion was seized upon by Lloyd Jones, who was present as a delegate, and was moved as a resolution recommending it to the Central Board. Toynbee tried to add to Acland's suggestion by emphasizing the need for a comprehensive scheme being drawn up by the Central Board rather than having each society and each teacher decide on his own program. "There were many other institutions making up for education, and unless co-operators could gather their forces and direct their attention to one point, they would not overcome that passion for dividend of which he had heard such constant complaints. The passion for dividend could only be overcome by a stronger passion for the cause."[25] Toynbee may have assumed that a program devised under the auspices of, and approved by, the Central Board was more likely to be based on, or at least contain, the principles he had advocated. The movement might also consider accepting, in addition to textbook writers, "special instructors" from the universities, a possibility that Benjamin Jones did not object to in his concluding remarks. The resolution adopted referred Toynbee's and Jones's papers to the various sections of the board "with a power to, and for the purpose of, drawing up a report on the whole question of education, which shall be sent out by the Central Board to societies as the outcome of our visit to Oxford and its University." In addition, Lloyd Jones's resolution based on Acland's suggestion was adopted.

In the course of the following year no action was taken in the direction of implementing the congress's resolution concerning a general report.[26] On the other hand Toynbee's and Jones's papers were distributed and discussed in various section conferences as well as in the *Co-operative News*.

Meanwhile Acland had some second thoughts on Neale's workingman's college. There existed, in his view, a serious danger that a cooperator who was sent to Oxford, having managed to acquire a sufficient knowledge of elementary Latin and Greek in order to satisfy university requirements, would, at the end of his studies, be lost to the movement and to his class.

Are they to return to the work which they left, or are they to become school masters, or ministers, or to join the ever increasing band of candidates for clerkships, who, attracted by the prospect of "respectability" and a black coat, often end up being far less educated, far less skillful, far less well off, far less independent, far less happy than many of the best of the artisan class, from which class they were not really rising, but falling.[27]

The ideal cooperator student was "a skillful artisan, with fair opportunities for good work, with a few hours in every week in the evening for self cultivation, a member of a good benefit society, a trades union, with a good balance in hand at the stores, and above all with a good wife and a house of his own." Such a man could be entrusted with a general education as offered by the universities, providing that he was willing to return, at the end of his studies, to his former life. Otherwise he "might simply become a discontented disappointed man, not strengthened, but weakened, by becoming a University man."

Acland felt that at least for the present it was best that the work should be conducted within the societies thereby enabling university lecturers to obtain first-hand knowledge of the movement while reaching the maximum number of cooperators. The first introductory lectures had been organized for the Christmas vacation and were to be given by Acland at the Manchester and Salford Equitable Society and at the Hebden Bridge Fustian Manufacturing Society.[28] "Is it too much to hope," Acland asked, "that in some future years there may be a demand here and there, from a group of societies, for a university man to go and spend a winter among them, and teach small classes of young cooperators week by week through the winter?"[29] This idea of a resident lecturer was to survive Acland in the Oxford extension as the ideal form by which Oxford might reach the nation rather than have the nation come to Oxford.

The differences with the Cambridge extension, which were partly ideological and partly the result of misunderstandings, came to the surface in a conference held on 20 September 1882 at Newcastle-upon-Tyne for the purpose of introducing the Cambridge extension system "to all associations of workmen, and particularly to co-operative societies,"[30] in a region in which Cambridge had already done some work. The differences between the Oxford and Cambridge approaches were apparent from their respective organization (Cambridge based its work on twelve-week courses consisting of a weekly lecture and class) as well as from their contents. R. D. Roberts of Clare College, Cambridge, stated that, in his view, a special cooperative educational program was too narrow an approach to adult education. It neglected science, an essential prerequisite for material progress, as well as culture, of which the ancient universities were the national guardians. Professor Stuart defined the object of cooperation as the bringing about of "a more equable distribution of wealth by the operation of natural causes." Therefore, except for specialized technical training, cooperative education should not be intrinsically different from the higher education offered to any other section of the working class. In words reminiscent of the educational philosophy of an older generation (e.g., Joseph Toynbee's) Roberts proclaimed that the aim of higher adult education was to "lay the higher truths before [the working-class's] gaze, and raise up in their minds the thought of a vast chain of cause and effect which bound the whole creation into one. . . . it would furnish a counter-attraction to those low, sensual indulgences which must be called the curse of their country, and it would cause them to take a still deeper interest, and to give a still deeper meaning to the world around them."

Toynbee, as might be expected, took exception to Roberts's interpretation of his scheme. In a letter to the *Co-operative News* he protested that it was his particular intention "to urge co-operators not to limit themselves to teaching the principles of co-operation [as might have been argued in the case of B. Jones's scheme], but to undertake a large, yet definite, part of education—the 'education of the citizen'—which was thoroughly in harmony with the traditions of their movement."[31] Cooperators should concentrate on one particular branch of education by which they would complement the work done by other educational agencies. Events seemed to justify Toynbee's insistence on a central educational policy. If the various societies were free to choose from among the various educational bodies, the scheme's essentially national character would never be realized.

The issue was further complicated in the Southern Section in which the Oxford educationalists had to contend with B. Jones's program. Jones, who had also thought in terms of a central policy, rejected Roberts's criticism. In a conference of the section he argued that his scheme merely suggested the educational priorities the movement should adopt, but his main concern was to ensure the autonomy of cooperative education. His immediate worry was not Cambridge but the danger of Oxford's excessive involvement. He at first argued that while Oxford and Cambridge teachers would be ideal contributors to cooperative education, the expense of engaging extension lecturers was more than southern societies could afford. It was therefore best that they find their teachers within their own ranks and train them themselves.[32] In reply, Acland pointed out that the courses he had previously suggested (in the *Co-operative News*) were not of the Cambridge extension type but much humbler affairs. He still hoped that a sufficient number of university men could be found who, like himself, would spend a few weeks among cooperators "and pass night after night meeting classes of co-operators, and helping them in their studies." Jones responded with a new objection, namely that, although university men were most welcome to contribute of their knowledge of "history and kindred subjects," the cooperators "must not forget that their care should be to learn thoroughly the principles and objects of co-operation. It was more important to working men to make history than to learn of what had been made."

Acland and his Oxford friends were placed in the delicate position of having to find a way in which the promotion of their scheme would antagonize neither the Cambridge extension nor B. Jones, who commanded considerable support in the Southern Section. Co-ordination with Cambridge was established at a meeting at Professor Stuart's rooms at Trinity College, Cambridge, in which Stuart, Acland, Toynbee, and H. S. Foxwell took part. It was agreed that the Oxford extension would officially support the Cambridge extension's efforts in the north while confining its involvement in cooperative education to instances in which demand was limited to "a humbler work than that of the University Extension Scheme in its complete form."[33] The semblance of common purpose and cooperation was further enhanced at a meeting held at Trinity College, Oxford, organized by the Oxford Committee of the Guild of Co-operators—Acland, A. Sidgwick, and Toynbee—and at which Roberts and Jones were guests.[34] The meeting's objective was to introduce the scheme to both senior and junior members of the university and, appropriately, the prevailing theme of all the addresses was that of cooperation and harmony. For a while the differences between the Oxford and Cambridge extensions were indeed solved by a simple division of labor helped by the limited resources and range of Oxford extension activities. The solution, however, was found unsatisfactory when in 1885 M. E. Sadler replaced Acland as the Oxford extension's secretary; hostilities were soon resumed.[35]

There remained the question of control over the operation of the education scheme in the Southern Section where the initiative was soon seized by Jones. At the section conference held on 28 October it was resolved that an attempt, "however humble," should be made by the section's societies to carry out "the system of education proposed by Mr. Jones's paper."[36] It was also recommended to the sectional board that an experimental teachers' training course should be started. However, Jones was not in a position to ignore completely the Oxford initiative. His main fear, as expressed in a circular addressed to the societies of the Southern Section, seems to have been that the societies as a rule would prefer university lecturers.[37] This fear may have fed on the enthusiastic response with which Acland's offer of a three-lecture course on "the systematic education of cooperators in their work as co-operators and citizens" was met, which had forced Acland to turn down some of the invitations.[38] Jones would have clearly preferred to have the Oxford committee relegated to a purely consultative position. However, he had to make allowances for its members' popularity as lecturers. It was finally agreed by the members of the Southern Section's board that, since they "feel a difficulty in procuring a university gentleman who has a sufficient acquaintance with the many details of co-operative work and practice," they would ask Jones to conduct the first teachers' training course, the syllabus for which was drafted by him and examined (and possibly added to) by the Oxford committee. At the same time the board also arranged for special lectures to be delivered by Oxford and Cambridge men (Stuart, Foxwell, Acland, and Toynbee).[39] In addition, a committee of four, including Jones and Acland, was appointed to consider the further implementation of cooperative education. The first teachers' training course was started at the Co-operative Wholesale Society, Whitechapel, on 31 January 1883 with an initial attendance of twenty-one pupils.[40]

The course's approved syllabus constituted something of a compromise between Jones's and Toynbee's concepts of the objective of cooperative education as understood by Jones.[41] It retained few of Toynbee's specific suggestions concerning the content of the course, but it did contain something of Toynbee's ideological position. The first lesson (out of fourteen) proclaimed equity to be "the keystone of co-operation" and cooperation as "a perfect form of civilisation," while lesson 2 contained a survey of the various benefits of cooperation to the nation. Lessons 2 and 3 considered the intellectual, moral, and social benefits of cooperation to the working class. Lesson 12 argued that the various existing forms of association, including trade unions, municipalities, and national government, were at best imperfect cooperatives. Finally, the last lesson, "The Co-operator as a Citizen: his Duties and his Attitude towards the Movements of his Time," aimed at demonstrating that perfect cooperation on the national level could only be accomplished through a general application of the cooperative principle of equity, hence the cooperator's duty to extend the application of his ideals. However, the course's main message was the desirability of reinvestment of profits in productive cooperation which was offered as the conclusion of various arguments. The general ideals may have been Toynbee's but the practical conclusion most likely to appeal to cooperators was Jones's.

Acland's work with the cooperative movement continued after Toynbee's death, although it was still some time before suspicions of condescension and paternalism were allayed.[42] His success was limited, and it was not until the congress of 1885 that Acland, on behalf of the Educational Committee of the United Board, could congratulate the movement for having enjoyed for the first time two full twelve-lecture courses given by a university lecturer.[43] Cooperative education failed to reach the national proportions Toynbee had envisaged, and it was only through Sadler's reorganized Oxford extension that some of Toynbee's social and political ideology reached a wide working-class audience.

8. Progress and Poverty

Toynbee's growing preoccupation with Henry George's *Progress and Poverty*, evident in the later Industrial Revolution lectures, was mainly due to the growing popularity of land nationalization among working-class organizations in both England and Ireland. In his 1881 pamphlet, *The Irish Land Question*, George confidently stated that Britain was ripe for agitation.[1] Nothing short of land nationalization could redress the imbalance between the material progress of the few and the poverty of the many. It was fallacious to suppose, as most English liberals did, "that in the democratization of political institutions, in free trade in land, or in peasant proprietorship, can be found any solution of the difficulties which are confronting them."[2] George was not the first to advocate a "total" solution of one sort or another, but in a period of agricultural depression, combined with growing Irish militancy and with the increasingly strident demand for the extension of borough franchise to England's counties, his doctrine had the appeal of simplicity and the promise of immediacy.

Unlike "standard" revolutionary socialism, the popularity of land nationalization was not confined to the small circles of London radicals and socialists, such as the positivists or the newly founded (1881) Democratic Federation. Some years later J. A. Hobson was to observe that as an extension lecturer he had found in the late eighties and early nineties "in almost every [extension] centre a certain little knot of men of the lower middle or upper working class, men of grit and character, largely self educated, keen citizens, mostly nonconformists in religion, to whom Land Nationalisation, taxation of unearned increment, or other radical reforms of land tenure, are doctrines resting upon a plain moral sanction."[3] By 1882 the popular support for land nationalization among workers was beginning to influence Trades Union Congress (TUC) politics as evident from the proceedings of the fifteenth annual congress held in Manchester, 18–23 September 1882.

The 1881 annual TUC, held in London 12–17 September, had unanimously adopted a relatively moderate resolution on land reform supporting a parliamentary move to facilitate "the acquirement by agricultural labourers of proprietory rights in the soil they cultivate" as well as the introduction of a bill providing cottagers and laborers with allotments of land.[4] At the same time the call for an increasingly independent political representation for the working class was gaining in popularity. The chairman of the Parliamentary Committee, William Crawford, stated that, while as a rule working men were on the Liberal side, workers "must be rigidly independent. Their actions must be above party considerations."[5] A similar blend of conformity and independence was present in Edward Coulson's presidential address. While asserting that the time for defensive strategies was over he stated, "We are not violent revolutionists, expecting an immediate political cure . . . or wishing to have everything arranged and provided for us by a paternal Government, but we are prepared to demand that no obstacles shall be placed by Parliament or the ruling classes in the way of our complete industrial independence."[6]

The exceptionally strident call in the 1881 TUC "not to trust to the political great guns and big wigs of the country, but to rely solely upon themselves to carry out and force upon Parliament the measures of which the country was in want," could be described as expressive of the mood of the 1882 congress.[7] In his presidential address Robert Austin attacked the Liberal government for the faults in the 1880 Employers' Liability Act, criticized Sir William Harcourt's reluctance to appoint workers as industrial subinspectors, and denounced war in Egypt as an extravagant expenditure "for the destruction of those people who have done us no harm."[8] The congress passed a resolution expressing the desirability and need for a larger measure of direct representation of labor in Parliament, adding, "The time has arrived when this question should pass from the region of abstract discussion to the domain of practical labour politics."[9] More significant, a relatively innocuous resolution calling for "extensive reforms of the land laws" was amended (by forty-nine to twenty-two) to the much more militant statement that "no reform will be complete short of nationalisation of land."[10]

The TUC's position on land nationalization was in line with its growing sympathy for Michael Davitt's Irish Land League agitation. The TUC had gone as far as adopting George's assertion that the Irish and English land problems and their solutions were essentially identical.[11]

Consequently, Toynbee's growing interest in George's work was coupled with an increasing preoccupation with finding a practical course of reform for both Irish and English rural problems. As of late March 1882 he had been examining, with Milner, George's solution and its possible alternatives.[12] Apparently dissatisfied with his findings and driven to investigate the Irish land system in further depth as well as the actual operation of the new Irish Land Act, Toynbee and his wife toured Ireland during August 1882. According to Davitt, the timing of Toynbee's visit was influenced by the press reports from the trials of the Joyce family murderers.[13] The Joyce family had been killed for fear that they would identify the murderers of two bailiffs who had been killed in January 1882 near Lough Masle in county Mayo, one of the centers of the Irish Land League agitation. Both the culprits and the witnesses were Gaelic-speaking peasants, members of a community that had been described by a sympathetic English traveler as "perhaps the least civilized of any in Ireland."[14] Four men, including one named Myles Joyce who apparently had been innocent, were found guilty and hanged, provoking a considerable outcry from Irish nationalists who condemned the execution as "judicial murder."

At first the Toynbees stayed with friends in a cottage in Killarney from where Arnold wrote to his sister Gertrude on 26 August 1882, "Beautiful as the scenery is, I have been more interested in the people. The Land Act is a great deal more intelligible to me after looking at peasants, holdings, and talking to peasants themselves. When I was at Oxford I worked hard at the history of the English Land Question, and I hope [very] much to be able to print something soon on both Ireland and England."[15] In a letter of the same date to his sister Grace (now Mrs. Percy Frankland) he added, "I am glad to be able to make the Land Act real to myself by cross-examining peasants and labourers. The disorder of the country is vivid enough to us. The other day a farmer was shot two miles from here and we attended his funeral, and a couple of hundred yards away lives an agent, protected by two policemen, who is to be shot next. The peasants tell you that murders will never cease till evictions cease."[16] Toynbee associated the Irish land agitation with George's theories and Davitt's Land League. He continued the same letter with the following comments:

I have known Mr. George's book for two years and have lectured on it at Oxford [in the Industrial Revolution course]. Recently I made the acquaintance of Mr. George himself. The work is remarkable as the first— or almost the first—American treatise on an economical subject that reflects American experiences. It is the product of a study of Ricardo's Theory of Rent and observation on "land grabbing" in California. Brilliant as it is, it is full of fallacies and based on a wrong method. . . . The work is getting generally known now because of Michael Davitt's Land Nationalization Scheme.

It is not clear where or when Toynbee had met George. In a diary entry dated 29 April 1882, Milner records having seen George "several times" during his English lecture tour. Toynbee may have met George during the same tour or possibly during George's subsequent (August–September 1882) tour of Ireland.[17] But, whatever the nature or circumstances of their meeting and despite Toynbee's empathy with George's motives, he could not accept the latter's theory. At the same time the problem's urgency and ominous nature required immediate consideration.

The sense of immediacy was greatly enforced by the misery Toynbee had witnessed in Connemara.

He saw people living actually on the mountains. They had a little patch of oats, potatoes, or barley, but they lived on the cattle and sheep which they fed on the mountain side. In one case, a very well intentioned, but indiscreet landowner had taken away this piece of pasture from the tenant, and let it to a grazier. It utterly ruined these people, because he took from them the mainstay of their life. The landlord spent large sums in giving them employment on his estate, but that by no means made up to them for the loss of the mountain waste.[18]

Toynbee may have found this situation analogous to the results of enclosures by English "improving" landlords.

On their way back the Toynbees stopped in Dublin where Arnold met Davitt. According to Davitt, Toynbee observed that "such a horrible crime [as that committed in Connemara] was due to the social and industrial condition of the peasantry . . . and also to the unnatural system of government, which concerns itself more with measures of defence for itself than with means for lifting the people it failed rightly to rule out of conditions of hardship and despair."[19]

Earlier the same year, following the Kilmainham treaty and his release from prison in May 1882, Davitt had been joined by George in addressing crowds in Manchester and Liverpool on behalf of the Land League.[20] He had cultivated contacts with the English trade unions and had been a supporter of the demand for independent labor political representation as expressed in the 1882 TUC (at which he was present).[21] His presence at the congress firmly bound the TUC's land nationalization resolution with the Irish Land League agitation. Despite their obvious differences, Toynbee had been shocked by what he regarded as the consequences of English policy in Ireland. In his history of the Land League, Davitt cites two letters from Toynbee on the Irish problem. On 30 December 1882, after informing Davitt of his intention to deal publicly with George's theory, Toynbee wrote, in reference to Davitt's description of distress in West Ireland in the *Freeman's Journal*, "I am not surprised at anything you say against the English government, under the circumstances, but I do wish you could win the [Liberal] Radicals to your side by showing that it is not hatred of England that actuates you but of English misgovernment."[22]

In the second letter, dated 16 January 1883, Toynbee proceeded to develop the theme of a possible cooperation between Irish reformers and English liberal radicals, a course of action Davitt himself was to adopt following Gladstone's later commitment to home rule.

The one thing I care for in the world is to soften a little the fierce enmity between England and Ireland. . . . If you would allow such a humble person as myself to co-operate with you I should be most grateful. I am not a politician, but a student who loves books, but I am dragged out of my seclusion by the turmoil that is going on around me. I cannot be quiet while this terrible crisis in the history of the English and Irish nations is before our eyes. On Thursday [18 January, the second "Progress and Poverty" lecture] I am going to speak on Ireland. I shall strain every nerve to make the English understand what is going on. My visit to Maamstrasna this summer opened my eyes.

With best wishes for your future and the future of Ireland.

The obvious bias of Davitt's work ought not to raise doubts concerning the authenticity of his account of Toynbee's sentiments. In his reference to Ireland in the lecture mentioned in his letter to Davitt, Toynbee repeated his position in terms that were even stronger than those used in his letters.

Mr. Davitt is right in saying that the labourers ought now to share in the reduction of rent which has taken place—for it was partly out of their wages that the excessive rent had been taken. The Irish Land Act of 1881 . . . does mark a great epoch in our history; but it is not an Act in which we can take any pride, for it was not the fruit of patient foresight, watching year after year to remedy the sufferings of a people; it was an Act snatched from us by crime and violence; . . . there is one class who are responsible—terribly responsible—I mean the Irish landlords (Hear, hear). I can hardly have temper to speak of them. Why did they imprison Michael Davitt? (Cheers.) Why have they goaded him to say mad things to the Irish people? Why have they put enmity between two great nations? Why have they driven a suffering race to pursue justice through crime? (Cheers.) . . . their power shall be taken away from them, and no class shall have it any more (Cheers).[23]

The TUC resolution in favor of land nationalization caused considerable alarm among liberal radicals bent on securing the perpetuation of the working-class–Liberal party alliance.[24] Concern was also evident within the cooperative movement. At the conference of the Southern Section that discussed the question of cooperative education, the chairman linked the subject of discussion with the surge of land nationalization popularity. "At the present time there was an immense socialistic movement going on all over the civilised world, and he was afraid unless there was a great increase of education that should direct and tone it down, it would end in a violent revolution, which would throw back for ages the progress of the working classes."[25]

For a while Toynbee's attention was diverted by other matters: the Oxford municipal elections, the new academic year, and new college responsibilities that were to lead to his anticipated election as a Fellow.[26] But with his defeat in the polls and his growing conviction of the necessity for popular political education he returned to the problem of formulating a detailed refutation of George's theories while providing a viable and comprehensive alternative. This presumably served to sidetrack him once again from his work on English

agrarian history from Tudor times, on which he had been collecting
material for some years and which was probably intended to furnish
the historical basis for his position on rural reform.[27] He went to the
extent of preparing copious drafts on George's work, which he used
for his two lectures on *Progress and Poverty,* delivered in the course
of Michaelmas term at the Palmerston Club.

From the drafts it is clear that at first Toynbee was somewhat uncertain as to the best way in which to deal with George's theory. The
obvious course was to use a line of reasoning basically similar to his
previous treatment of some of the "old" economists. This approach
suggested two obvious themes: a demonstration of the link between
George's theory and the unique circumstances that had inspired it,
circumstances that were not currently existent in England, and a
factual refutation of George's arguments concerning the existing cor-
relations among rent, capital, and wages (or, progress and poverty)
in England. However, since George was a contemporary theorist,
Toynbee was uncertain of the adequacy of a refutation of his theories
solely on the basis of current facts. George claimed to have revealed
the underlying universal principles of the relations among rent,
capital, and wages wherever private property in land existed. Refutation of the theories' factual application in any particular case,
whether contemporary England or elsewhere, might shake it but
would not necessarily disprove it entirely. At one point, with this
problem in mind, Toynbee wrote:

I think there will be but little doubt in the minds of most persons that
the average wealth of the whole middle class and of the whole working
class as well is greater than it was 40 years since. These facts alone are
enough to prove that Mr. George's theory of the progressive degradation
of the capitalist and workman class does not at any rate apply to England.
But I will now briefly explain the causes of the relation between rent,
interest and wages at . . . various periods.[28]

As it happened, it took Toynbee another sentence to realize that a detailed historical survey of English conditions was not practical, and
the draft was discontinued.

In questioning George's facts Toynbee regarded his own position
as invulnerable, as he often did when considering the factual faults
of deductive theory. "I will . . . test Mr. George's theory by experience. . . . It was a just remark of Mr. Cliffe Leslie's that one of the
principal views of the deductive method was that men were encour-

aged by it to omit the last and most important stage, the verification of conclusions by experience. Had Mr. George tested his conclusions he [would have] probably hesitated before publishing his book. I will now do the book wh[ich] he ought to have done."[29]

However, since this approach soon proved impractical, Toynbee was forced to attempt a theoretical refutation using his imperfect command of the deductive method. Thus Toynbee's criticism of George was meant to contain a demonstration of George's inconsistencies, his theories' invalidity, and his factual errors. By the latter Toynbee meant both the facts George himself had used in his analysis of conditions in California and historical and contemporary figures regarding the relations among rent, capital, and wages in America and in England with some reference to India, Ireland, and the continent.[30]

As might be expected, Toynbee was at his best in dealing with the factual inaccuracies of George's theories. However, when he came to analyze George's theoretical faults the result was often confusion. At one point Toynbee referred to George's admission that in an economically isolated area of cultivation (i.e., a "new land"), "wages will be determined by what the labourer can get working for himself on the land last taken into use," that is, on the margin of cultivation.[31] He then argued that George explained the drop in wages that followed the occupation of new lands through the operation of diminishing returns "activated" by the need to cultivate poorer lands.[32] In fact, George had argued that, when poorer lands came into cultivation as the result of increased demand for agricultural product, wages fell not because of the land's lower fertility but because of the increase in rent. Hence wages did drop not for natural reasons but because a larger proportion of the product was appropriated by the landowner in the form of rent.[33] P. H. Wicksteed was later to add in George's defense that Toynbee assumed that in a "new land" the peripheral uncultivated lands would be left unoccupied awaiting the need for extended cultivation caused by an increase in population. In fact, Wicksteed maintained, the lands would be occupied in anticipation of cultivation, thereby creating land speculation and ensuring that when the need arose the previously uncultivated land would bring in rents.[34]

Toynbee appears to have confused George's distinction between real wages ("wages as a proportion") and nominal wages ("wages as a quantity") in arguing that George did not explain the appearance of tramps and the fall of wages in a new country.[35] George had in fact stated that nominal wages might remain stable while rent rose, whereas real wages would drop. Toynbee further argued that George did not deal with the possibility of "tenure in large quantities" continuing despite taxation, whereas George had maintained that if each holder of land had to pay the whole rent to the state it would not be profitable for him to occupy more than he could cultivate.[36] George, therefore, did not ignore the question of the future of large farms but rather felt that they would naturally diminish in size.

On a different point Toynbee repeated his previous statement about Ricardo having been the "founder of two new systems of socialism," Lassalle's, through his theory of wages, and George's, through his theory of rent.[37] Elsewhere he stated that "Ricardo's theory of rent . . . which as far as California or any new country is concerned, is true."[38] However, it had been only partly understood by George, hence the latter's faulty analysis of Californian conditions. Wicksteed was later to argue that the theory Toynbee had attributed to Ricardo as the theory of rent valid in all new countries was in fact not Ricardo's but essentially George's, a claim that admittedly overlooked the occasional inconsistencies in George's theory.[39]

It might be argued that Toynbee himself was not entirely consistent in his criticism. George envisaged the state appropriating rent through taxation, thereby becoming "the agency by which the common property was administered for the common benefit."[40] The benefits to the industrial worker would, in the main, be derived from his share in the common property as allotted to him by the state, for example, through various services aimed at raising his standard of living (i.e., his real wages). At one point Toynbee stated that, while the revenue from the nationalization of rent would go to the state, "it would not benefit wages."[41] Elsewhere he argued at some length that the actual total income derivable from the confiscation of ground and agricultural rent would not exceed £60 million per annum, a sum hardly worth risking a "whole civilisation" for, regardless of how it was distributed.[42] It might, in addition, be noted that at this point Toynbee appears to have abandoned his previous prediction of the inevitable decline in rent that would render nationalization superfluous.

Part of Toynbee's difficulties were undoubtedly due to the large areas on which he was in agreement with George (a point noted and emphasized later by Wicksteed). He had been in sympathy with the fundamental grievances expressed by George as well as by most of the socialist writers. He had found George's book to have been one of many similar works "inspired by a vision of human misery" with "human injustice for its theme" and could not therefore dismiss it out of hand.[43] Toynbee also avowedly rejected the "old" economists' denial of hope for the human race.[44] But he was also determined not to "sacrifice my intellectual conscience by supporting a fair, but delusive panacea."[45]

Beyond his general sympathy with George's motives Toynbee's work reveals an agreement on many substantial issues. Whereas in the Industrial Revolution lectures he had unequivocally stated that the law of diminishing returns was universally valid,[46] he now came around to George's view and conceded that, at least in respect to new countries, the true law was that of increasing returns.[47] He was also in agreement with George when he stated that "when industries become monopolies [e.g., the London water companies] they should be undertaken by the state."[48] Both were confirmed free traders. Toynbee even admitted the validity of the application of George's theory to Ireland in which, indeed, "rent has lowered wages,"[49] to India, and to a certain extent to the south of England (mainly Dorset and Wiltshire).[50] Like George, Toynbee was wary of peasant proprietorship.[51] Finally, although he rejected the single tax solution, Toynbee was inclined to accept that more should be done to tax the rich's unearned increment through a graded income tax.[52] He virtually admitted that they deserved to be heavily taxed, while there remained the question of the most practical way of doing so without losing sight of the main course of progress. Toynbee and George may have been in greater agreement than Toynbee had initially been prepared to admit, but it was Toynbee's main contention that George's suggestions, if adopted, would not provide a total solution to the problems of industrial society. The scope of the problem was much wider and the solutions required much more complex. The full or partial appropriation of the landed unearned increment could at best be considered part of a program, certainly not its sole component.

The manner in which current issues came to dominate Toynbee's thoughts is apparent in a speech delivered on 8 January 1883 (three days before the first "Progress and Poverty" lecture) at a meeting

organized by the Newbury Liberal Club. Toynbee opened his address on land and franchise reforms by stating that

he was pleased to address such an audience, assembled not for the purpose of mere political excitement, but to obtain instruction (hear, hear).
The questions with which the Government had to deal were daily becoming more difficult because they were more important and pressed
more closely on the interests of the people (hear, hear), and when they
dealt with questions affecting the conditions of the people it required the
energies of the highest intelligence. It was a little unfortunate that as
some people were only religious on Sundays, some of them were only
politicians at election time (laughter), but if they really were to deal
with these questions they must be politicians every day of their lives
(hear, hear). They must carefully watch the course of events, and study
each question, turning what light they could upon it, and making use of
what experience they had (hear, hear).[53]

His own experience, he added, included (since 1881) his work as
Balliol's Senior Bursar. This experience had brought him closer to
problems of estate management and had enabled him to question
land agents on various matters, incorporating the information thus
collected in his "Progress and Poverty" lectures.

Toynbee was not alone among Oxford Liberals in addressing himself to the question of land reform. It was generally agreed that urgent change was made both inevitable and desirable by recent circumstances, including the Irish land reforms and the English system
being placed "on its trial not only by the progress of democratic
ideas, but also by the inevitable effect of agricultural depression the
severest and most prolonged [of] which has occurred within living
memory."[54] It is therefore not surprising that the Newbury meeting
was something of a Balliol affair. Toynbee was joined on the platform by his Balliol contemporary, William Henry Grenfell, the
former MP for Salisbury, and by J. L. Strachan-Davidson. It was
generally agreed that one immediate step toward the reform of rural
conditions was the extension of the franchise to the counties. A
resolution to that effect was moved by Strachan-Davidson (and seconded by Toynbee) linking the extension of the franchise to a reform
of land laws "as soon as possible." It was argued that the two issues
were linked in a manner resembling the connection between the
1867 franchise reform and the 1870 Education Act, hence "the grant

of suffrage to the labourer would be followed by a serious attempt to ameliorate his condition." Strachan-Davidson proclaimed reform to be a measure superior and preferable to revolution. "The tradition of the Liberal party had been to resist revolution by the timely removal of grievances." A step toward reform could be seen in the Irish Land Act that, by allowing the formation of a class of peasant proprietors, had created a class that "would have something to lose, and might be trusted to defend it."

Like most of his fellow radicals (as well as Henry George) Toynbee defined the land problem as "the concentration of land in a few hands," the result of a process he had described in lecture 5 of the Industrial Revolution. However, rather than limit himself to a discussion of the system's iniquities and their historical origin (as he had done in that lecture and as Brodrick would do in his lecture to the Junior Reform Club), Toynbee widened the scope of his investigation. He tied the misery of the rural laborer in with the growth of England's urban population, leading to the concentration of more than half of the urban population in London alone. The result was "a very serious and sinister political problem, enormously affecting the life of rural districts." The need for an urgent amelioration of the agricultural laborers' adversity should be considered as part of a wider effort to solve the problems of rapid urbanization that were seemingly getting out of control.

Toynbee had come to admit that in the instance of the agricultural laborer Henry George had been right: poverty had indeed followed progress. Whereas in the Industrial Revolution lectures, he had produced figures from Forfar in order to prove that the real wages of agricultural laborers had historically risen,[55] he now stated categorically (later limiting his observation's applicability to the south of England, thereby regaining consistency with his Forfar observations) that "the fact was, and an awful fact too, that whilst the wealth of England had increased rapidly, whilst great fortunes had been made in trade, whilst landowners had been getting richer, and farmers had made great fortunes, the condition of the labourer had been getting worse and worse."

In focusing on the plight of the agricultural laborer Toynbee had joined a number of Oxford dons who actively supported Joseph Arch's efforts to recruit farm laborers in the vicinity of Oxford for the National Agricultural Labourers Union (NALU),[56] and at least some of his Oxford contemporaries came to regard him as an authority on the matter.[57]

As may be surmised from his historical survey of the causes of rural distress, Toynbee regarded it as due mainly to a combination of political and natural reasons (namely bad harvests). Economic factors appeared to him to be subservient to political ones; hence political measures (i.e., the franchise) were more likely to effect an economic change.[58] The standard liberal solution had been free trade in land leading gradually to the development of a class of peasant proprietors: the resurrection of the yeomanry and the equivalent of a rural middle class. However, by then, peasant proprietorship had been abandoned by the TUC since it had declared in favor of land nationalization. Toynbee therefore set out to offer a sufficiently comprehensive and effective program for reform that would be more attractive than both the dangerous solution advocated by George and the standard free trade solution.

Rather than concentrate on measures calculated to affect directly the free trade in land, such as legislation abolishing primogeniture, Toynbee suggested a number of measures that would, in his view, diminish the social and political attractions of large-scale land ownership (whereas George had aimed at a diminution of its economic attractions). These included, in addition to the county franchise, the abolition of the game laws, the transference of local government powers to county boards (that were likely to be controlled by the agricultural laborers' votes), and, in the "Progress and Poverty" lectures, the abolition of the House of Lords.[59] As a result of these measures, "men would cease to care to own estates in several counties, amounting in extent to twenty, thirty, forty, and fifty thousand acres. . . . the desire, the passion to buy land, for political influence might wane." If, in addition, the agricultural land rent would continue to fall (as predicted in lecture 12) the historical trend toward the concentration of land ownership would be reversed (as in the United States, where the capitalists tend to invest in land for the purpose of speculation only). The end result would be similar to that hoped for by George, since it would "become impossible for men to own land unless they cultivated it."

These political reforms were to be supplemented by additional measures aimed at a more direct and immediate improvement of the agricultural laborers' conditions, including the discontinuance of the enclosure of common and waste lands by placing them in the hands of the projected county boards. In addition, in compliance with Arch's demands, each laborer should be enabled to purchase his house and a plot, half an acre in size. Public control over public land would allow experimentation in peasant proprietorship, possibly following the Prussian example.[60] As for subsidized housing and allotments, these would be made available by the state by means of a graded income tax. Another measure aimed at the strengthening of the agricultural laborers' independence would be the formation of provident medical societies (an issue that Toynbee had raised in a previous speech), which would free the laborer from dependence on parish medical aid.

Much of what could and should be done depended on the goodwill and the cooperation of the farmers. In the same way that Toynbee had hoped to strengthen the (by now somewhat frayed) alliance between the urban middle and working classes, he felt that the revitalization of rural England depended on the farmers' transferring their allegiance from the landlords to the laborers. Although he realized that at present "the great mass of farmers did throw in their lot with the landlords," he argued that "if the farmer were to be successful, he must throw in his lot with the labourer." If the laborers were not helped, rural decline would continue. At the same time the farmer could hardly hope for any significant help from the landlords, especially since it was not in the latter's interest to secure the farmers' investment in land by allowing security of tenure. The landlord's was a doomed cause, whereas the possible improvement in the laborers' conditions and the offer of higher wages would benefit the rural community as a whole. In an appeal to the contracting rural middle class—the farmers—Toynbee emphasized the relative ease with which change could be effected. "When he went into their great cities and saw the misery, destitution, and appalling wretchedness, he felt that he was in the presence of a great fate, and that it would be an enormous difficulty to raise these people; but when he went into the country and saw the cottages and the labourers themselves, . . . [he] felt that it was in the power of the farmers and landowners by only opening their eyes and determining to do justice, to remove this great evil."

By his own admission the main, and more complex, problem was that of the urban industrial working class. So far Toynbee's public appearances had been confined mainly to Oxford and to some north-

ern cities in which, as a rule, he had addressed audiences receptive
to his brand of radical liberalism. It had led him to believe that
popular political education was simply a matter of making people
listen to reason, the appeal of which they could hardly resist. Once
the people were in possession of the basic facts and were made aware
of the causes of present conditions they could not fail to concede
that reform along liberal lines was the only true and effective course
of progress. This, he believed, applied equally to middle-class and
working-class audiences. Yet not since his first debate at the Tower
Hamlets Radical Club had he confronted an audience of radical
working-class socialists who might prove hostile to his gospel of liberalism. An opportunity, or perhaps a challenge, of that nature presented itself in the late autumn of 1882 in an invitation from Uni-
tarian minister Philip Henry Wicksteed to deliver his lectures on
"Progress and Poverty" in London.[61]

The initiative for the arrangement of the lectures had come from
radical circles in London. It was at first suggested that the lectures
should take place under the auspices of the Democratic Federation,
apparently with the idea of producing a confrontation between
George's views, represented by the federation, and his critics. But
H. M. Hyndman, president of the Democratic Federation, objected
to antagonizing radical liberals who he considered to be allies (Toynbee being a self-proclaimed radical socialist) and therefore vetoed
the proposition.[62] The invitation was therefore issued by Wicksteed,
whose own interest in economics had been initially stimulated by
reading *Progress and Poverty*, and the lectures were set for January
1883.

There were those who questioned the advisability of Toynbee confronting a radical London audience. A correspondent of Phelps won-
dered whether he had much of a chance of being heard by "a
benighted flock led by partisan opponents who will follow their
leaders."[63] On the other hand there were those who urged him to
"show up that wicked book."[64] In any event Toynbee himself felt he
was in full command of his subject. Confidently, he wrote to Grey,
"I shall criticise him [H. George] from the point of view of the new
school of economists, and as an extreme Radical I shall express great
sympathy with his ideals. Both his theoretical and practical arguments are full of extraordinary oversights, and his whole scheme of
social regeneration is retrograded."[65] Not quite aware of what awaited
him he continued, "I shall like to get a good audience of all classes.

. . . I was very reluctant to turn away from writing just now, and should be sorry to throw away energy on an indifferent audience. . . . If we want the workman to listen we must criticise him from a radical point of view." In a similar vein he wrote to Davitt shortly before his first lecture, "I shall criticise Henry George from the point of view of a Social Democrat, and shall try to show that his theory of economic progress is to a very large extent mistaken. At the same time, I am myself in favour of very sweeping measures of social reform, but, then, I wish to see them justified on their own true grounds."[66]

The first lecture, delivered at Saint Andrew's Hall, Newman Street, on 11 January 1883, went well enough. It attracted a number of prominent radical reformers, including Professor Edward Spencer Beesley, the positivist, who chaired the meeting, and Alfred Russel Wallace, president of the Land Nationalisation Society.[67] There was some press coverage and a shorthand writer was employed (probably by Grey), whose notes were to be used for a pamphlet based on the lectures (which were delivered from sketchy notes).[68] Beesley, in his introduction, made it clear that the organizers had not arranged it in order to launch a crusade against George but merely to have his theory discussed by a political economist who was competent to furnish a serious and detailed response to *Progress and Poverty*. The organizers chose Toynbee because they

were well aware that he does not belong to that old narrow school of Political Economy the professors of which seem to think that the object of their so called science is to persuade working men to take less money, and to enable those who were rich already to get much richer still (cheers). He belongs to a broader and newer school, which, to tell the truth, takes a much humbler view of Political Economy than those who thought that all problems could be solved by it; and I know him sufficiently well to be able to say that there is no adherent of Mr. George in this room who feels a more earnest desire than Mr. Toynbee does—who wishes more to do what is desirable—to remedy those great inequalities in the social condition of the people which everyone feels constitute the most painful problem of the present generation (Hear, hear).[69]

The differences between the new and the old school of political economy were a subject close to Toynbee's heart. He treated it in both lectures in some detail, repeating some of the arguments as well as some of the phrases he had used in the past such as "the long and bitter controversy between economists and human beings has ended in the conversion of the economists."[70] The old economists had been pessimists who clung to the deductive method, refusing to acknowledge that the world has changed and that since Ricardo the material conditions of the people had in fact improved.[71] The new economist, on the other hand, "now dares to say that the end of his practical science is not wealth, but man; and further, he owns that his intellectual theories have also undergone a vast change."[72] Toynbee rejected the universality of the old deductive theories, confining their application to the "partial and provisional," dependent on the presence of clearly stated preconditions. Instead he increasingly came to rely on the "patient and vigilant" assembly of historical and contemporary facts.

Having stated unequivocally where his sympathies lay, Toynbee's detailed and occasionally qualified criticism of George was received with few interruptions. At the end of the lecture "loud and continued cheers" were recorded, and the first discussant, A. R. Wallace, admitted that he found himself in agreement with Toynbee on many points, even when the latter disagreed with George. Although Wallace "was an enthusiastic admirer of Mr. George . . . still he [George] had made great errors in some of the practical conclusions he had arrived at from his admirably deduced general principles."[73]

The audience's favorable reaction was partly due to the expectations Toynbee had raised toward the end of the first lecture concerning his own position, the subject of the second lecture. He had, in fact, gone further than he may have intended in indicating the anticipated role of the state in his vision of social reform. "I admit that we cannot wait for the time when higher ideals will control men's self-interest, and that the economists if they admit that the economic harmonies are to a large extent a fiction, are bound to admit the necessity for more administration and control. That is true. The era of free trade and free contract is gone, and the era of administration has come."[74] The new era had begun with Gladstone's 1881 Irish Land Act "which extended the protection of the State, which is the organised power of the community for good, not merely to women and children but to men."[75] Although Gladstone may have been unaware of the ideological significance of his policy he had, in fact, "committed the Radical party to a socialist programme."[76] Socialism was defined as the extension of state protection to workers, most of whom could not be considered free agents. These rather radical statements were qualified by the often-repeated pledge to avoid "undermining that old independence, that habit of voluntary association." Nevertheless, Toynbee promised his audience a comprehensive "programme of administration" dealing with working-class wages, dwellings, insurance, and leisure, a program that would demonstrate how "without revolution and without socialism, in the continental sense, we shall be able to do something towards that better distribution of wealth which we all desire to see."[77]

In addition, Toynbee inserted at the end of his first lecture a note on the moral character of his vision of reform. Reform could not be a simple mechanical course of action. It required patient and rational corporate effort. The new type of administration could be successful only if it was infused with a sense of "devotion to the community." As indicated elsewhere Toynbee had rejected the possibility of a sufficiently rapid and comprehensive moral transformation of the nation as unrealistic, and he did not regard it as essential for the first phases of reform. He had believed, and had acted on his belief, that in initiating reform much could be done by individual action motivated by a determination "to do all that in them lies to bring about the great event for which the people have longed for so many centuries . . .—the reign of social justice."[78] Yet although action did not depend on an initial moral change, such a change was an integral and crucial part of the regeneration of humanity. Otherwise change would have little, if any, meaning. He envisioned an age in which "there will come a purer faith, a faith which, cleared of superstitious control, shall make devotion to the community no longer a troubled and uncertain refuge from doubt, but a source of a pure and tranquil inner life."[79] It was this view of the moral significance of reform that enabled him to write in between lectures to his uncle, Henry Toynbee, "you could, I think, consider me a Christian, though I do not hold a great many of the doctrines of Christian Theology."[80]

The platform at the second lecture (delivered on 18 January) was shared by Lord Aberdare, Arthur Cohen, MP, Henry Broadhurst, MP, John Passmore Edwards, MP, A. R. Wallace, and the Reverend Stewart Duckworth Headlam, who had just (December 1882) lost his last curacy and had been refused a license to preach as a result of his radical political activities. The wide interest in Toynbee's lecture seems to indicate that it may very well have been regarded as an important contribution to a much anticipated radical program for the Liberal party. Whether or not Toynbee realized what was expected of him he gradually became conscious that the audience was different than those he had previously encountered. A reporter noticed in the galleries "a good many working-men, some of whom during the evening indicated by somewhat boisterous interruption their sympathy with Mr. George's views."[81] At one point, while discussing the future prospects of cooperative production, a subject always well received in the north, Toynbee remarked almost in exasperation, "There is one remedy which has been much spoken of and dealt with in Lancashire and Yorkshire, but, again, is little understood in London. That is the difficulty of dealing with you London workmen: you lead a peculiar life; you have a sort of civilisation of your own; you have a history of your own; and I, talking about the workman's life in Lancashire and Yorkshire, have sometimes been surprised to find that workmen in London are as ignorant of it as if—well, as if they belonged to the middle class."[82] This was an observation unlikely to curry favor with a crowd of working-class socialists.

Toynbee's popular lecturing technique called for the incorporation of local examples and observations in his general arguments. Accordingly, he referred in the course of the second lecture to the peculiarities of London economic conditions. He went as far as admitting that on the matter of rent and wages London proved to be the exception to the general rule. Rent was much higher than anywhere else since artisan dwellings were situated in London on land that could otherwise be used for warehouses. Therefore rent was determined not by the value of land as used for dwellings but by the value of land as it might have been used for warehouses.[83] In other places, on the other hand, where the system of 99-year, and even 999-year, leases prevailed, rents, even when on the increase, could not diminish profits or wages (to the extent that wages depended on profits).[84] As for wages, although the wages of London artisans were "in a certain measure" higher than elsewhere, they did not compensate for the higher cost of living.[85]

Toynbee admitted that London working men had suffered considerably from these disparities, hence the immense popularity of George's theories.[86] However, Toynbee was uncertain whose fault it was. He made the tactical mistake of arguing that

hundreds of labourers and artisans will prefer to take lower wages and live in London, than live elsewhere. Men so prefer the excitements and the attractions of city life, that they are willing to accept a lower money wage in order to obtain a higher social advantage, and, therefore, the labourers and artisans of London get lower money wages in the main, because they are anxious to share the life of the place. And the question is, can you remedy the evil from which they suffer—the evil which is produced by their own voluntary movement to a large extent.[87]

Such a statement came alarmingly close to the old economists' blaming the poor for their poverty, and it was clearly not what an audience of London radicals had expected to hear in the way of a comprehensive reform program. Toynbee quickly qualified his argument by pointing out that to a certain extent the move of many of the workers to London had not been voluntary but had been the result of the draw effected by the growth of London capital and commerce, but that the argument was at all voiced demonstrates the tenuity of the hold Toynbee had on his audience.

The first part of the second lecture dealt primarily with the inapplicability of George's theory to English conditions. Toynbee ended his discussion of *Progress and Poverty* by pointing to the dangers inherent in George's solution while conceding the desirability of achieving a similar effect by means of taxing rent. He then turned to the problem of raising wages. He first established that to all practical purposes there was no material reason why wages should not or could not rise.[88] This he followed with some of his standard suggestions on the means of achieving a rise: self-help through trade unions, which, in turn, would facilitate the creation of boards of conciliation; productive cooperation, whose best chance seemed to lie in "trades in which small capital is required," such as the nail trade; and middle-class support through the mobilization of public opinion.[89] Although these may have appeared to the audience to fall short of an adequate alternative to land nationalization, a new note of militancy is apparent in Toynbee's views. He had already professed his faith in a new state administration, dismissing the common objections that assumed an inherent inefficiency in any bureaucracy. He repeated the TUC's 1882 condemnation of cooperative societies that underpaid their workers.[90] In addition, to his standard self-help suggestions he added "international co-operations of workmen" (e.g., through the "much misunderstood" First International).

At this point in the lecture Toynbee paused to explain why in his view a change in workingmen's attitudes toward international cooperation "between men of different races, different languages, different ideas and prejudices,"[91] constituted a prerequisite to any future International. But by now his audience was becoming restless, and Toynbee's wording only resulted in a confusion: "It [the International] broke down because workmen were not yet fit to co-operate (Oh, oh!): that is, they were not yet fit for international co-operation. (A Voice: 'Revolution, not co-operation,' and some disorder.)"[92]

It may have been Toynbee's mistake that, having noticed the audience's impatience, he did not concentrate on a more concise and succinct presentation of his program. Instead, he constantly resorted, in the course of an already long lecture, to repetitious and digressive sermons on the necessity for a change in working-class moral attitude toward its responsibilities and on the dangers of revolutions, in which he employed a tone that may well have served to further antagonize his listeners.

Remember that the material change you want can only be got by the development of higher moral qualities. That is the thing which I am afraid a great many of you do not understand. You do not realise what a subtle and delicate and complicated thing civilisation is. Civilisation has not been built up by brute force, as I told you before; it has been built up by patience, by self sacrifice, by care, by suffering; and you cannot, and you will not, obtain any great material change for the better unless you are also prepared to make an effort to advance in your moral ideas.[93]

Despite all interruptions and regressions Toynbee pressed on. He described in some detail his views on rural reform, a subject on which his London audience might have been content with a brief outline. As a result he was left with little time or strength to elaborate on his suggestions for the improvement of urban working-class dwellings. These included the enforcement of existing laws by means of better inspection, including setting up vigilance committees with a combined working- and middle-class representation,[94] the subsidizing of housing by municipal authorities through buying land and letting it to building companies at low rates,[95] and the preservation and development by local authorities of public open spaces. To these he briefly added two further suggestions concerning working-class conditions: state-subsidized insurance by Friendly Societies that he thought would help "in time to diminish pauperism" and the setting up of urban recreation centers to be financed by guilt-ridden landlords.[96]

As the lecture drew to an end, the weary Toynbee became increasingly emotional. He realized that he had lost his hold on the audience, and in a last effort to win it over he turned from the details of his program to a direct and personal appeal to his listeners.

Now I turn to the workmen. Some of you have been impatient here this evening; you have shouted for revolution, but I do not think that that is the feeling of the great mass of the people. What I do feel is, that they are justified, in a way, in looking with dislike and suspicion on those who are better to do. We—the middle classes, I mean, not merely the very rich—we have neglected you; instead of justice we have offered you charity, and instead of sympathy, we have offered you hard and unreal advice; but I think we are changing. If you would only believe it and trust us, I think that many of us would spend our lives in your service. You have—I say it clearly and advisedly—you have to forgive us, for we have wronged you; we have sinned against you grievously—not knowing always; but still we have sinned, and let us confess it; but if you will forgive us—nay, whether you will forgive us or not—we will serve you, we will devote our lives to your service, and we cannot do more. It is not that we care about public life, for what is public life but the miserable, and waste of barren controversies and personal jealousies, and grievous loss of time? Who would live in public life if he could help it? But we students, we would help you if we could. We are willing to give up something much dearer than fame and social position. We are willing to give up the life we care for, the life with books and those we love. We will do this, and only ask you to remember one thing in return. We will ask you to remember this—that we work for you in the hope and trust that if you get material civilisation, if you get a better life, you will really lead a better life. If, that is, you get material civilisation, remember that it is not an end in itself. Remember that man, like trees and plants, has his roots in the earth; but like the trees and plants, he must grow upwards towards the heavens. If you will only keep to the love of your fellow men and to great ideals, then we shall find our happiness in helping you, but if you do not, then our reparation will be in vain.[97]

A sympathetic reporter described the meeting as possessing "a gladitorial interest."[98] Another observer described the audience as "of a critical, not to say rather refractory, character."[99] Some of those present were obviously sympathetic to Toynbee's views, but those who were not confronted him with some of the fiercest criticism he had ever encountered. It was noted at the time that the questions asked after the lecture indicated "disappointment with the conclusions of the lecture, a strong sympathy with schemes for recognising a common right in the land of the country, and an opinion that the lecturer had failed to show that what he said would be inexpedient would not be just."[100] Passmore Edwards, probably aware of Toynbee's exhaustion, suggested that a separate meeting for questions be arranged, to which Toynbee readily agreed. However, Beesley did not close the meeting, thereby allowing a barrage of criticism, some of which went to the length of questioning Toynbee's own integrity. One of the speakers, a Mr. Kitts, doubted whether anything could be accomplished without a revolution since, contrary to Toynbee's fervent assurances, the upper class's attitude was not changing nor was it likely to. "If Professor Toynbee were not of the cultured classes, he would know that it is a fact, that in the City of London and in the outlying districts, the working classes find it hard to put proper food into their stomachs, the primary cause being the excessive and exorbitant rents that they have to pay." In his view, he concluded, the best the landlords deserved was "to be flogged at the cart's tail."[101]

Rev. Stewart Headlam, as well as some others of those present, were highly incensed by Toynbee's rejection of land nationalization on grounds of its inexpediency, after having virtually admitted its justice. Some came close to suspecting Toynbee of representing the interests of the propertied classes, accusing him of reducing the question of injustice to a matter of expediency and then dismissing it as impractical. Headlam scathingly stated, "We are willing to meet such gentlemen as the lecturer on the score of mere injustice, if he and his friends like; but it will perhaps be to their advantage if we take the simple ground of expediency, and say we will take the land as it is, without demanding compensation from those from whom we have a right to demand it."[102] A Mr. Campbell regarded Toynbee's utilitarian approach as "an insult to intelligent men," and a Mr. Barton asked whether injustice, even if expedient, could ever result in good.[103] It was obvious that Toynbee's own program as well as his moral message had made no impression on them.

Headlam also took exception to Toynbee's comments on London laborers that once more demonstrated Toynbee's failure to make his meaning clear to the audience. "I would ask Mr. Toynbee with reference to what I must say was the somewhat supercilious way in which he spoke of the morals of the London workmen, whether his experience of Oxford is not that the morals of Oxford (I can speak for Cambridge myself) are certainly a good deal lower than the morals of the East-end of London?" Regardless of what Toynbee tried to say, his audience, impatient and hostile, chose to misinterpret it. Exasperated and exhausted he rose to answer. He began by assuring the audience that he would try to answer all of its questions at a future meeting, only to be heckled by an unnamed listener, "Don't evade them."[104]

Nevertheless Toynbee made a final effort to leave his hearers with a vision of a sufficiently radical and immediate goal that, if accepted, would at least be a step in the right direction. It was essential that they realize that their best and safest course of action lay in conventional politics. Once they became determined to advance in the right direction nothing could stop them. They would find that the obstacles they have insisted upon as insurmountable except by means of a revolution would crumble before them.

You can get universal suffrage, and then you will find that the rich will be forced to consider you ("Forced!"). Yes, forced if you like, but not by direct physical force. They may be influenced by fear; many of us are; some of us are better for being afraid, and sometimes some of us are the worse. I think the rich have been the better for being made afraid by the poor. It has purified their minds, and they have seen things they never saw before. But if you want to do all these things, do first one very simple thing—get universal suffrage.[105]

The alliance of capital and labor against the landowners had, in the past, won the repeal of the Corn Laws. "You may trust in future to the same alliance, and obtain similar victories." A vote of thanks was moved by Llewellyn Davies and Passmore Edwards and the meeting ended.

Toynbee's friends were to recall that he had looked exceptionally tired that winter. Phelps was to reflect that "his thin worn face had given his friends a great cause for alarm,"[106] while Gell recalled Toynbee's almost frantic mental activity as having "gradually but relentlessly worn out the body; strength has been steadily dwindling since Christmas or earlier."[107] A reporter present at the lecture had commented in retrospect that Toynbee had not been in a state of health fit to undertake the pressure of addressing a hostile audience.[108] Following the lecture, Toynbee was taken to his mother-in-law's house in Wimbledon in a state of nervous collapse.

9. Death and After

It appears that Toynbee's views on reform were not entirely his own brainchild. Milner records as early as 5 December 1881 long talks with Toynbee at Oxford on the latter's lectures on socialism (i.e., "Are Radicals Socialists?").[1] Toynbee seems to have recruited Milner to help in developing what he hoped would be accepted as a comprehensive radical program, that, in turn, would provide him with a platform when he entered politics. Beyond the formulation of doctrine Milner lent a hand in helping to propagate it. During December 1882 he delivered a series of six lectures on socialism in the East End that bear the mark of Toynbee's influence not only in the choice of subject and main arguments but also in the use Milner made of the concept of the industrial revolution: "a revolution more momentous than any political change."[2]

Milner argued that as a result of this revolution, the "industrial world is converted from a graduated democracy into a narrow oligarchy, and as the small man sinks into the position of a mere labourer the big man rises gradually above labour altogether. The gulf between them becomes wider and wider." He believed that healthy societies contained an element of socialism (defined as the means by which they provided for their weakest members). As a result of the industrial revolution the "socialistic" element "has gone out of the constitution of society, and we have as yet nothing to take its place," hence the need for a doctrine of social radicalism.

Milner's arguments are similar, if not identical, to those stated by Toynbee in his more moderate addresses (including the Industrial Revolution lectures). Like Toynbee, his alternatives to land nationalization included municipal ownership of land to which he added a supplementary clause meant to ensure that municipalities could not relinquish land they already owned. However he did not go to the relative extremes of state intervention and the "new administration" advocated by Toynbee in his last lectures. Since preparations for Toynbee's London lectures had begun as early as November 1882, it is likely that Toynbee and Milner, as well as some of their closer associates such as Grey, regarded their lectures as part of a collective effort to stem the growth of revolutionary socialism by furnishing a sufficiently attractive alternative. This possibility might be considered in connection with Toynbee's firm commitment to radical politics which, in view of his appearance in Newbury and the presence of MPs at his London lectures, may have gone beyond Oxford municipal politics. While reiterating his admiration for Gladstone's leadership, the general gist of his political statements seems to suggest an attempt to join the radical effort to force on the Liberal party a program of social reform. Not surprisingly, his views on land reform closely resemble the unofficial Radical Program that was to appear later in 1883 in the *Fortnightly Review*.

Toynbee's lectures may well have been regarded by his supporters as a definitive statement of their political and social creed. Furthermore, it is possible that Toynbee's impassioned pledge of total commitment to the cause of working-class amelioration might have been initially intended not merely as a personal statement but as a political one as well, representative of a group of like-minded Liberals. This might explain the relatively wide notice the lectures received as well as the presence of some prominent radicals in the audience and on the platform. The initial plan had called for the publication of the lectures shortly after their delivery. The matter seems to have been of some urgency. While Toynbee was, it was hoped, convalescing from his breakdown, his wife, with Milner's help, took charge of preparing the lectures for publication as a pamphlet.[3] It was Milner's initial suggestion that, in order to save time, the lectures should be printed "just as uncorrected reports of the lectures with a prefatory note very clearly stating this and the reason for it."[4]

When the lectures were published later the same year they were prefaced by a note by Milner explaining that it had been Toynbee's intention to prepare them for publication by using as a basis the shorthand writer's account, recomposed and supplemented by additional statistical detail. Under the circumstances the published version was unrevised with no more than "the most trifling and obvious corrections" made by Milner. This, however, was not an entirely accurate account of the editing process. It was Toynbee's professed wish that Foxwell, who had seen the initial reports in the *Bradford Observer,* should undertake to correct some of the reporter's factual errors and make certain that they did not recur in the published version.[5] Charlotte Toynbee informed Milner of her husband's wish, but it was clear that the latter was in no condition to insist upon the way in which the matter was handled. In a long letter to Milner, in which Mrs. Toynbee discussed various editing problems, it became clear that she had resolutely taken the preparation of the pamphlet into her own hands. "This is writing as if he were quite a dummy poor dear fellow but only yesterday he talked to me about the sentimental passage at the end which he said he would not have put in if he had not been so dead weak. But when he begins to talk of these things we have to hush him up, he will be quite satisfied with anything *you* do when he gets well I am sure. Applications for the lectures [to be delivered elsewhere] still continue and come in."

The Toynbees remained at Mrs. Toynbee's mother's at Wimbledon while Phelps took over his Oxford teaching responsibilities.[6] At first all were certain of eventual, if slow, recovery. The main problem appeared to be prolonged sleeplessness, which was quite unaffected by drugs.[7] A London doctor attending him "did not see any danger of lengthened illness, in fact [he] treated his nervous prostration with much less seriousness than one would have supposed," but by early February Toynbee's state remained unstable. In her letter to Milner of 7 February Mrs. Toynbee described it as "the least little bit better but it will be a longer illness than we thought for I fear. When he gets a fairly good night he is better and his head stronger, then perhaps he won't sleep for 36 hours or more, then his poor head is quite weak. . . . It is very trying." There was a question of the possible advantages of a sanatorium, but it was felt that for the time being he had best remain where he was. Less than a week later Mrs. Toynbee wrote to Milner, "He had a good night Sat. and was a bit better yesterday, then a dreadfully bad night last night and is not so well today, and so it goes on, but still perhaps we only need patience."[8]

By then, Charlotte, rather than wait for her husband's recuperation, decided to proceed independently with the matter of publication. It may have been that Foxwell was unable to complete the proofreading as quickly as she wished. In any event, she soon transferred full editorial responsibility to Milner, explaining that "what Arnold wished Mr. Foxwell to attend to at first was the *dates* in the first lecture—but of course you can do this. I suppose Mr. Foxwell did not like to touch another man's work. Unless you wish it, don't trouble about asking Mr. Marshall. I am sure Arnold can trust your judgement as to whether the thing is worth printing as it is. I fancy you would feel like myself almost over anxious about his reputation."[9]

The extent of their efforts to ensure Toynbee's "reputation" becomes clear from Milner's editorial policy. It may be argued that his omission of the discussions at the end of each lecture, the audience's reactions, and Toynbee's confused reference to the wages of London's laborers were legitimate editorial decisions intended to preserve the lectures' cohesion while bringing them closer to their originally intended form. There were also some factual additions and changes made, based on the notes Toynbee had placed at Milner's disposal. Yet some of the passages were clearly politically embarrassing. Milner chose to drop Toynbee's diatribe against the Irish landowners and watered down his demand for the abolition of the House of Lords by changing it into a recommendation for reform. These changes were meant to tone down Toynbee's occasional radical outbursts and were done in agreement with Mrs. Toynbee.

Nevertheless, despite Milner's editing, the lectures remained too radical for his taste, especially in view of his later association with the Liberal Unionists and imperial policy. They still contained a firm statement in support of Gladstone's Irish policy as well as the concluding declaration, "We shall try to rule India justly. We shall try to obtain forgiveness from Ireland. We shall try to prevent subject races from being oppressed by our commerce, and we shall try to spread to every clime the love of man."[10] Milner had publicly placed Toynbee on a pedestal, and it would have been a considerable embarrassment to him if Toynbee's memory were to be associated with views that might be interpreted as anti-imperialist or in favor of Irish home rule.[11] It is therefore not surprising that the "Progress and Poverty" lectures, which had been appended to the first printing (May 1884) of the first edition of the *Industrial Revolution,* were omitted from all later reprints and editions, the first of which (December 1886) appeared after the Home Rule crisis.

After a deceptive improvement Toynbee's health continued to deteriorate. At the beginning of March, Mrs. Toynbee informed Phelps:

I fear I have nothing to say that will give you pleasure to hear. . . . He has been worse and not better lately, after making a start [and] enjoying being out of doors the sleeplessness returned with some persistence [and] has made him as weak as a baby. Fancy five doses of chloral [hydrate] in one night taking no effect [and] I am beginning to fear the doctors will perfectly stupify him with their endeavours. . . . There is no doubt the doctors are getting rather anxious at his protracted illness [and] are kind enough to hint at possible paralysis—which may God indeed forbid![12]

Three days later she added, "Whether he can possibly come out from it all with sound mind [and] body God only knows."[13] With a similar fear in mind Toynbee's brother William wrote to Milner, "Dearly as I love and admire the dear noble fellow, if he is only to be spared from a long servitude of suffering I would rather a thousand times that he were gently taken as he would be now; for he is quite happy and placid, and without a trace of pain."[14] By then Toynbee's family and friends were beginning to lose hope.[15] Exhausted and worn out by his insomnia, Toynbee developed "brain fever" (i.e., meningitis)[16] and on 9 March 1883, "his constitution then worn to a thread, [he] sank beneath the exhaustion of the fever," and died.[17]

Toynbee's friends naturally associated his illness and death with the traumatic experience of the second "Progress and Poverty" lecture. In a letter written a day after Toynbee's death, Gell told Grey that Toynbee's restlessness following the lecture was the result of his mind harping "forever upon the miseries and misfortunes of the poor and wretched."[18] The theme was later developed by F. C. Montague in his description of Toynbee's last days. "His mind, wandering and unstrung, turned again and again to the one preoccupation of his life; to the thought of all the sin and misery in the world. At times a strange unearthly cheerfulness broke through his gloom. He constantly asked to lie in the sun—to let the light stream in upon him; murmuring 'Light purifies—the sun burns up evil—let in the light.' "[19]

The connection between the lectures and Toynbee's death was

accepted even by none-too-sympathetic observers. *The Economist's* reporter observed that "Mr. Toynbee was willing to die for the masses, and it would seem that, in a very real sense, he has done so." He continued to lament such wasteful sacrifice, arguing, "The cause of the poor is better aided by influence and teaching husbanded by care through a long lifetime, than by spurts of feeling, however noble, which practically end in an early grave."

Curiously enough, it was Charlotte Toynbee who in retrospect questioned the significance of the sequence of events. In 1895 she wrote to E. Abbott, who was then collecting material for the Jowett biography, "I am always a little annoyed to have it stated . . . that Arnold died as it were after those lectures on Progress and Poverty which of course is exaggeration—I believe his breakdown w[oul]d have come just as surely without them."[20] Indeed Charlotte's attitude betrayed an element of bitterness at her loss. It was almost as if Toynbee had been responsible through his mindless devotion to other causes for her personal tragedy.[21] With time a shade of impatience crept into her memory of that impractical young man. Compare Montague's overgenerous observation on Toynbee's habit of never writing his lectures—"Clear copious and rapid as a speaker, he wrote slowly and with a certain effort. He found the labour of composition much more severe than the labour of thought. . . . he committed nothing to paper until he had fully elaborated it in his own mind"[22]— with Mrs. Toynbee's curt comment: "He never wrote if he could possibly help it or if there was any chance of talking instead."[23]

Shortly after his death Toynbee came to be identified with two popular late Victorian middle-class images: the prophet and, to a larger extent, the martyr. Men of vision, preferably pessimists such as Carlyle or Ruskin, were often, occasionally in their own lifetime, declared prophets. Some were prophets of doom, others of hope, but they were all claimed to have a profound insight into the age and its problems and a vision of a better more perfect world, whether in the past or in the future. Some, like Ruskin, seem to have accepted the role and even acted it out by adopting a prophetic manner in their wrathful denunciations of modern society, by gathering bands of disciples, and by displaying a tendency toward symbolic gestures (such as Ruskin's North Hinksey project). Toynbee's early death meant that he never acquired the prophet's proper sagacity, which usually came with more advanced age, and he also lacked the wrath of the prophets of doom. However, he did match the biblical image of the prophet consumed by his own fire, a modern Jeremiah in whom God's words were "in my heart as a burning fire shut up in my bones . . . and I could not stay."[24]

The other popular image that was soon used to describe Toynbee was that of the modern martyr. Late Victorians had cultivated their own cult of martyrdom complete with modern English martyrs. The martyrs furnished modern society with an enlightening and elevating example combining selflessness, piety, and a heroic effort to serve England and English society. In a predominantly religious and romantic age the martyrs and the prophets provided an apprehensive middle-class England with heroes whose spiritual superiority and courage were perhaps more representative than Smiles's practical and industrious heroes of a previous, more self-assured generation. They furnished an example of confident piety that, in an age of growing doubt concerning England's commercial superiority and the validity of the orthodox liberal creeds, bolstered faith in the soundness of middle-class values and the class's ability to cope with rapidly changing circumstances in a decisive, if not a particularly practical, manner. Missionaries such as Livingstone and Patteson strengthened England's faith in its moral (compared to material) strength, while General Gordon's death popularized the moral dimension of empire building. In one popular account of their martyrdoms their lives were described as fulfilling the recurring need for an "analogy." It was emphasized that they were thoroughly modern heroes: "The 'spirit of the age' breathes through them."[25]

Similarly, internal problems required their own modern martyrs. Edward Denison had been hailed as one,[26] and his memory was soon to be associated with that of Toynbee's, both having fallen in the struggle for the same cause.[27] The theme of the modern martyr of the internal (as opposed to imperial) variety had even penetrated children's literature, furnishing a simple message on both the desired social attitude and personal conduct in an age of growing consciousness of social problems. A curiously fitting example which may have fed on the imagery of Toynbee's martyrdom may be found in *Olive Roscoe or the New Sister,* one of the works by the popular children's author, Evelyn Everett Green. One of the story's heroes— Basil Roscoe, son of a mine owner—has been suffering from poor health ever since he rescued some miners from a collapsed pit. His selfless conduct in the event had led to the miners looking up to him as their natural leader and friend. "Basil had never been like a master to them, but as a friend and comrade and a leader of their own choosing. His influence had not been weakened by frequent appearances amongst them."[28] In one of the story's climaxes the miners, in the course of an industrial dispute, try to employ pressure on the mine owner by starving the pit ponies. In a personal and highly emotional appeal Basil succeeds in persuading the miners to stop their strike and feed the ponies. When the miners of the neighboring pits learn of the collapse of their previously united front they attempt to force the reclosure of the Roscoe mine. In the course of a fight that breaks out between the two groups of miners Basil collapses and is taken home in an unconscious state while the victorious miners return to work with the hope that the news of the strike's end will help Basil to recuperate. Basil's sacrifice is summed up by his father:

Basil has stopped the strike. It was a blow struck just in the very nick of time by the one man who could strike it. It has cost him dear; it may cost him dearer yet, and all of us too. Yet I would not wish it undone. . . . He alone of all men in the world could do what he did, and he did it fearlessly, in the spirit of perfect self sacrifice—not counting the cost so that he might save the men from a lasting sin and disgrace.[29]

In keeping with the plot's requirements Basil survives, but the message of his near-martyrdom is clear. It is in the power of individuals whose character embodies the virtues of moral uprightness and dedication to their fellow man to provide an example and leadership that the working classes will follow. It was the duty of the middle and upper classes to provide such leadership. The challenge was to each individual to assume the responsibility inherent in his social position. The working class would not fail to respond to such a message even to the extent of its transcending class interests. Toynbee's memory almost instantly assumed the form of such an "analogy," proving most attractive to young Oxford men.

Milner set the tone of most of Toynbee's obituaries and memoirs when he stated, "His spoken words will not soon be forgotten, and the influence of his original mind and noble character will live on in many."[30] Milner emphasized the contemporaneous importance of Toynbee's thought, describing it as "the modern philosophic spirit that shrinks from a breach with the past," dedicated to "the duty of social union—the alliance of good men of all classes for promoting a better distribution of wealth." He also made the point of representing Toynbee's death as an act of self-sacrifice: Toynbee had dedicated his life to social reform "in the restless struggle to promote which, by word and deed, he wore himself out and died." Milner depicted Toynbee as a modern prophet who, when talking on social reform, "looked like one inspired." Consequently, all obstacles in the path of progress "seemed to shrivel before the fire of his enthusiasm." The obituary was dominated by the recurring image of the prophet consumed by his own fire. Toynbee's words, when addressing northern crowds, "struck fire," his spirit was like a "keen flame" that "burned too brightly to burn long," and so on. In his summary of Toynbee's heritage, Milner concluded, "His memory remains to rebuke selfishness and silence cynicism, to strengthen faith in individual goodness and in the possibility of general progress, and to hold high the standard of social duty and the growing perplexities of our modern life."

The prophet image was also evident in Phelps's obituary of Toynbee. In his description of Toynbee's appeal, Phelps stated that it was the "combination of high principle, and, in its best sense, deep sentiment, which gave to his own statement of his ideas an irresistible force, and hence it sometimes happened that those who had heard him found in endeavouring to reproduce his ideas that they had lost the secret. This led them to speak of him as a visionary."[31] Phelps portrayed Toynbee as having been, in addition to a prophet, a leader of men, possibly conjuring the biblical image of the judge providing a confused and distraught people with political and moral leadership. "His friends had hoped that he might do a great work in the world, that he might raise the level of political questions, and initiate social reforms, and by the strength of his deep religious convictions be the preacher of a great spiritual revival."

Montague in his obituary developed the analogy theme. Toynbee's life had been a lesson to all who sought guidance in the confusion of the modern world, and his death was an almost inevitable consequence of his faith. "To feel all the anguish of our race, and yet know that for the race there is no easy way of salvation; this is a burden far too heavy for human strength. Nevertheless it is this feeling and this knowledge which distinguish the sincere reformer from the dreamer and from the charlatan."[32] His life in relation to his fellow man was described as nothing short of saintly. "He brought solace to the sick, strength to the weary, hope to the dispirited. Men came to him for practical advice and for spiritual consolation; and he sent none empty-handed away. . . . He conferred many benefits; but he put men under no obligation." Finally, like Milner and

Phelps, Montague stressed the guidance Toynbee's sacrifice offered to the living.

> No words can tell what we lose in losing our comrade and our guide. Deafened by the din of the importunate world without, and distracted by the insatiable cravings within, few of us can ever listen to the voice of reason, lead our true life, or fulfil our proper destiny. How many soever our harassed and baffled years, how few soever the years of the wise and brave, it is they who have lived, not we. Yet in the thought of such lives we find our strength! The memory of an Oxford student who freely gave up his life to help his fellow-citizens will long live in the hearts of all Oxford men, to silence a cynical despair and to shame an Epicurean indifference. His example will perpetually remind us of the service a great University might render to a great nation![33]

Montague's obituary, which was clearly aimed at a younger generation of Oxford men, was followed by a poem by J. W. Mackail entitled "Salve Aeternum." Mackail too adopted as his theme Toynbee saintliness: "For a soul more pure and beautiful our eyes / Never shall see again." He had Toynbee join a long line of ancient heroes who had died in their prime: "The equal hands of unrelenting fate / Struck down the best and dearest even thus, / Thousands of years ago." Although Mackail stopped short of actually proclaiming Toynbee a saint in the Christian sense, this soon became a relatively common association. P. H. Wicksteed, in his sympathetic but critical commentary on the "Progress and Poverty" lectures, referred to "the lesson of his martyrdom."[34] Albert Mansbridge proclaimed him a modern saint and prophet,[35] stating that "in deep, silent, indirect ways his influence is making him an ever-present name."[36] His martyrdom even assumed some of the trappings of iconolatry. The *Co-operative News* of 7 April 1883 published an advertisement by Messrs. Hills and Saunders who "have agreed to furnish a quantity fearte-de-visite size photographs of the late Mr. Toynbee at such a price as shall enable every admirer of him to secure at a nominal cost [8 d.] a tangible momento." Finally, Toynbee's sister, Gertrude, in a published collection of Joseph and Arnold Toynbee's letters, carried the martyrdom image to its limits. "Arnold was akin to the saints and the prophets in his power of spiritual appeal and in the revelation his presence made of his beautiful inner life. . . . We went to see his face in death, it was exceedingly beautiful, without any trace of suffering. We took our last farewell when we laid him to rest in our dear father's grave. . . . You cannot think of death there, and the words come borne in upon you: 'He is not here; he is risen.' "[37]

For a time it became quite common for young Oxford, and especially Balliol, men to attribute an early determination to serve society to Toynbee's influence regardless of whether they had had any direct contact with him or not. R. R. Marett attested to having in time come "to regard Toynbee's work as a kind of answer to doubt."[38] Cosmo Gordon Lang, who knew Toynbee by sight only, wrote that, upon leaving Oxford, he had been "genuinely eager" to serve society "with the memory and example of Arnold Toynbee before me."[39] Cosmo Lang had come up to Balliol in Michaelmas 1882 and Marett only after Toynbee's death. It may therefore be safely assumed that his "example" had been largely an image created by his friends, many of whom were young dons (D. G. Ritchie tutored Lang, and R. L. Nettleship tutored both Lang and Marett), given a more concrete form by the various Toynbee memorials.

About a month after Toynbee's death a number of his friends who were away from Oxford, including Gell and Milner, asked A. L. Smith to organize a meeting at Oxford in order to consider a suitable memorial.[40] At the meeting (held on 15 April), which was chaired by William Markby, it was agreed that a subscription should be raised for a memorial with a sum of not more than £100 earmarked for the publication of any of Toynbee's writings "that might be found in an adequate condition."[41] Various schemes were suggested as suitable memorials, and it was finally agreed that the money collected should be used to "endow lectures on social economics, to be delivered in Oxford, and, if possible, elsewhere." It was later announced that the lectures, to be named the Toynbee Lectures, would be delivered by people of "ability and practical experience who sympathise with the spirit of Mr. Toynbee's work."[42] It was hoped that the lectures "may exert a lasting influence and tend to promote zeal for the study of social questions, as well as union between various classes in the cause of social reform." The meeting elected a committee of London and Oxford men, including some undergraduates, one of whom was Michael Ernest Sadler, to serve as cosecretaries, and a bank account was opened under the name, Toynbee Memorial Fund. At the same time, the Toynbee family and some of his closest friends privately commissioned artist J. E. Boehn to produce a medallion depicting Toynbee's profile. The work, which cost £110, was completed in 1885 and was placed in Balliol.[43]

For the rest of the academic year and the following long vacation the question of the memorial's final form was left undecided while the money was being collected.[44] This was still the case in the autumn of 1883 when a development in public opinion resulted in a suggestion for the adoption of a different scheme as the official Toynbee Memorial. In October 1883 the Reverend Andrew Mearns published *The Bitter Cry of Outcast London,* the unexpected popularity of which brought living conditions in the East End to popular attention. Public opinion had already been, to some extent, prepared by C. R. Sims's articles in *Pictorial World* which had helped to bring out the need for immediate action in dealing with the conditions in London's slums. Mearns, a Congregationalist, made one significant suggestion concerning the approach to the problem. He argued that the situation's acuteness did not allow for sectarian differences. It called for a coordinated effort that would transcend the sectarian rivalries embodied in the numerous and often competitive religious missions. "In each district a Mission Hall will be erected, or some existing building transformed into a Hall having appliances and conveniences requisite for the successful prosecution of the Mission. Services and meetings of all kinds will be arranged and as far as possible an agency for house to house visitation organized."

Meanwhile, in the East End the local committee of the London extension lectures had run into some difficulties. The London Society in general had been under severe financial strain, having managed to raise only £500 to cover an annual expenditure estimated at £1,000.[45] The Whitechapel extension committee had been seeking a permanent center for extension work as it had failed to gain possession of the Beaumont Institution.[46] In view of the unlikelihood of the London Society's being able to provide financial help, the committee was on the lookout for a solution that would not require major expenditure on its part. Some of the extension work had been carried out locally by a small number of university graduates working in collaboration with some of the younger local clergymen. The university men chose to reside temporarily in the East End while, as a rule, pursuing a professional career elsewhere in London. Five of these young graduates settled around 1880 in a disused pub in Leman Street, where they established a bachelor household that came to be known as the Friary.[47] Some of the graduates, including two Glaswegians (B. F. C. Costelloe and James Bonar), had been in the East End for some years and, as they were about to leave, it was locally felt that replacements should be found. With this need in mind the Reverend S. A. Barnett addressed on 25 May 1883 a meeting of the Oxford Palmerston Club chaired by M. E. Sadler.[48] In addition, Barnett had been in touch with G. C. Moore Smith, who represented a group of undergraduates at Saint John's College, Cambridge, who were seeking an alternative to the conventional college-city missions. Barnett suggested to them the setting up of a communal residency in the East End similar to the Friary.[49]

Beyond the immediate problem of securing the continuity of extension work, Barnett, as well as some of Toynbee's friends such as P. L. Gell, were eager to ensure that middle-class East End settlers would continue to provide local leadership and guidance in forwarding municipal reform in matters such as working-class housing. Those acquainted with the conditions in slums such as the East End realized that the local inhabitants could not be realistically expected to act independently or to be able to exert sufficient pressure on the local authorities in order to force them to take action. In his pamphlet, *The Municipal Responsibilities of the "Well to Do,"* Gell argued, "The whole English system is based upon the assumption of a resident leisured class who can undertake the responsibility of the local administration. . . . in the poorer districts of London neighbourhoods are already springing up where there is not a resident with the surplus of energy, of time, or of ability requisite to work our local institutions. The clergy alone stop the gap."[50] In his view forming a bureaucracy to deal with the problem was analogous to hiring mercenaries for one's defense. The only solution was for "the wealthy middle class deserters from the commonwealth . . . [to] take up again their civic responsibilities. . . . It is their duty to labour personally at the improvement—material, moral, and spiritual—of the masses, by whose labours alone their leisured life is rendered possible."

In practical terms such local leadership could, if at all, be provided only by the permanent presence of a core of highly motivated and educated young men rather than by an irregular and uncoordinated voluntary effort. Gell admitted that "hitherto the conditions of bachelor life in Whitechapel were not inspiring. Men want the society of their comrades and work the better for it." A permanent settlement could furnish a social as well as a professional center for all who might be interested in such work. Friends would come to visit the settlers, their corporate effort would be more easily noticed, and it

would, one hoped, attract other volunteers. Gell was referring specifically to the East End and the idea of a permanent settlement had
been developed through his association with Barnett. It is not at all
clear whose idea it was originally or, indeed, whether it had been an
individual's inspiration (as Mrs. Barnett seemed to believe).[51] In
any event, with its conception sometime in the autumn of 1883 it
occurred to Gell that the funds necessary for the establishment of a
settlement that, consequently, would solve the problem of the extension committee, might be found in the Toynbee Memorial Fund. It
would require a change in the committee's view that, it was hoped,
Gell as a member of the committee might be in a position to effect.
Thus within Oxford the settlement idea was first known as Gell's
scheme rather than Barnett's.

One of the first converts to Gell's scheme was S. Ball, who had
initially expressed hopes that the fund would be used to start a hall
at Oxford, possibly along the lines suggested a year earlier at the Co-
operative Congress. In a letter to Gell, Ball admitted that "the idea
of a Hall in E. *London* has not occurred to me. I hardly know what
to think of it but if I am convinced of one thing it is that the lecture
scheme will . . . fall miserably short in the way of performance, it
cannot but be so."[52] Some days later Ball wrote to Barnett, "Do you
approve Gell's scheme with regard to the *'Toynbee memorial'*. If so,
could you prepare a plan for so disposing it—I mean with regard to
an *East London Hall*—so that people may have a clear view of it."[53]
It was agreed that Gell and Barnett would draw up a detailed plan
that would be ready by 17 November, the date on which the fund's
committee was to determine the memorial's final form.

The main and most important opponent of a redesignation of the
fund was Mrs. Toynbee. The reasons for her objection to Gell and
Barnett's idea are not entirely clear. In a letter to Phelps she argued
somewhat vaguely that Arnold might have been suspicious of a "hall"
in view of his preference for personal contact. "I am not saying
whether he would have cared for the scheme of a formal settlement.
I feel rather that he would have been suspicious of the brick and
mortar part of it and feared a waste of money [an objection probably
more appropriate to herself]. . . . it seems too hazardous—don't you
think so?"[54] She appears to have resented the delay in announcing
the foundation of a memorial, and she certainly favored the lecture
scheme.

Another consideration, in Milner's case, was a certain resentment of Barnett's insistence on the money being used exclusively for the East End. In his view Barnett was "simply a professional grabber for the East End. Why the dickens should the thing be specially for the East End. Oxford certainly, Bradford, Newcastle, any other of the towns that received Toynbee well and he was fond of have more claim. You see, if we do upset the lecture scheme we shall only have some other d—d thing."[55] Consequently, Milner and most of the other committee members decided to stick to the original plan.

As arranged, Barnett presented the settlement scheme at an open meeting convened at Ball's rooms at Saint John's College, Oxford, on 17 November 1883.[56] Following an examination of the inadequacies of college missions Barnett suggested, as an alternative, that colleges purchase one of the large East End houses that had formerly been the residences of the wealthy and could, therefore, provide ample sleeping quarters and reception rooms. Such a house could then be entrusted to a college graduate who would serve as a salaried director. It was expected that such a hostel would appeal to other graduates "working in London as curates, barristers, government clerks, medical students, or business men [who] would be glad to make their home in the house for long periods," as well as to those wishing to spend parts of their vacations undertaking local work in return for bed and board. The director would cultivate contacts with the local community that would enable him to assign to each settler the work for which he was best qualified. Full-time settlers might find work in parish activity, as visitors for the cos, as managers of industrial and general elementary schools, as members of sanitation committees, etc. Part-time settlers might take classes, join political clubs, and help run cooperative and friendly societies. Older and more experienced settlers might take up more official positions in community life such as vestry men, poor law guardians, schoolmasters, and representatives to, or even workers for, local government. Consequently, an East End residency might serve as a useful training for public life.[57]

Through direct and friendly contact the settlers would offer the community an example of a "higher standard of man's life." At the same time their own attitude toward society's less fortunate members would be brought up against the test of reality.

It will be something if they are able to give to a few the higher thoughts in which men's minds can move, to suggest other forms of recreation, and to open a view over the course of the river of life as it flows to the

Infinite Sea. . . . It will be something, if thus they give to the one class the ideal of life, and stir up in the other those feelings of self respect, without which increased means of livelihood will be useless. It will be more if to both classes they can show that selfishness or sin is the only really bad thing. . . . Not until the habits of the rich are changed, and they are again content to breathe the same air and walk the same streets as the poor, will East London be "saved."

Rather than wait for the reluctant fund committee to change its mind it was initially agreed that an independent effort should be made to implement the scheme either through a single college or through a combination of a number of colleges, but in any event not by the university as a whole.[58] The scheme had been simultaneously presented at Cambridge, and it was announced that further action would be coordinated by Sedley Taylor and William Cunningham at Cambridge and A. Sidgwick and A. H. D. Acland in Oxford. The expectation at Oxford was that "the 'settlement' might serve as a home of the University Extension and Lecture classes, but it might be more generally described as a school or centre of social work." This emphasis on educational work may have been contrary to Barnett's initial intention, but it was also closer to the general purpose of the memorial, that is, the endowment of educational work on the lines of Toynbee's efforts in popular education. It was Barnett's view that while the settlers' work could be described as primarily educational in the widest sense of the word, such a designation did not fully represent "the larger and moral work of the settlers."[59]

Despite the pressure exerted by the supporters of the settlement scheme the members of the fund committee chose to postpone their decision. Various alternatives were still being discussed, including a hall in Oxford, the lecture scheme, a university prize, an extension prize, a mosaic "in some crowded thoroughfare in a large town," and the East End settlement.[60] Rather than decide, the committee chose to distribute a circular among the fund's subscribers asking for their views on the matter. Since answers were due back only on 1 January 1884 the younger supporters of the settlement scheme, rather than wait for the committee's decision, chose to proceed independently.[61] At the initial meeting in Ball's rooms two undergraduate secretaries had been elected: M. E. Sadler and C. G. Lang.[62] They now began to recruit undergraduate support for the settlement.

The enthusiasm with which the settlement scheme was met was

largely due to the support of an increasingly influential group of young dons who were roughly of Toynbee's age. Two of them— S. Ball and A. H. D. Acland—had founded small societies of undergraduates, namely the Social Studies Club (started by Ball during Michaelmas 1883, possibly as an extension of the settlement meeting in his rooms in November) and the Inner Circle, dedicated to the discussion of social problems in a manner similar to Toynbee's "Regeneration of Humanity" Society.[63] Their support of the settlement scheme provided Barnett with a sympathetic undergraduate audience whose enthusiasm and dedication were primarily responsible for the eventual successful launching of the scheme independently of the fund committee's deliberations. By the time the committee finally agreed to endorse the lecture scheme its caustic comment that a settlement "as yet could not provide a sufficient nucleus for a Hall in London" did nothing to dampen the undergraduate enthusiasm for the scheme.[64]

Barnett brought the scheme to the attention of the general public by publishing a version of his 17 November paper in the *Nineteenth Century* in its February 1884 issue. Barnett added a final touch to the settlement scheme by christening it "Toynbee Hall" at a sermon delivered at a memorial service to Toynbee at Balliol on 10 March 1884. As it happened the idea of a settlement proved unexpectedly popular. The hall was soon followed by the founding of Oxford House in Bethnal Green which laid a greater emphasis on the settlers' contributions to the community's religious life.[65] A survey of settlements published in 1898 listed some thirty-seven institutions (including a Toynbee House in Glasgow started by E. Caird).[66] In it Toynbee Hall was proclaimed the "Mother of Settlements," founded "as a memorial of Arnold Toynbee, and as a practical outcome of his teaching."[67]

Thus, although not the "official" memorial, Toynbee Hall soon came to be regarded as *the* Toynbee memorial, a fact effectively recognized by Milner and Mrs. Toynbee who joined its general committee by autumn 1884.[68] Toynbee, then, was appropriated as the patron saint of a movement that, while reflecting some of his ideals, cannot be described as their perfect expression. When Lang professed to have been inspired by Toynbee's example he, in fact, meant Barnett's interpretation of Toynbee's example as embodied in the settlement movement. Although the appropriation of Toynbee's name was mainly due to Barnett's realization of its popular appeal, the eventual result was that all parties concerned, including Toynbee's family and closest friends, came to regard the settlement movement as an apt memorial to Toynbee's spirit. Hence later references to Toynbee by those directly involved in the work of Toynbee Hall tended to emphasize the significance of his short stay in the East End and his attachment to local social work. In one such reference J. J. Mallon claimed in 1939 that "Apostle Arnold" had thought of joining his Friary friends but was prevented from doing so by his deteriorating health.[69] Finally, it should be noted that indirectly Toynbee's spirit came to influence the hall in a significant way. The involvement of some of its residents in local political and labor activity (e.g., Hubert Llewellyn Smith in the dockers' strike) may be attributed to the ideal of political involvement that Toynbee had helped inculcate among Oxford undergraduates as well as fellow dons.

The lecture scheme may have been closer to Toynbee's views, but as a memorial it was a relative failure, entirely overshadowed by Toynbee Hall. On 21 March 1884 the memorial fund was officially reconstituted as the Toynbee Trust. It was to be managed by a committee whose main function was to appoint occasionally "some competent person . . . to give a course of systematic instruction in Political Economy, arranged primarily for the working classes, in some important centre of industry on a plan similar to that adopted in the University Education Extension scheme."[70] The lecturer was to reside wherever the lectures were to be delivered for a period of four months, of which three would be spent lecturing. In addition he was expected to undertake during his period of residency a special study of local economic conditions. Upon the completion of the courses and the term of residency the lecturer would deliver at Oxford one or more lectures based on his findings. His remuneration was to be £100, the equivalent of one-third of a junior lecturer's average annual income. An additional resolution passed by the committee to arrange for an annual memorial lecture at Oxford by "some eminent man" was never acted upon.

Despite the availability of funds, the trust encountered two major difficulties: it lacked the organization to arrange the courses, and it found it difficult to agree on suitable lecturers. The trust was in principle a modified attempt to realize the concept of a residential district lecturer as propounded in connection with cooperative education. In the absence of a suitable response from within the cooperative movement and since some of the committee's members had been closely associated with either the Oxford or the Cambridge extension organizations the trust was eventually forced into a dependence on these bodies both for the provision of suitable candidates and for the organization of courses. In due course three Oxford extension lecturers were appointed as Toynbee Trust lecturers: L. L. Price (twice), H. Ll. Smith, and W. A. S. Hewins, as was one Cambridge extension lecturer: W. R. Sorley. Under the auspices of the trust, Price, Smith, and Sorley conducted their first independent research projects, the results of which were published with the trust's help.[71] Hence the lectureship provided for Price and Smith a vital boost in the initial stage of their professional careers. The trust finally ceased to function due to the committee members' loss of interest.[72] In 1892 the remaining funds were transferred to the care of the Toynbee Hall Council which continued to manage them as a research fund for work done at Toynbee Hall.[73]

Another body that was to claim Toynbee as its patron saint was the Oxford extension movement. Until 1885 most of Oxford's extension work, as organized by Acland, was aimed at cooperative education. It offered mainly short courses given by Acland and a few young graduates, including M. E. Sadler.[74] As might have been expected, Toynbee was declared shortly after his death a great believer in the cooperative movement. In a lecture delivered by Acland at Woolich on "Brotherhood and Citizenship" he attested that Toynbee had "considered the co-operative movement the greatest social movement of modern times, and one which if its programme was fairly carried out, would more fully develop the universal brotherhood of man than anything hitherto attempted."[75] Toynbee was soon acknowledged as one of the movement's prophets, as one official history stated, "both [James] Stuart and Toynbee addressed co-operative congresses and so became the guides and prophets of co-operative education for a whole generation."[76]

By 1885 it was becoming obvious that the Oxford extension lecturing was not likely to reach a national scale of operation by confining its operation to the cooperative movement. Sadler, who in 1885 succeeded Acland as secretary of the extension, undertook to reorganize its work on lines similar to those developed at Cambridge, while retaining much of the ideology and spirit of the work done by Toynbee, Acland, and A. Sidgwick for cooperative education. A strong emphasis was placed on courses in political economy, and short six-lecture courses were offered with all the "trimmings" (certificates, examinations, prizes, etc.) with the hope of stimulating interest in the extension among local committees who were otherwise reluctant to commit themselves to a full, Cambridge-style, twelve-lecture course. Consequently, the reorganized Oxford extension inherited the controversy with Cambridge concerning the nature and form of extension work.

Toynbee's memory as a pioneer and prophet of adult education was frequently conjured by Sadler as well as other extension workers during the 1880s and early 1890s.[77] In one instance an extension student speaking at a conference of extension students argued that Toynbee's pledge to the working classes at the end of his second "Progress and Poverty" lecture was being fulfilled by the extension movement.[78] In another instance Hudson Shaw, one of the Oxford extension's most popular lecturers and a Balliol friend of Toynbee's, invoked Toynbee's name in order to reprove the extension movement for having become "very largely a middle class movement." In his view, "the chief intention of Arnold Toynbee and Professor Stuart in connection with the University Extension movement was that the Universities should make the working men sons of the Universities."[79]

Thus Toynbee's memory was transformed, molded, and romanticized by popular myth and through its appropriation by various organizations and movements, each giving it meaning in accordance with its own needs. All except Toynbee Hall have either faded into insignificance, disappeared altogether, or been entirely transformed with the result that Toynbee in popular memory is by now solely associated with Barnett's Toynbee Hall.

In the two remaining areas of Toynbee's public activity—church reform and Oxford municipal politics—his impact was even less durable. Contrary to his own hopes the Church Reform Union (CRU) abandoned any attempt to inspire a popular movement. Phelps, who had shared Toynbee's ambition of transforming the CRU into a popular organization unifying all the various bodies committed to church reform, would remember Toynbee as a man who might have become a "great religious reformer."

If the time is ever to come when the Church will throw off its dogmatic shackles and enter upon its great work as the Saviour of the world, we shall miss him then. He was never so great as when he showed the smallness of the differences among Christians compared with their points of union—or as when he sketched the future of the church as it might be in the time of Christian toleration and yet of Christian zeal.[80]

But by 1883 the CRU was no more than a parliamentary committee, having realized that it was incapable of sustaining any other form of prolonged action.[81]

The involvement of Oxford dons in municipal and national politics did not begin or end with Toynbee but he certainly contributed to the emergence of municipal politics as a sphere of political action acceptable to Oxford dons as well as young graduates. Toynbee's place as a North Ward Liberal candidate was unsuccessfully filled by Sir G. K. Rickards, who was introduced to the ward's Liberals in a meeting chaired by Nettleship and addressed by Phelps.[82] Rickards (1812–89) had matriculated at Balliol in 1829 before transferring as a Scholar to Trinity; he had also been a Fellow of Queen's College and an undistinguished Drummond Professor of Political Economy (1851–57). At the time of his candidacy he had just resigned from his post of counsel to the speaker of the House of Commons and had moved back to Oxford. Despite his lack of success as a candidate the link between university economists and municipal politics survived.[83] In 1896 the economist Edwin Cannan, another Balliol man with only a Pass degree, was elected to represent the university on the town council. He was soon joined by J. Carter, one of the first editors of the Oxford-based *Economic Review* and a future mayor of Oxford. For a time there had also been some attempts to recruit from among the Liberal Oxford dons of Toynbee's circle candidates for Parliament but without any success.[84]

At the time of his death, Toynbee had just begun to establish a professional reputation. He was probably closest in his economic views to H. S. Foxwell, who described him in a letter to Walras dated 30 December 1882 as *"very able, more or less a socialist."*[85] Foxwell, a compulsive book collector, helped Toynbee to collect some of the pamphlets and books used for the Industrial Revolution lectures.[86] Foxwell shared Toynbee's aversion to the "old" economists as well as his insistence on considering the moral dimension of economic and social problems. In his 1887 survey of contemporary English economists Foxwell claimed that Toynbee had come closest to forming current opinion and founding a school, if not having actually achieved it. "The influence of such a man . . . was extremely strong within the circle to which it reached. . . . The more economic tendency of Toynbee's influence is better traceable in the humanized policy of charity organization, in the new attitude of Oxford to the Co-operative and University Extension movements, and in the tone of the press which is largely guided by Oxford men."[87] In a similar vein, J. K. Ingram referred to Toynbee's published papers as worthy of attention despite their fragmentary and unfinished form, "both for their intrinsic merit and as indicating the present drift of all the highest natures, especially amongst our younger men, in the treatment of economic questions."[88]

Another note of appreciation, although somewhat critical, was sounded by P. H. Wicksteed in a three-part article discussing Toynbee and Henry George.[89] Wicksteed repeated in a mild form some of the criticisms of Toynbee's position that had been voiced by the audience in the course of his last lectures. But the main gist of his article was an attempt to minimize the differences between Toynbee and George who were, in his view, "one in spirit." Wicksteed accepted Toynbee as representative of a new school of economists and was therefore able to note with considerable optimism that

opinions may differ as to the extent and intensity of material suffering, but all will agree that a great amount of material suffering exists which can be and ought to be removed. All will agree that the problem is one of distribution, not of production. Opinions will differ as to the relative importance of rent on the one hand and of the various practical monopolies so powerfully dwelt on by Mr. George himself (Bk III, ch. IV.) on the other, but all will agree that rent is *amongst* the funds that absorb the earnings of labour without benefiting the labourer. Opinions will differ as to the extent to which rent, while diverting to private pockets what is by right a public and impersonal fund, also positively lowers personal wages, but all will agree that under many circumstances—not imaginary, but actual—it does so lower them; and I cannot see how anyone can escape the conclusion that wherever there is land speculation it must act in the same direction. And if this is so then Mr. George is right in principle, and the question is, at most, only one of degree.

However, Foxwell, Ingram, and Wicksteed were not the ones to determine Toynbee's reputation as an economist. Alfred Marshall, who would soon come to dominate English theoretical economics, had met Toynbee, probably through Jowett, and had been invited by the latter to fill the vacancy created at Balliol by Toynbee's death. He remained there for four terms until his election to the Cambridge chair vacated by Fawcett's death. Marshall made it clear that, despite Toynbee's numerous merits, he hardly qualified as an economist. In his introduction to the first publication of the Toynbee Trust, Marshall recalled that "on the few occasions which I met him, the talk ran chiefly on social and economic questions. He was always brilliant in thought, eager in speculation; but his intellect, fresh and vigorous as it was, was not the chief part of him: the leading controlling strain of his character was emotional."[90] This approach to economics may have been acceptable to Foxwell or Wicksteed, but it was certainly not acceptable to Marshall. Marshall's low opinion of the value of Toynbee's economic work is brought into relief by his proclaimed admiration for Toynbee's character and spirit. He pronounced Toynbee "the ideal representative of the medieval saint; . . . St. Francis, the founder of a new order, the leader of a new and more direct attack on the evils of the age."

Marshall, possibly aware of the power of the Toynbee myth, attempted to bring Toynbee back into the fold of neoclassicism by claiming that with time Toynbee had "somewhat changed his attitude towards the earlier economists" and that he had gradually "settled himself down to work very much on the old fashioned lines." It is unclear where Marshall got this impression which can be supported by Toynbee's work only by means of very selective reading or a misunderstanding of his confused essay on Ricardo. It may have been inspired by Jowett's view, which is close to the truth, that Toynbee was not always consistent in his appreciation of Ricardo.[91] But whatever the origins of Marshall's observation it effectively helped to neutralize the possible effect of Toynbee's attack on the "old" economists. He had been pronounced by the foremost economist of the late nineteenth century as a closet neoclassicist; his work could be described as primarily historical and therefore of little bearing on theory. There remained little any other neoclassicist could say of him, as demonstrated in Luigi Cossa's 1893 edition of *An Introduction to the Study of Political Economy,* in which Marshall's appreciation of Toynbee was reproduced unquestioningly.[92] Fortunately, though, for Toynbee his professional reputation was in retrospect to be based on his contribution to the early development of the study of economic history. By the time economic history came to be recognized as an independent or semi-independent scientific discipline Toynbee was redesignated an economic historian and it is as such that he is referred to in later histories of economic thought.

While Marshall may have been unable to take Toynbee seriously as an economist, a young generation of Oxford economists, some of whom were also historians, accepted Toynbee's views on economics as their own professional point of departure. This is evident from their early work and is conveniently demonstrated in L. L. Price's discussion of Toynbee in the last chapter of the early version of *A Short History of Political Economy in England from Adam Smith to Arnold Toynbee,* which was based on Price's extension lectures and was completed in December 1890.[93] Price had been an undergraduate at Trinity College, Oxford (1881–85), where he had been a contemporary of Sadler. He had received his initial training in economics from Marshall while the latter lectured at Balliol. Following his graduation Price was appointed the first Toynbee Trust lecturer, which helped to launch him on a short but successful career as an extension lecturer. Although Price was to emerge during the early 1890s as an ardent defender of Marshall against the criticism of the relativists (including his Oxford contemporaries, Ashley and Cannan), it is clear that he was not a fully converted Marshallian. By the mid-1890s he began to move back toward the Oxford position, described in his chapter on Toynbee in a manner that makes his own sympathies clear.

Price completely overlooked the significance of the *Industrial Revolution* lectures as a framework for historical research. Instead he concentrated solely on Toynbee's concept of the nature of economics and the economist's role in society. Price repeated with approval Toynbee's rejection of the economist's supposed impartiality as advocated by Cairnes (and Marshall). He maintained that the attempt to distinguish between the science of economics and the art of statesmanship or philanthropy "is open to the danger of pushing the distinction between theory and practice too far, and of underrating the influence exercised by our speculative opinions on our practical action," a view that was reflected in Price's own work.[94] Price found that Toynbee's reforming zeal had not led him to dispense with theory: "He wanted more rather than less economic study, but it must be study which, without being soulless or passionless, took into consideration the varied interests of human life, and issued in practical action."[95] This position was generally accepted by Oxford's young economists as representative of the true relation between scientific research and civic duty.

Another important feature in Toynbee's work commented upon

by Price was his position regarding the "old" economists and the history of economic thought. Price had correctly identified Toynbee as a relativist inasmuch as he had maintained that, in view of the constant change in material and human conditions, the laws describing their relations required constant examination and frequent modification. The work of the "old" economists reflected a very specific and transient combination of circumstances. "All these economists were led by facts, which were especially prominent in their own time, to construct theories based upon this prominence; but other facts have since come into prominence, and the theories require alteration."[96] Price himself was not an extreme relativist. He admitted the need for occasional modifications in classical theory (e.g., in Ricardo's theory of rent), but as a rule he did not accept the claim of complete invalidity of past theories and the need for their constant and thorough replacement. Nevertheless, relativism of one sort or another is evident at the core of the economic thought of all young Oxford economists, with its ultimate and impressive expression in Edwin Cannan's *The History of Theories of Production and Distribution 1776–1848* (London, 1893).

Price, whose first independent research, undertaken as a Toynbee Trust lecturer, was into forms of industrial arbitration (a subject close to Toynbee's heart), had, possibly in retrospect, attached some importance to Toynbee's occasional attempts at formulating a wage theory. In a response to a debate between Ashley and Cannan occasioned by his work on industrial conciliation Price pointed out that, although economic theory could determine the limits of wage settlements as decided by the workers' standards of comfort and the capitalists' and employers' average rate of profits, it could not determine theoretically at what precise point between these two limits the actual settlement would be made.[97] In his review of Toynbee's contribution to economics Price attributed to Toynbee the observation that, within the two limits of wage settlement, one could distinguish the factors determining the actual point of compromise as including public opinion, removal of legal restrictions (e.g., on workers' combinations), legal protection, and power of combination. Price credited Toynbee with showing "how, led by the influence of facts, we have departed in our theories of wages from the comparatively inelastic conception of a 'wages fund.' "[98] From Price's as well as his Oxford contemporaries' work it is clear that they all had inherited a strong bias against the wages fund theory that, in some instances, was extended to most of the "old" doctrines. Within Oxford Toynbee was accepted as an authoritative critic of these doctrines, and during the young economists' academically formative years they were often content to accept his criticism as the definitive statement on the matter.

Finally, Price ended his book (in its early version) with a description of Toynbee's social philosophy, giving it the appearance of being the final and therefore, in a progressive science, the best expression of the economist's social conscience. Price emphasized Toynbee's retention of the traditional liberal values of self-help and individualism, which were to be supplemented rather than replaced by state help. In this he contrasted Toynbee's position not only with the radical socialists but also, and perhaps more important, with the older generation of Liberals represented by Fawcett. Toynbee, then, had come to represent the new liberalism, seen to have rendered T. H. Green's philosophy into practical politics. The Toynbee alternative to old liberalism was demonstrated by Price by a review of Toynbee's real and presumed positions on a number of current issues. On national education Price thought that "while Toynbee might have viewed with favour proposals for 'free education,' they would have aroused the distrust, and encountered the opposition of Fawcett as tending to weaken individual responsibility, and discourage voluntary effort."[99] On factory laws, "while Toynbee approved, Fawcett disliked and opposed, their extension to adult women, for fear that it would undermine individual independence."[100] Finally, on Toynbee's general approach to state intervention, "his socialism might be more correctly described as the complement than the opposite of the individualism to which Fawcett inclined."[101]

Price's description of Toynbee's work provides the main outline of the nature of Toynbee's intellectual influence on young Oxford. There remains however his more specific influence as a historian, best discerned in the work of his most outstanding student, W. J. Ashley. Ashley accurately summed up Toynbee's place in shaping the views of the next generation of Oxford economists when he observed that Toynbee's importance as an economist was not necessarily dependent on his originality or lack of it. Ashley thought that it was clear "that both in his discussion of theory and in his practical proposals he did but follow other men—Comte, Cliffe Leslie, Walker, Bagehot, Mundella, Sedley Taylor. . . . But a man's importance is to be measured not by his consistency nor by the bulk of his writings, but by the impression he has been able to produce."[102] Ashley repeated much of Price's evaluation of Toynbee's work but with a slightly different emphasis. He stressed Toynbee's interest in "the historical investigation of social development, and of the direct examination of existing phenomena" rather than his allowing for a synthesis of theory and practical needs. (That both should have cited Toynbee as an authority on the status of theory is indicative of the importance they attributed to his work.) Ashley also credited Toynbee with being "the first professional economist in England to distinctly recognize the element of good in the scientific socialism of to-day, and to see in a cautious extension of the functions of the state one of the most effectual preventatives of revolution"—this from a fervent admirer of the German school.[103]

As an undergraduate at Balliol (1878–81), Ashley had been tutored by A. L. Smith and J. F. Bright. His first choice for specialization had been medieval constitutional history. Having been greatly impressed by Toynbee's lectures he sought advice from Toynbee as to how he might develop his growing interest in economics. Toynbee recommended that Ashley "take some one subject e.g. Wages, and, beginning with Adam Smith, read in chronological order what each noteworthy English economist has said upon the subject, and see if you can make out the way in which various doctrines have arisen and been modified." It was Ashley's view that Toynbee had been the first professional teacher of economics (i.e., unlike Bagehot, who did not hold an academic position) to make "the historical *development* of theory" the governing principle of his teaching. Although he did not follow Toynbee's advice, the relativist approach to theory (placing it as an historical agent within a wider context of historical circumstances) is evident in his *An Introduction to English Economic History and Theory,* the first part of the first (and only) volume of which was dedicated to Toynbee's memory.[104]

Following his attendance of Toynbee's lectures Ashley was invited to join a fortnightly essay class on English classical economic doctrines.[105] In it the relativist approach to theory was developed, later to be described by Ashley as a "dynamic as contrasted with the static view of economic theory and fact." Ashley identified the historical and relativist approach to economics with his own social philosophy and the search for the scientific principles of social and economic reform. He combined Toynbee's influence with a Comtist view of the scope and aim of historical research, which was becoming prevalent among a young generation of Oxford historians (e.g., A. L.

Smith). In a letter to his future wife Ashley stated that, in the search for the historical laws of progress, it was the economist's duty to examine "modern industrial life *in the piece.* We can leave to the Cambridge people hair-splitting analysis of abstract doctrine." Thus Toynbee's influence on his star pupil transcended Ashley's academic pursuits. When describing it in retrospect Ashley, not untypically, confused Toynbee's growing radicalism with many of his friends' (including his own) later advocacy of Liberal Unionism. In a letter to Lujo Brentano in 1913 he wrote, "I was brought up a strong Liberal and many of my most intimate friends are strong Liberals; but since I began to care for Social Reform under Toynbee's influence I have been indifferent towards the claims of the Liberal party just because the party has never, in any deep sense, been fundamentally the party of social reform."[106] In time Ashley was recognized as Toynbee's most significant disciple. In a testimonial in support of Ashley's 1891 unsuccessful candidacy to the Drummond chair Brentano expressed his satisfaction for having found in Ashley's work "the elevated views which distinguished Toynbee."[107]

Ashley and Bolton King used their lecture notes as the basis of the published version of the Industrial Revolution lectures.[108] However, the collection of papers and fragments that, in addition to the lectures, constitute Toynbee's published works was edited by Milner.[109] It is therefore reasonable to assume that it was Milner's decision to omit some of Toynbee's popular addresses and some fragments. In some instances the decision may well have been taken on general technical grounds. Some fragments were deemed of little interest, and some addresses were repetitious of statements made in the lectures and addresses that were published. But some, such as the Newbury speech or Toynbee's early enthusiastic advocacy of free trade, may have become a potential source of political embarrassment for Milner and were therefore ignored without so much as a reference to their existence. Milner may well have acted in this matter on his own. Charlotte Toynbee was certainly quite vague as to an editorial policy. In a letter to Grey she admitted, "It was difficult rather to know exactly which [addresses] to publish—his friends might perhaps have liked more, . . . He [Toynbee] had an idea of reproducing some of the popular addresses in a cheaper form—perhaps one or two more than will be contained in this volume."[110] Consequently, Milner's editorial policy may well have determined Toynbee's later reputation, for, with time, as the memory of the fiery social reformer faded, it was replaced by the impression left by Toynbee's concept of England's industrial revolution.

Whenever economic historians have come to deal with Toynbee's contribution to the study of the English industrial revolution they have usually referred to his periodization of the revolution and to what has come to be known as the pessimistic view of the social consequences of industrialization. A third reference, concerning the employment of "revolution" as descriptive of an economic process, belongs to a debate that seems to have faded with the general acceptance of the term "industrial revolution," for which Toynbee is commonly credited. On the question of periodization it has been argued that Toynbee's point of departure—1760—is unacceptable. J. U. Nef would have us start the historical narrative of the industrial revolution in the mid–sixteenth century; some scholars would have it moved back only to 1740; some later scholars would prefer to see it moved forward to the 1780s.[111] It is also generally accepted that, during the eighteenth and nineteenth centuries, England had gone through economic revolutions that did not end in 1850. Hence Toynbee's periodization is generally regarded as outdated, which is not quite fair to Toynbee. A more generous appreciation of Toynbee's periodization appeared in Ashley's 1914 lectures on the "Economic Organization of England," in which he stated that

what to Toynbee and Mantoux was "the industrial revolution of the eighteenth century" has become in the mouths of their popularisers "the industrial revolution."

The qualification . . . is that the changes between, let us say, 1776 [not 1760] (when Adam Smith published the Wealth of Nations and James Watt perfected the steam engine) and 1832 (the date of the first Reform Bill), did but carry further, though on a far greater scale and with far greater rapidity, changes which had been proceeding long before. No great period is in actual fact sharply cut off from that which precedes and follows it.[112]

That Toynbee did not attempt a precise periodization is borne out by a more careful examination of his work. Although his survey of pre-industrial England is dated 1760, he also argued that the nature of the age is best expressed in The Wealth of Nations (1776), which aimed at "the substitution of industrial freedom for a system of restriction." Since free competition was regarded by Toynbee as one of the main prerequisites of the revolution, it may be argued that

Ashley's interpretation of Toynbee was closer to the mark than that of subsequent scholars. As for the upper date limit of the revolution it is not at all clear that Toynbee had in fact set one. While the initial course outline set 1832 or thereabouts as the upper date limit, Toynbee had added in the course of the lectures a fourth phase of industrialization marked by J. S. Mill's *Principles of Political Economy* (1848). Toynbee's concept of the revolutionary nature of the revolution was based on a theory of the political consequences of industrialization. It precluded setting a historical end to the revolution prior to the completion of the process of the redistribution of wealth and political power, which would redress the imbalance created by industrialization. Rather than set a time limit to the process he aimed at constantly updating his description of it.

Toynbee also cannot be clearly labeled as either an evolutionist or a revolutionist. In his philosophy he was clearly an evolutionist and, while he regarded some of the effects of industrialization as violent and sudden, his view of its causes seems to synthesize the evolutionary and the revolutionary. Toynbee could not have foreseen the findings of modern scholarship or know of some of the facts on which the later periodization debate is based. His concept of industrialization as dependent on the institution of free competition may have been mistaken,[113] but he should not be blamed for false periodization whatever its origins.[114]

A similar misunderstanding has identified Toynbee with the pessimists' camp, which regards industrialization as having had a disastrous effect on the standard of living and on the working conditions of the working class.[115] Toynbee had indeed come to consider the first phases of industrialization as having resulted in a significant deterioration in the conditions of the working class. Although he had initially maintained that in some sectors of the labor market conditions since the days of Adam Smith had improved, he had gradually adopted a bleaker view of labor conditions. He attempted, however, to reconcile the evidence of partial material improvement with growing working-class dissatisfaction by arguing that a modicum of improvement had often resulted in growing expectations. Hence, the state of labor's dissatisfaction, while justified, was not entirely based on a case of unremitting exploitation. Ideologically, therefore, Toynbee certainly was not a pessimist. In his last Industrial Revolution lecture he abandoned his earlier "catastrophe" view of the consequences of industrialization, replacing it with a more linear vision of progress. Pre-industrial conditions had had their mean side and in some respects industrialization had replaced one type of misery with another, but there was one significant difference: industrialization also provided the means for redressing that misery. Toynbee was essentially an optimist. His main thesis was that in the long run industrialization had made working-class progress possible. It had freed the laborer from the confines of pre-industrial static society and had given him unprecedented power through which he would, with time, change the distribution of industrially produced wealth so as to secure his just portion of it. That the process was neither immediate nor automatic was explained by Toynbee's concept of the nature of progress and historical change, which required an increasing degree of rational corporate action. Progress was dependent upon both the ability to act collectively and the comprehension of collective interests and aims. The misery caused by the industrial revolution had served a purpose in forcing the working class onto the path of progress.

On the other hand, if economic historians are to be blamed for having long been preoccupied with the problems of distribution and consumption while taking increase in output for granted, Toynbee may be held at least partly responsible for it.[116] His main interest certainly was the problem of unequal distribution. Initially an ideological concern, it stemmed from the combination of general historical circumstances and the course of his individual intellectual development (which determined his choice of subject for scientific investigation). He set out to provide a social and political ideology with scientific proof. The nonscientific aspects of his work were regarded by him as meritorious rather than condemnable. A preoccupation with the question of unequal distribution (with its strong link to current political, social, and economic issues) was to survive Toynbee's death in the work of the next generation of Oxford economists. It was given a methodological and ideological justification and was later infused into the London School of Economics by Cannan and W. A. S. Hewins. In addition, by becoming one of the main bones of contention with Marshall and his supporters it probably helped the economic historians and dissenting economic theorists (such as Cannan, Foxwell, and Smart) to define their own scientific positions.

It has been commonly acknowledged that, despite the faults of the *Industrial Revolution* lectures, Toynbee's contribution to the development of economic history as a scientific discipline has been considerable.[117] This was largely due to the significance of his concept of the industrial revolution. As an economist Toynbee had adopted a dynamic rather than a static view of the nature of economic relations. As economic relations changed, so did the economic laws describing them, but economic change in itself was only part of a greater process of social and political change, the pattern of which could be identified and formulated as the general laws of progress. Toynbee did not regard the course of English history as being categorically determined by economic relations. Therefore the general laws of progress transcended the occasional laws of economics. The general course of English history had been described by Macaulay as that of constant progress, a continuous Glorious Revolution that could only be seen for what it was by adopting an overall perspective. Progress was essentially political—a point he wished to demonstrate in his *History*—and political progress entailed all other form of progress: "from the auspicious union of order and freedom, sprang a prosperity of which the annals of human affairs had furnished no example."[118] Thus, while Europe was racked by the political turmoil of 1848, Macaulay confidently asserted, "In all honest and reflecting minds there is a conviction, daily strengthened by experience, that the means of effecting every improvement which the constitution requires may be found within the constitution itself. . . . It is because we had a preserving revolution in the seventeenth century that we have not had a destroying revolution in the nineteenth."[119]

Toynbee accepted the premises of Macaulay's view of the general course of English history. His own great contribution to the development of historical thought was in indicating a way in which liberal historiography could combine with a dynamic view of economic relations, allowing for a wider perspective of English history within a unified philosophical framework. The combination had brought English historiography a step closer to the Comtist ideal of an all-encompassing science of human activity that at the time had become increasingly popular. This apparently simple conceptual and methodological synthesis of history and "new" economics is the key to Toynbee's influence on the writing of English history. Marx and Engels regarded industrialization as inevitably resulting in a political revolution similar to the French Revolution. Politically as well as philosophically their view of English history, determined by static economic laws, was unacceptable to the mainstream historians of nineteenth-century England. On the other hand, Mill had considered industrialization as an isolated process of rapid economic change that was not placed within a specific historical context. J. E. Thorold Rogers, the best-known English economic historian of the age, was essentially a classicist whose interpretation of history was based on static economic laws, an approach that was quickly becoming outmoded.[120] Jevons helped to set the economists' sights on industrialization as a specific historical development, but it was Toynbee who united the "new" economics with history, fitting them into the larger ideological framework of new liberalism. His synthesis offered the young liberals a scientific method complete with acceptable ideological postulates for the analysis of current problems (which appeared to provide viable and morally acceptable solutions). Some young liberals were so impressed by Toynbee's teachings that they partly or even wholly abandoned previous academic interests and dedicated themselves to a scientific study of social problems. It is from that generation on that one can speak of economic historians as a group of academics sharing a scientific discipline.

The popularity of an idea is commonly explained by the readiness to accept it.[121] In a review of J. R. Seeley's *The Expansion of England,* John Morley, then a leading radical liberal, wrote in *Macmillan's Magazine* (1884):

If the expansion of England was important, not less important were other changes vitally affecting the internal fortunes of the land that was destined to undergo this process. . . . There would be nothing capricious or perverse in treating the expansion of England over the seas as strictly secondary to the expansion of England within her own shores, and to all the causes of it in the material resources and the energy and ingenuity of her sons at home. Supposing that a historian were to choose to fix on the mechanical and industrial development of England as the true point of view, we are not sure that as good a case might not be made out for the invention of Arkwright, Hargreaves, and Crompton as for the acquisition of the colonies; for Brindley and Watt as for Clive and Hastings.[122]

Toynbee's potential remained largely unrealized, but his lectures on, and his concept of, the industrial revolution demonstrated how such a history of England's material progress might be written.

Finally, Toynbee demonstrated, in a manner acceptable to historians, the importance of economic developments in influencing the course and nature of political and social change. While economic factors were not presented as sole determinants of historical change neither were they completely subjected to political factors. Hence it might be argued that Toynbee's was the first English research project in economic history proper, in the sense that his narrative of historical economic development is not dependent for its causal cohesion on a political narrative, as in the work of Rogers or William Cunningham.[123] Furthermore, Toynbee influenced the reperiodization of English history with the result that most surveys of modern English history, both political and social, begin with industrialization or its consequences rather than with the Glorious Revolution. In this final respect Toynbee's contribution to English historiography was not merely in widening the perspective of historical scholarship. It has, in addition, helped to effect changes in perspective, in choice of subjects, and in choice of historical evidence—all of major importance in shaping modern historical thought.

Notes

Chapter 1

1. Gertrude Toynbee, *Reminiscences and Letters of Joseph and Arnold Toynbee* (London, n.d.), p. 10.
2. Arnold J. Toynbee, *Acquaintances* (Oxford, 1967), p. 2.
3. Some years later his lecture notes were inserted in Bisset Hawkins, *Germany, the Spirit of her History, Literature, Social Conditions, and National Economy* (London, 1838). The lectures were reproduced in H. G. Fiedler, ed., *A. W. Schlegel's Lectures on German Literature from Gottsched to Goethe; Given at the University of Bonn and taken down by George Toynbee in 1833* (Oxford, 1944). It was the editor's view that the work of Hawkins and Toynbee deserves more attention than it has received (p. 12).
4. Entry under "Toynbee, Joseph" in the *Dictionary of National Biography* (hereinafter referred to as DNB).
5. G. Toynbee, *Reminiscences*, pp. 9–10.
6. Arnold Toynbee, *Lectures on the Industrial Revolution of the Eighteenth Century in England. Popular addresses, notes, and other fragments* (1884; reprint, London, 1927), p. 216.
7. A. J. Toynbee, *Acquaintances*, pp. 7–11.
8. Capt. H. Toynbee, *The Basest Thing in the World and Other Papers* (London, 1891), p. vii.
9. G. Toynbee, *Reminiscences*, p. 165.
10. H. Toynbee, *The Basest Thing*, p. 32.
11. A. J. Toynbee, *Acquaintances*, p. 3.
12. C. J. Holmes, *Self and Partners* (London, 1936).
13. Ibid., p. 8.

14. A. J. Toynbee, *Acquaintances*, p. 34.
15. Chadwick to J. Toynbee, 15 April 1845, 22 April 1845, Chadwick papers, University College, London; G. Toynbee, *Reminiscences*, pp. 20–22, 79; Gertrude Toynbee, *Joseph Toynbee F.R.S. Aural Surgeon* (London, 1908), p. 3.
16. Joseph Toynbee, *Beneficence in Disease* (London, 1865), pp. 18–19.
17. Ibid., p. 27.
18. G. Toynbee, *Joseph Toynbee*, p. 3.
19. Joseph Toynbee, *An Address delivered at the Italian Gratuitous School* (London, 1841).
20. G. Toynbee, *Reminiscences*, p. 39.
21. Joseph Toynbee, *Hints on the Formation of Local Museums* (London, 1863).
22. G. Toynbee, *Reminiscences*, p. 56.
23. J. Toynbee, *Local Museums*, p. 64.
24. G. Toynbee, *Reminiscences*, pp. 65–66.
25. Ibid., p. 73.
26. MS by Mrs. Arnold (Charlotte) Toynbee, Toynbee papers, Balliol College, Oxford, p. 15.
27. See G. Toynbee, *Reminiscences*, pp. 31–32.
28. Ibid., p. 44.
29. Ibid., p. 89.
30. James Hinton, *The Mystery of Pain* (London, 1866; reprint 1912), pp. 50–51.
31. Ibid., p. 94.

Chapter 2

1. Information provided by Miss Margaret Toynbee.
2. Gertrude Toynbee, *Reminiscences and Letters of Joseph and Arnold Toynbee* (London, n.d.), p. 101.
3. Ibid., p. 110.
4. Ibid., pp. 104–5. See also p. 120.
5. Ibid., p. 101.
6. F. C. Montague, *Arnold Toynbee* (Baltimore: Johns Hopkins University Studies in Historical and Political Science, 1889), pp. 5–6.
7. G. Toynbee, *Reminiscences*, p. 94.
8. Ibid., p. 38.
9. Ibid., p. 94.
10. MS by Mrs. Arnold (Charlotte) Toynbee, Toynbee papers, Balliol College, Oxford, p. 2.
11. Montague, *Arnold Toynbee*, p. 14.
12. Mrs. S. A. Barnett, *Canon Barnett, His Life, Work, and Friends* (London, 1918), 1:303.
13. Charlotte Toynbee's MS, p. 3.
14. Ibid., pp. 3–4.
15. G. Toynbee, *Reminiscences*, pp. 95–96.

16. Ibid., p. 58.

17. Ibid., p. 59.

18. Ibid., p. 64.

19. A. Toynbee to P. L. Gell, December 1873, Gell family papers.

20. G. Toynbee, *Reminiscences*, pp. 74, 93. The Reverend J. M. Brackenbury was a member of the Wimbledon Museum Committee of which
Joseph Toynbee was treasurer.

21. Montague, *Arnold Toynbee*, p. 6; R. L. Nettleship, "Arnold Toynbee,"
Co-operative News, 17 March 1883.

22. Charlotte Toynbee's MS, p. 25.

23. G. Toynbee, *Reminiscences*, p. 57.

24. Ibid., pp. 61–63.

25. Ibid., p. 96.

26. Ibid., p. 123.

27. Charlotte Toynbee's MS, p. 4.

28. G. Toynbee, *Reminiscences*, p. 96.

29. Ibid.

30. Charlotte Toynbee's MS, p. 7.

31. G. Toynbee, *Reminiscences*, p. 97.

32. Montague, *Arnold Toynbee*, pp. 7–8.

33. G. Toynbee, *Reminiscences*, p. 112.

34. Lord A. Milner, "Reminiscence," in A. Toynbee, *Lectures on the Industrial Revolution of the Eighteenth Century in England. Popular
addresses, notes, and other fragments* (1884; reprint, London, 1927),
p. xv. In 1879 he recommended Macaulay's essays to his sister Lucy as
"very brilliant indeed and never tedious" and his *History* as "wonderfully attractive and winning." Toynbee papers.

35. G. Toynbee, *Reminiscences*, p. 98.

36. See ibid., p. 211; *Industrial Revolution*, pp. 261–62.

37. G. Toynbee, *Reminiscences*, pp. 166–74.

38. Ibid., p. 4.

39. Ibid., p. 98.

40. The letter, dated 8 September 1871 and sent from East Lulworth, is
reproduced in part in Charlotte Toynbee's MS, pp. 7–8; B. Jowett,
"Memoir," in the first editions (1884, 1886, 1890) of A. Toynbee,
Industrial Revolution, p. xx; and in Montague, *Arnold Toynbee*,
pp. 8–9.

41. A. M[ansbridge], "An Oxford Talk about Arnold Toynbee," *Commonwealth* 1, no. 1 (January 1896).

42. First authorized version published in 1643. All references in the text
refer to the 1955 Cambridge University Press edition.

43. Jowett, "Memoir," pp. xx–xxi; Montague, *Arnold Toynbee*, p. 16.

44. Charlotte Toynbee's MS, pp. 12–13.

45. A. Mansbridge, "An Oxford Talk."

46. C. J. Holmes, *Self and Partners* (London, 1936), pp. 53–55.

47. A. Mansbridge, "An Oxford Talk."

48. G. Toynbee, *Reminiscences*, pp. 109–10.

49. G. Toynbee, *Reminiscences*, pp. 109–10.
50. Montague, *Arnold Toynbee*, p. 10.

Chapter 3

1. Gertrude Toynbee, *Reminiscences and Letters of Joseph and Arnold Toynbee* (London, n.d.), p. 115.
2. W. M. Hardinge, "Some Personal Recollections of the Master of Balliol," *Temple Bar* 103 (October 1894), p. 179.
3. Leonard A. Montefiore, "Undergraduate Oxford," in Montefiore, *Essays and Letters* (London, 1881).
4. Lord A. Milner, "Reminiscence," in A. Toynbee, *Lectures on the Industrial Revolution of the Eighteenth Century in England. Popular addresses, notes, and other fragments* (1884; reprint, London, 1927), p. xiii.
5. Milner to P. L. Gell, 7 March (c. 1874), Gell family papers.
6. F. C. Montague, *Arnold Toynbee* (Baltimore, 1889), p. 12.
7. MS by Mrs. Arnold (Charlotte) Toynbee, Toynbee papers, Balliol College, Oxford, pp. 21–22.
8. Ibid., p. 32.
9. Ibid., p. 9.
10. Montague, *Arnold Toynbee*, p. 12.
11. Charlotte Toynbee's MS, pp. 9–10.
12. Milner, "Reminiscence," p. xiv.
13. Charlotte Toynbee's MS, p. 9. Also A. Mansbridge, "An Oxford Talk about Arnold Toynbee," *Commonwealth* 1, no. 1 (January 1896).
14. C. E. Vaughan, "Balliol Five and Twenty Years Ago," *South Wales and Monmouthshire University College Magazine* 11 (March 1899).
15. Frederick Rogers, *Labour, Life and Literature* (London, 1913), p. 85.
16. Milner, "Reminiscence," p. xiv.
17. A. R. MacEwen, "Benjamin Jowett," lecture delivered in New College, Edinburgh [c. 1901 or 1902], G. A. Oxon MS, Bodleian Library, c. p. 360.
18. Charlotte Toynbee's MS, p. 32.
19. Ibid., p. 33.
20. Milner to Gell, 7 March [c. 1874], Gell family papers.
21. A. Mansbridge, "An Oxford Talk." On Nettleship's relativism, see A. C. Bradley, "Biographical Sketch," in R. L. Nettleship, *Philosophical Remains* (London, 1901), p. xlii. See also Toynbee to Falk, 13 July 1873, Toynbee papers, Balliol College, Oxford, in which Toynbee recommends Nettleship's essays on Browning.
22. Milner, "Reminiscence," pp. xviii–xix.
23. A case might be made for the more precise nature of Nettleship's influence by comparing the philosophical terminology employed by Toynbee in Toynbee to Gell, 25 February (1876), Gell family papers, and in some of the fragments included in the *Industrial Revolution* (e.g.,

on "definiteness" and "definition," p. 270, and on the concept of the "Fall," p. 263) with passages from Nettleship's works (e.g., in *Philosophical Remains*, pp. 195, 270, 217, respectively).

24. Toynbee to Evans (master of Pembroke College), 3 January 1874, Jowett papers, Balliol College, Oxford.
25. Montague, *Arnold Toynbee*, p. 10.
26. Toynbee to Gell, December 1873, Gell family papers. The examiners were the Reverend J. F. Bright and R. Laing, both Balliol lecturers.
27. An attitude that appears to have been somewhat reinforced by his friends. See Gell to Toynbee (n.d.), Jowett papers.
28. Charlotte Toynbee's MS, pp. 23–24.
29. Toynbee to Gell, December 1873, Gell family papers. See also Toynbee to Jowett, 23 December 1873, Jowett papers.
30. Toynbee to Gell, December 1873, Gell family papers.
31. Hardinge, "Some Personal Recollections."
32. This dating of Jowett's offer is based on a passage in Toynbee to Jowett, 23 December 1873, Jowett papers, in which Toynbee stated that he had not notified the Master of Pembroke of Jowett's offer sooner since he had not been certain whether it would still hold after the results of the examination became known.
33. Evans to W. Toynbee, 7 December [1873], Jowett papers.
34. Jowett to A. Toynbee, 19 December 1873, 21 December 1873, Jowett papers.
35. Toynbee to Jowett, 23 December 1873, Jowett papers.
36. Jowett to Toynbee, 2 January [1874], Jowett papers.
37. Toynbee to Evans [draft], 3 January 1874, Jowett papers.
38. E. Abbott and L. Campbell, *The Life and Letters of Benjamin Jowett* (London, 1897), 2:66.
39. Lord Salisbury to Toynbee, 20 March 1874, Jowett papers.
40. Note by Charlotte Toynbee (probably for the use of E. Abbott), Jowett papers.
41. In the case of J. R. Anderson, see A. R. MacEwen, "Preface," in J. R. Anderson, *The House of Bondage* (Edinburgh, 1908), p. viii.
42. A. Mansbridge, "An Oxford Talk."
43. B. Jowett, "Memoir," in A. Toynbee, *Industrial Revolution* (1884, 1886, 1890). Cf. Rev. T. Fowle to Phelps, 12 March 1883, L. R. Phelps papers, Oriel College.
44. Charlotte Toynbee to Phelps, 9 April 1883, Phelps papers.
45. In Montague, *Arnold Toynbee*, p. 14.
46. [H. D. Rawnsley], "Ruskin and 'the Hinksey Diggers,'" *Atlantic Monthly* 85 (April 1900).
47. David S. Caird, *Life and Times of Alexander Robertson MacEwen D.D.* (London, 1925), p. 52. See also A. J. Ashton, *As I Went On My Way* (London, 1924), pp. 79–80.
48. Caird, *Life and Times of A. R. MacEwen*, p. 57.
49. [Rawnsley], "Ruskin and 'the Hinksey Diggers.'"
50. For Ruskin's letter to Acland, dated 28 March 1874, see E. T. Cook

and A. Wedderburn, *The Works of John Ruskin 1874–1889* (London, 1905), pp. xli–xlii; and Cook, *The Life of John Ruskin* (London, 1911), 2:187–88.

51. Caird, *Life and Times of A. R. MacEwen*, p. 58.
52. [Rawnsley], "Ruskin and 'the Hinksey Diggers.' "
53. A comprehensive description of the project may be found in ibid. and in Caird, *Life and Times of A. R. MacEwen*.
54. E. P. Poulton, *John Viriamu Jones and other Oxford Memories* (London, 1911), p. 246.
55. Caird, *Life and Times of A. R. MacEwen*, pp. 58, 62.
56. [Rawnsley], "Ruskin and 'the Hinksey Diggers.' "
57. G. Toynbee, *Reminiscences*, pp. 174–75.
58. L. Montefiore to family [c. Autumn] 1874, Montefiore papers, Moccata Library, University College, London.
59. Derrick Leon, *Ruskin, The Great Victorian* (London, 1949), p. 433.
60. See entries in J. Evans and J. H. Whitehead, eds., *The Diaries of John Ruskin 1874–1889* (Oxford, 1959).
61. Cook, *The Life of John Ruskin*, p. 189.
62. Ibid., p. 191; and [Rawnsley], "Ruskin and 'the Hinksey Diggers.' "
63. Milner to Marianne Malcolm, 1 November 1874, Milner papers, dep. 653, fols. 38–39, Bodleian Library.
64. Milner to M. Malcolm, 15 November 1874, ibid., dep. 653, fols. 42–44.
65. Milner, "Reminiscence," p. xvi.
66. Charlotte Toynbee's MS, p. 26; G. Toynbee, *Reminiscences*, p. 125.
67. J. Ruskin, *Unto This Last* (London, 1862), sec. 48.
68. Ibid., sec. 69.
69. Montefiore, "Undergraduate Oxford."
70. Toynbee, *Industrial Revolution*, pp. 182–83.
71. Ruskin, *Unto This Last*, sec. 55.
72. "Trade and Industry," *Bradford Daily Telegraph*, 6 January 1880.
73. He had been proclaimed as one of Ruskin's "warmest admirers and ablest pupils" in W. G. Collingwood, *The Life of John Ruskin* (London, 1900), p. 309.
74. See letters in the Montefiore papers from 1873; and [A. Milner], "Memoir," in Montefiore, *Essays and Letters*, p. xiv.
75. Milner to M. Malcolm, 25 October 1874, Milner papers, dep. 653, fols. 35–37.
76. Montefiore to family, [c. Autumn 1874] Montefiore papers; Charlotte Toynbee's MS, p. 26.
77. Milner to M. Malcolm, 1 November 1874, Milner papers, dep. 653, fols. 38–39. It should be noted that at the same time at least Montefiore and Toynbee continued their work on the North Hinksey project.
78. Milner, "Reminiscence," p. xviii.
79. Ashton, *As I Went On My Way*, p. 61. See also Walter Sichel, *The Sands of Time* (London, 1923), p. 126; H. Kingsmill Moore, *Reminiscences and Reflections* (London, 1930), p. 114; John St. Loe Stra-

chey, *The Adventure of Living* (London, 1925), p. 128; and Vaughan, "Balliol Five and Twenty Years Ago."

80. Lewis R. Farnell, *An Oxonian Looks Back* (London, 1934), p. 15.

81. W. G. Hiscock, *The Balliol Rhymes* (Oxford, 1939), p. 27, first performed in 1881.

82. Ashton, *As I Went On My Way*, p. 62.

83. James Bryce, *Studies in Contemporary Biography* (London, 1903), p. 97. See also Rev. P. A. Wright-Henderson, *Glasgow and Balliol and other Essays* (Oxford, 1926), pp. 44–45; and H. A. L. Fisher, *An Unfinished Autobiography* (Oxford, 1940), p. 50.

84. A. C. Bradley, in his preface to the first edition of T. H. Green, *Prolegomena to Ethics* (Oxford, 1883), pointed out that those "unaccustomed to metaphysical and psychological discussions" could study Green's ethical views by turning directly to the book's last two parts.

85. Benjamin Jowett, *Sermons Biographical and Miscellaneous* (London, 1899), p. 214.

86. T. H. Green, *"The Witness of God" and "Faith."* *Two Lay Sermons* (London, 1883). They were eventually published by Charlotte Toynbee.

87. G. Toynbee, *Reminiscences*, p. 124. Also in Montague, *Arnold Toynbee*, pp. 19–20.

88. Montague, *Arnold Toynbee*, p. 21.

89. Ibid.

90. Green, *Two Lay Sermons*, p. 91.

91. *Oxford Chronicle and Berks and Bucks Gazette*, 27 December 1879.

92. Mrs. S. A. Barnett, "The Beginnings of Toynbee Hall," in S. A. and H. O. Barnett, *Practicable Socialism*, new ser. (London, 1915); Mrs. S. A. Barnett, *Canon Barnett, His Life, Work, and Friends* (London, 1918), 1:302ff.

93. Montague, *Arnold Toynbee*, pp. 24–25; Charlotte Toynbee's MS, p. 27; Barnett, *Canon Barnett*, p. 309.

94. G. Toynbee, *Reminiscences*, pp. 117–18. An undated letter by Toynbee from the Lake District refers to the 11 July 1875 issue of the *National Reformer* as "published yesterday."

95. From a notebook quoted in Charlotte Toynbee's MS, p. 28.

96. Ibid., pp. 28–29. He was especially fascinated by the face of one of the angels in the pieta by Francesco Francia, the upper part of the altarpiece from the chapel of Saint Anne in Saint Frediano in Lucca, which depicts the dead Christ, the Virgin, and two angels.

97. Rogers, *Labour, Life and Literature*, p. 96.

98. W. Besant, *All Sorts and Conditions of Men* (new ed., London, 1883), pp. 190ff. The club is thinly disguised as the Stepney Advanced Club.

99. *National Reformer*, 11 July 1875.

100. Vaughan, "Balliol Five and Twenty Years Ago."

101. Letter appended to Jowett, "Memoir," and to Charlotte Toynbee's MS, p. 30. See also Toynbee to Falk, 9 November 1876, Toynbee papers, in

which Toynbee declared that he would consider it proof of Falk's friendship "if you will give me any opportunity you find of speaking to working men."

102. [J. Bonar], *The Adam Smith Club, An Address by the President* (London, 1884).

103. G. Toynbee, *Reminiscences*, p. 125.

104. Milner, "Reminiscence," p. xxi.

105. Toynbee to Gell, February 1876, Gell family papers.

106. G. Toynbee, *Reminiscences*, pp. 127–28.

107. Ibid., p. 100; A. J. Toynbee, *Acquaintances* (Oxford, 1967), pp. 21ff.

108. *Oxford Magazine*, 22 January 1931, pp. 332–33.

109. Toynbee to Milner, 27 March 1876, Milner papers, dep. 25, fols. 30–31. Toynbee to his mother, 8 March 1876, Toynbee papers.

110. G. Toynbee, *Reminiscences*, p. 129; Arnold to William Toynbee, 6 November 1846, MS Eng. Lett. e. 199, fol. 188, Bodleian Library.

111. G. Toynbee, *Reminiscences*, p. 138.

112. Ibid., pp. 144–45.

113. Ibid., pp. 139–40.

114. Ibid., p. 154; Milner to Gell, 23 December 1877, Gell family papers.

115. Balliol College Register (English), 1875–1908. The tutorship of Lord Russell was dropped when it became apparent that he would require the services of a trained coach.

116. Sir Michael O'Dwyer, *India As I Knew It, 1885–1925* (London, 1925), p. 20.

117. Charlotte Toynbee to Phelps, 7 March 1883, Phelps papers.

118. Balliol College Ledger, Junior Bursar, 1880–1885; Charlotte Toynbee's MS, p. 34. In 1883 A. Marshall regarded an annual income of £300 as sufficient for the needs of a bachelor Fellow, including four months of traveling abroad and books. See A. Kadish, "Marshall on Necessaries and Travel. A Note on a Letter by Marshall to the *Pall Mall Gazette*," *History of Economic Thought Newsletter* (Spring 1981).

119. Barnett, *Canon Barnett* 1:306. See also A. Toynbee to H. Toynbee, 11 August 1878, Toynbee papers; and Toynbee to Mrs. Penny, [c. Summer] 1878, ibid., in which Toynbee described Charlotte as being, mentally, "exactly of my age."

120. Poulton, *John Viriamu Jones*, p. 70.

Chapter 4

1. Toynbee to Gell, December 1873, Gell family papers.

2. Ibid., 25 February [no year].

3. A similar sentiment is expressed in Milner to Marianne Malcolm, 27 February 1874, Rendel papers. Upon winning the Hertford Scholarship Milner wrote, "I feel that I have a very great deal to thank God for, and that once more there is reposed in me a great trust. These things stagger one at first. One does not realize them. One can only hope that with the practical realization of success may come also a profounder

feeling of duty." Cf. Toynbee to Mrs. Penny, 23 December 1878, Toynbee papers: "Political Economy is for me the disclosure of the highest problems of life. . . . Without it the Gospel of Jesus fills me with despair."

4. Toynbee to Gell, 31 August [no year], Gell family papers.
5. For a contemporary summary of the views for and against disestablishment and disendowment, see S. Buxton, *A Manual of Political Questions of the Day*, new ed. (London, 1891), pp. 59ff. See also E. C. Mack and W. H. G. Armytage, *Thomas Hughes, The Life of the Author of Tom Brown's Schooldays* (London, 1952), pp. 198–99.
6. For the main arguments for reform, see Albert Grey and Rev. Canon Fremantle, eds., *Church Reform* (London, 1888).
7. The Master of the Temple, ed., *Recollections of Fremantle* (London, 1921), p. 92.
8. Mrs. S. A. Barnett, *Canon Barnett, His Life, Work and Friends* (London, 1918), 1:22ff.
9. W. H. Fremantle, *Lay Power in Parishes, the Most Needed Church Reform* (London, 1869), p. 4.
10. *Memoir of the Reverend T. W. Fowle, M.A.* (Oxford, 1903).
11. Deborah Wormell, *Sir John Seeley and the Uses of History* (Cambridge, 1980), pp. 18ff.
12. Fremantle to Tait, 7 June 1870, Tait papers, vol. 167, fols. 140–47, Lambeth Palace.
13. *Church Reform Union* (1 December 1870). Pamphlet in Fourth Earl Grey papers, Dept. of Palaeography and Diplomatic, Durham University.
14. This, in Fremantle's view, remained the cornerstone of church reform. Fremantle to Tait, 20 May 1873, Tait papers, vol. 92, fols. 127–30: "With it, I see hardly anything that might not be accomplished. Without it the church will continue to be a clerical set."
15. Mack and Armytage, *Thomas Hughes*, p. 200.
16. Hughes to Grey, 27 May 1879, Grey papers.
17. Hughes to Barnett, 31 December 1878, Barnett papers, vol. 1466, Lambeth Palace. Hughes took it upon himself to put the Oxford men "in touch with Davies, Fremantle and such . . . as may be found game for another dash at millenium."
18. Charles Llewellyn Davies, ed., *From a Victorian Post Bag; Being letters addressed to the Reverend J. Llewellyn Davies* (London, 1926), pp. 31–32.
19. Toynbee to Barnett, 19 January 1879, Barnett papers, vol. 1466.
20. Ibid., 2 February 1879.
21. *Oxford Chronicle*, 22 May 1880. See the report on laying the foundation stone of the New Congregational Chapel and School building in Cowley Road.
22. Notes for an address on church reform delivered at a conference at Merton College, 7 December 1881, T. H. Green papers, Balliol College. Report in the *Oxford Chronicle*, 10 December 1881.
23. It is only in view of their common position on church reform that the

Balliol rhyme on Toynbee seems to make any sense.
What finance and trade and coin be
Learn of me, for I am Toynbee:
Green and I our faith have plighted
To a sepulchre re-whited.
W. G. Hiscock, *The Balliol Rhymes* (Oxford, 1939), p. 8.

24. "The Ideal Relation of Church and State," in Toynbee, *Industrial Revolution,* pp. 249–58.

25. G. A. Oxon 4° 600, b. 146, Bodleian Library.

26. Charlotte Toynbee's MS, pp. 35–36.

27. A. Milner, "A Retrospect of Ten Years," in *The Toynbee Journal and Students Union Chronicle,* 1 September 1886.

28. Milner to Gell, 1 March 1880, Gell papers.

29. Recollections by Bruce and by Montague, Milner papers, dep. 667, fols. 229, 218–19.

30. Toynbee to Barnett, 17 June 1879, Barnett papers, vol. 1464.

31. D. G. Ritchie, *Philosophical Studies* (London, 1905), p. 6.

32. See Charlotte Toynbee's MS, pp. 40–41.

33. See Toynbee to Rendel, 5 February [1882], Rendel papers, on Rendel's engagement: "May you be as happy in your married life as I have been happy in mine!"

34. Lack of interest should not be confused with ignorance. See Charlotte Toynbee to Phelps, 9 April 1883, Phelps papers; Charlotte Toynbee to Grey, 2 January [1884], Grey papers, on Toynbee's letters before their marriage, which while "charming as illustrative of his character seldom contained any discussion of topics of general interest."

35. Arnold J. Toynbee, *Acquaintances* (Oxford, 1967), p. 35.

36. Toynbee to Gell, October 1879, Gell family papers.

37. Ibid., Milner to Gell, 1 March 1880.

38. Ibid., Toynbee to Gell, 15 August and 24 August 1880.

39. Ibid., Milner to Gell, 24 August 1880.

40. Hughes to Grey, 27 May 1879, Grey papers.

41. Ibid., 20 July 1879. It was included in the CRU's annual report for 1880.

42. Toynbee to Gell, 16 November 1879, Gell family papers.

43. Grey and Fremantle, *Church Reform.*

44. Toynbee to Grey, 13 June 1880, Grey papers. Grey was clearly regarded by Toynbee as an ally. Two months later he described him to Gell (Toynbee to Gell, 15 August 1880, Gell family papers) as "especially a most interesting and encouraging fellow."
    At the time Rev. Dr. Edwin Abbott was at the City of London School and a member of the CRU Council.

45. Reported in *Supplement to the Leicester Chronicle and Leicestershire Mercury,* 20 October 1880, p. 5; and the *Leicester Daily Post,* 29 September 1880.

46. Milner to Gell, 20 October 1880, Gell family papers.

47. Toynbee to Grey, [c. Autumn 1880], Grey papers.

48. Toynbee, *Industrial Revolution*. An original copy may be found in the Barnett papers, vol. 1463. See also Toynbee to Grey, 19 April [1881], Grey papers.

49. Toynbee to Gell, [c. early 1881], Gell family papers.

50. *C.R.U. Annual Report for 1881*, Grey papers. Other branches were founded at Bristol (with Barnett's brother as secretary), Manchester, Newcastle, Tamworth, and Lancashire.

51. Toynbee to Gell, 5 December 1880, Gell family papers. Coworkers at Oxford included S. Ball, T. H. Green, and A. Robinson.

52. Toynbee to Grey, 11 February and 21 February 1881, Grey papers.

53. "Free Trade and Protection," *Bradford Chronicle and Mail*, 6 January 1880; "Trade and Industry," *Bradford Daily Telegraph*, 6 January 1880.

54. On the misinterpretation of Ricardo, see J. E. Cliffe Leslie, "Political Economy and Emigration," *Fraser's Magazine* (May 1868).

55. The currently accepted figures for 1880 are 44 percent foodstuffs, 39 percent raw materials, and 17 percent manufactured goods (F. Crouzet, *The Victorian Economy* [London, 1982], table 60, p. 351).

56. "Trade [and] Industry, The Law of Wages," *Bradford Daily Telegraph*, 8 January 1880; "Trade [and] Industry," *Bradford Chronicle*, 8 January 1880. The lecture was repeated in February 1882 at Firth College, Sheffield, and reproduced in Toynbee, *Industrial Revolution*, as "Wages and Natural Law."

57. The subject was later dealt with in lecture 11 ("The Wage Fund Theory," in Toynbee, *Industrial Revolution*).

58. "Ricardo and the Old Political Economy," in Toynbee, *Industrial Revolution*, p. 174.

59. See ibid., p. 180, where Toynbee refers to "a more recent economist" who replaced Mill's concept of the "wages of superintendence" with the "earnings of management."

60. Ibid., p. 174.

61. *Bradford Chronicle*, 8 January 1880.

62. *Bradford Daily Telegraph*, 8 January 1880.

63. *Bradford Chronicle*, 9 January 1880.

64. In a later lecture he would single out Carlyle's *Past and Present*.

65. *Bradford Chronicle*, 6 January 1880.

66. J. E. Cairnes, *Essays in Political Economy, Theoretical and Applied* (London, 1873); Toynbee to Grey, 5 October 1880, Grey papers.

67. *Newcastle Daily Chronicle*, 9 August 1880.

68. Ibid., 13 August 1880.

69. Ibid., 16 August. See also 17 August and 24 August 1880. The whole exchange appears to have been triggered by a course on political economy arranged through the Durham University Extension Scheme and delivered at five mining villages with an aggregate attendance of over thirteen hundred miners. The course was financed by donations from colliery proprietors, the Miners' Union, and private persons, and was

delivered by W. M. Moorsom, previously of Trinity College, Cambridge, and a superintendent of a department of the London and North Western Railway works at Crewe. See University Library, Cambridge, B.E.M.S. 22/1. Judging by a previous course by Moorsom his economics were unabashedly orthodox. See *Crewe Guardian*, 20 March, 3 April, 10 April 1875, and 26 February and 25 March 1876.

70. *Newcastle Daily Chronicle*, 19 and 21 August 1880.
71. Ibid., 17 August 1880.
72. Ibid., 21 August 1880.
73. Ibid., 8 September 1880.
74. Pringle to Grey, 16 September 1880, Grey papers.
75. Ibid., Moorsom to Grey, [n.d.].
76. Ibid., Toynbee to Grey, 13 September 1880.
77. Ibid., 18 September 1880.
78. Toynbee papers, Balliol. Undated MS beginning 'There is no one,' etc.
79. Toynbee, *Industrial Revolution*, p. 143.
80. Ibid.
81. Ibid., p. 139.
82. Ibid., p. 146.
83. Ibid., pp. 145–46.
84. Ibid., p. 147.
85. Ibid.
86. Ibid., p. 148.
87. Ibid.
88. Ibid., p. 154.
89. Ibid., p. 157.
90. Ibid., pp. 157–58.
91. Ibid., p. 143.
92. *Bradford Chronicle*, 1 February 1881; and "Industry and Democracy," in Toynbee, *Industrial Revolution*.
93. Toynbee, *Industrial Revolution*, p. 193.
94. *Oxford Chronicle*, 28 February 1880.
95. See also Charles Fenby, *The Other Oxford; The Life and Times of Frank Gray and His Father* (London, 1970), p. 39.
96. Milner papers, dep. 667, fol. 229. See also J. Saxon Mills, *Sir Edward Cook, K.B.E.* (London, 1921), pp. 42–43.
97. *Oxford Chronicle*, 20 March 1880.
98. Ibid., 27 March 1880.
99. With him was elected his co-candidate, Joseph W. Chitty, QC. Due to the local party's financial difficulties the Tories managed to put up only one candidate: A. W. Hall, the brewer, otherwise known as the "Little Squire," who had won one of the city's seats in the Tory victory of 1874. In 1880 he came at the bottom of the poll.
100. See C. O'Leary, *The Elimination of Corrupt Practices in British Elections* (Oxford, 1962), pp. 145–47. Hall's act was generally regarded as a breach of common etiquette. See Fenby, *The Other Oxford*, p. 32.

101. *Oxford Chronicle*, 1, 8 May 1880.
102. Of the university Liberals, T. H. Green and J. E. Thorold Rogers campaigned on Harcourt's behalf.
103. *Oxford Chronicle*, 15 May 1880.
104. The leader of the local Liberal party, Richard "Dickie" Carr, opposed the petition and most Tories appeared confident that the Liberals would not dare to bring their dirty linen out in the open. See Fenby, *The Other Oxford*, p. 45.
105. *Oxford Chronicle*, 5 June 1880.
106. Ibid., 9 April 1881 (Supplement). The commissioners were Lewis M. Care, Hugh Cowie, and Edward Ridley. Their deliberations took thirty-eight days.
107. Ibid., 16 April 1881.

Chapter 5

1. "Industry and Democracy," in Toynbee, *Industrial Revolution*.
2. There may have been some personal contact or at least indirect knowledge of each other. Henry Crompton's sister was married to the Reverend J. Ll. Davies. Another sister was married to Professor E. S. Beesley, a fellow positivist. For an example of a positivist use of "revolution," see E. S. Beesley, "The Social Future of the Working Class" (1868), in E. Frow and M. Katanka, eds., *1868: Year of the Unions* (London, 1968).
3. Henry Crompton, *Industrial Conciliation* (London, 1876), p. 30.
4. Ibid., p. 3.
5. G. Toynbee, *Reminiscences*, p. 112.
6. E.g., as expressed in "On the Philosophical Method of Political Economy," in *Hermathena* 2 (1876).
7. Crompton, *Industrial Conciliation*, p. 2. Cf. Cliffe Leslie, "On the Philosophical Method of Political Economy": "The whole economy of every nation . . . is the result of a long evolution, in which there has been both continuity and change, and of which the economical side is only a particular aspect or phase."
8. Crompton, *Industrial Conciliation*, p. 164.
9. Ibid., p. 4.
10. Ibid., p. 7.
11. Ibid., p. 50.
12. See Anna Bezanson, "Early Use of the Term Industrial Revolution," *Quarterly Journal of Economics* 36 (1922); and George N. Clark, *The Idea of the Industrial Revolution* (Glasgow, 1970).
13. Lord Macaulay, *The History of England from the Accession of James the Second* (London, 1913), 1:2.
14. In *Macmillan's Magazine*, August, September, and October 1870.
15. J. S. Mill, *Principles of Political Economy* (London, 1848), bk. 3, chap. 17, sec. 5.

16. The reference is in W. S. Jevons, *The Coal Question; An Inquiry Concerning the Progress of the Nation, and the Probable Exhaustion of Our Coal-mines,* 2d ed. (London, 1866), p. 206.

17. Ibid., p. 367.

18. Ibid., pp. 206–7.

19. Ibid., p. 226.

20. See Herbert Heaton, "Industrial Revolution," in *Encyclopaedia of the Social Sciences* (New York, 1932), 8:3.

21. Michael Angelo Garvey, *The Silent Revolution* (London, 1852), p. 15.

22. Ibid., p. 129.

23. Ibid., pp. 160–61.

24. The term was used several times in pt. 4, chap. 15.

25. F. Engels, *The Condition of the Working Class in England* (London, 1892; Moscow, 1977), p. 40.

26. Ibid., p. 52.

27. Ibid., p. 55.

28. See "Sir James Mackintosh's History of the Revolution," in Lord Macaulay, *Reviews, Essays and Poems* (London, n.d.), pt. 2, p. 118.

29. Ibid., p. 119.

30. C. R. Fay, *English Economic History, Mainly since 1700* (Cambridge, 1940), p. 8.

31. Toynbee, *Industrial Revolution,* p. 201.

32. Ibid., p. 204.

33. Ibid., p. 212.

34. Ibid., p. 215.

35. Ibid., p. 216.

36. Ibid.

37. *Bradford Chronicle,* 1 February 1881. See also Toynbee to Grey, [n.d.], Grey papers: "I am so glad you have been caught by the pure and deep enthusiasm of Mazzini. In years to come I hope his name will become a household word with the people."

38. Toynbee, *Industrial Revolution,* p. 217.

39. Ibid., p. 218.

40. Toynbee to Grey, 13 January 1881, Grey papers.

41. *Bradford Chronicle,* 1 February 1881.

42. Toynbee to Grey, [c. February 1881], Grey papers. In one of the fragments reproduced in the *Industrial Revolution,* Toynbee wrote, "To make a political speech is like being carried up a flight of steps by the pressure of a crowd" (p. 274).

43. Toynbee to Barnett, 7 May [1881], Gell family papers.

44. W. H. Fremantle to Grey, 2 July 1880, Grey papers.

45. Ibid., Toynbee to Grey, 7 August 1881.

46. Ibid., Toynbee to Grey, 2 October 1881.

47. Grey to Phelps, 9 February 1882, Phelps papers. It was precisely Grey's emphasis on institutional reform that led a critic in the *Morning Post,* 27 January 1882, to accuse the CRU of an attempt to reduce the church to a religious cooperative society for good works. Such a church would

be "a mere political device, a creation of economists, an organisation for the promotion of certain social benefits chiefly in the connection with the working classes, a machinery, in short, to do part of the work of parliament."

48. Gell to Grey, 31 January 1882, Grey papers.
49. Ibid., Toynbee to Grey, [c. late January or early February 1882].
50. Toynbee suggested S. Ball while Gell supported E. T. Cook, neither of whom got the job. Toynbee to Grey, 2 October and 6 November 1881; Gell to Grey, 6 September 1881, Grey papers.
51. S. Ball to Grey, 18 November 1881; and Toynbee to Grey, 18 November 1881, Grey papers. For an account of the conference, see Charlotte Toynbee to Grey, 9 December 1881, Grey papers; and the *Oxford Chronicle*, 10 December 1881.
52. Toynbee to Seeley, 4 June 1881, Seeley papers. For Seeley's position on "social religion," see *A Paper Read before the University College Students Christian Association* (London, 29 October 1867).
53. Toynbee to Grey, [n.d.], Grey papers.
54. See Cliffe Leslie, "On the Philosophical Method of Political Economy": "The laws of which it [economic evolution] is the result must be sought in history and the general laws of society and social evolution. . . . [Economic development] is in fact, a social evolution, the economical side of which is indissolubly connected with its moral, intellectual, and political sides."
55. Toynbee to Seeley, 4 August 1881, Seeley papers.
56. See Milner papers, MS Milner dep. adds. 1, fols. 13–14, Milner to Wise, in which he assured Wise that lectures for the Tower Hamlets University Extension Society on free trade "would draw like anything at the present time and are sorely needed."
57. Toynbee to Grey, 17 November 1881, Grey papers.
58. See Cecil Headlam, ed., *The Milner Papers, South Africa, 1897–99* (London, 1931), p. 12. In a letter dealing with Professor Neumann's lectures, Milner wrote to Toynbee from Tübingen (5 October 1880), "The doctrine of Free Trade, he regarded precisely as you do, not as a supreme principle of economic morals, but as a statement of fact. Whether or not home industry was to be protected depended upon the circumstances of each country."
59. Toynbee to Grey, 18 November 1881, Grey papers.
60. Percy Corder, *The Life of Robert Spence-Watson* (London, 1914), p. 165. For Spence-Watson's reasons for arranging such lectures, see Spence-Watson to Seeley, 17 August 1880, Seeley papers.
61. The Newcastle version was reproduced in Toynbee, *Industrial Revolution*, pp. 219–38. The opening comments were not reported when Toynbee gave the same address at Leicester (*Leicester Chronicle* [supplement], 1 April 1882) or at Bradford (*Bradford Daily Telegraph*, 19 January 1882).
62. Toynbee, *Industrial Revolution*, p. 219.
63. E.g., J. Morley, *On Compromise* (1874; London, 1933), pp. 137–38.

64. Toynbee, *Industrial Revolution*, p. 220.
65. Ibid., p. 225.
66. Toynbee referred to Lange and Brentano as authorities on the matter. See also Ernst von Plener, *The English Factory Legislation: From 1802 till the Present Time*, 2d ed. (London, 1973).
67. See Charles A. Barker, *Henry George* (New York, 1955), p. 390. In reference to Toynbee's criticism of Henry George, H. M. Hyndman wrote to George, "I disapprove of attacking allies and Toynbee calls himself a Radical Socialist."
68. Toynbee, *Industrial Revolution*, p. 225.
69. Ibid., p. 229.
70. Ibid., p. 233.
71. Ibid., p. 237.
72. T. H. Green, "Liberal Legislation and Freedom of Contract," *Oxford Chronicle*, 26 February 1881.
73. See John Barnett, *A Social History of Housing 1815–1970* (London, 1980), p. 155.
74. Toynbee, *Industrial Revolution*, p. 236.
75. Ibid., p. 238.
76. Ibid. Cf. Gladstone's first principle of foreign policy in the third Midlothian speech.
77. The surviving version of the course is based on notes taken by William James Ashley and Bolton King which were collated with the notes of other students and Toynbee's own. The latter were mostly references to various sources and cover only the first lectures.
78. Toynbee, *Industrial Revolution*, p. 5.
79. Ibid., p. 2.
80. J. S. Mill, "On the Definition of Political Economy; and on the Method of Investigation Proper to It," in Mill, *Essays on Economics and Society. Collected Works of John Stuart Mill* 4 (Toronto, 1967).
81. Toynbee, *Industrial Revolution*, p. 3.
82. Ibid., p. 4.
83. That is, if one accepts Professor Samuel Hollander's interpretation of Mill's position as an apologia for Ricardo's abstract method. S. Hollander, "On J. S. Mill's Defense of Ricardian Economics," paper read at the History of Economic Thought Conference at Oxford, September 1981.
84. Best exemplified by E. A. Freeman's dictum, "History is past politics, politics is present history."
85. *Oxford Chronicle*, 12 March 1881.
86. Ibid., 19 March 1881.
87. Toynbee, *Industrial Revolution*, pp. 5–6.
88. Ibid., pp. vi–vii.
89. H. S. Maine, *Ancient Law* (1861; London, 1905), pp. 150–51. See also J. W. Burrow, " 'The Village Community' and the Uses of History in Late Nineteenth Century England," in Neil McKendrick, ed., *His-*

torical Perspectives (London, 1974); and J. W. Burrow, *A Liberal Descent* (Cambridge, 1981).

90. E.g., Brodrick in the *Oxford Chronicle*, 4 February 1882.
91. Toynbee, *Industrial Revolution*, p. 5.
92. Ibid., p. 111.
93. Ibid., p. 112. Toynbee appears to have overlooked Maine's fundamentally different notion of progress, i.e., that "the stationary condition of the human race is the rule, the progressive the exception" (H. Maine, *Ancient Law*, p. 30).
94. Toynbee, *Industrial Revolution*, p. 112.
95. Ibid., p. 121.
96. Ibid., p. 74.
97. Ibid., p. 86.
98. Ibid., pp. 129–30.
99. E.g., ibid., pp. 132n, 134n.
100. On the latter he cited Adam Smith as his authority, ibid., p. 51.
101. Ibid., p. 33.
102. Ibid., pp. 131–32.
103. Ibid., p. 35.
104. Ibid., p. 36.
105. Ibid., p. 42.
106. Ibid., p. 43.
107. Ibid., p. 44.
108. Ibid., p. 48.
109. Ibid., p. 50.
110. Ibid., p. 51.
111. Ibid., p. 53.
112. Ibid.
113. Ibid., p. 54.
114. Ibid., p. 57.
115. Ibid.
116. Ibid., p. 61.
117. Bagehot concluded that "What . . . a student will find in Adam Smith is a rough outline of sensible thoughts; not always consistent with themselves, and rarely stated with much precision, often very near the truth, though seldom precisely hitting it" (Walter Bagehot, *Economic Studies* [London, 1880], p. 119).
118. Ibid., p. 117.
119. It has been suggested, erroneously in my view, that Toynbee may have abandoned his essay on Ricardo partly because Bagehot had covered the same ground (Toynbee, *Industrial Revolution*, p. vi).
120. Ibid., p. 62.
121. Ibid.
122. Ibid., p. 63.
123. Ibid., p. 123.
124. Ibid.

125. Ibid., p. 65.
126. Ibid., p. 66.
127. Ibid.
128. Ibid., p. 67.
129. Ibid., p. 72.
130. Ibid., p. 73.
131. Hence a possible explanation of the discrepancy in Toynbee's statements on Malthus and Godwin, ibid., pp. 73–74, 86.
132. Ibid., pp. 74–75.
133. Ibid., p. 75.
134. Ibid., p. 84.
135. Ibid., p. 79.
136. E.g., ibid., pp. 87n, 88.
137. Bagehot, *Economic Studies,* p. 136.
138. Toynbee, *Industrial Revolution,* p. 6.
139. Ibid., pp. 89–90.
140. G. Toynbee, *Reminiscences,* p. 161.
141. Toynbee, *Industrial Revolution,* p. 92.
142. Ibid., p. 93.
143. Toynbee papers, "Notes on the Moral Condition of Normandy." The following passages are all taken from these notes.
144. Toynbee, *Industrial Revolution,* p. 95.
145. Ibid., pp. 95–96.
146. Ibid., p. 95.
147. See H. George, *Progress and Poverty* (1879; London, 1908), p. 97, "The tendency to increase, instead of being always uniform, is strong where a greater population would give increased comfort, and where the perpetuity of the race is threatened by the morality induced by adverse conditions, but weakens just as the higher development of the individual becomes possible and the perpetuity of the race is assured. In other words, the law of population accords with and is subordinate to the law of intellectual development."
148. Toynbee, *Industrial Revolution,* p. 100.
149. Ibid., p. 99.
150. See Henry Sidgwick, "The Wages Fund Theory," *Fortnightly Review* (February 1879), p. 411.
151. Toynbee, *Industrial Revolution,* p. 102. At Firth College, Toynbee emphasized the effect of the availability of vast tracts of uncultivated land in America while ignoring the efficiency argument. This deviation from his previous argument was in keeping with his criticism of Henry George and his observation concerning the link between wages in California and the accessibility of natural treasures. See ibid., p. 188.
152. Ibid., p. 103.
153. Ibid., p. 104.
154. Ibid., p. 105.
155. Ibid., p. 106. Toynbee appears to have completely overlooked the po-

litical implications of a general strike and regards it as merely another possible weapon that might be employed in the future course of industrial relations.

156. Ibid.
157. Ibid., p. 109.
158. Ibid., p. 113.
159. Ibid., p. 118.
160. Ibid., p. 119.
161. F. C. Montague, *Arnold Toynbee* (Baltimore, 1889), p. 51. See also G. Toynbee, *Reminiscences*, pp. 163–64.
162. Toynbee, *Industrial Revolution*, p. 122.
163. Ibid., p. 120.
164. Ibid., p. 136.
165. Ibid., p. 126.
166. Ibid., p. 127.
167. Ibid., p. 128.
168. Ibid., pp. 128–29.
169. Ibid., p. 131.
170. Ibid., p. 133. Cf. Lujo Brentano, "On the History and Development of Gilds," in Toumlin Smith, *English Gilds* (London, 1970), p. cxcviii.
171. Toynbee, *Industrial Revolution*, p. 133.
172. Ibid., p. 134.
173. Sedley Taylor, *Profit Sharing between Capital and Labour; Six Essays* (London, 1884). Essays 1, 2, and 5 were published in the *Nineteenth Century* during the period 1880–82. See also W. Stanley Jevons, *On Industrial Partnerships* (London, 1870).
174. Taylor, *Profit Sharing*, p. 250.
175. Toynbee, *Industrial Revolution*, p. 133, mentions only two schemes as worthy of consideration.
176. Ibid., p. 135.

Chapter 6

1. Bodleian Library, G. A. Oxon. b. 165, statement by L. R. Phelps, 30 April 1888. Of the thirty-five guardians, the mayor, the Vice Chancellor of the university, and ten aldermen served ex officio. Eleven guardians were elected by the incorporated parishes, two by the convocation of the university, and two by Christ Church. The town representatives did not always take the university-appointed guardians seriously. In one instance an alderman remarked in A. L. Smith's presence that it appeared to him a good thing for dons to "'elp people over the Long Vacation when work was slack" (Smith to Phelps, 2 September 1883, Phelps papers).
2. *Oxford Chronicle*, 6 November 1880.
3. Ibid., 11 December 1880. Wise replaced T. H. Ward.
4. Ibid., 19 March 1881.

5. Ibid., 5 November 1881.
6. See MS by W. A. Spooner, "Notes for Autobiography," chap. 5, New College Archives.
7. *Oxford Chronicle*, 17 March 1883. Both in the cos and on the Board of Guardians there were those, mainly among the town's representatives, who took a lenient view of outdoor relief. At one time Spooner wrote in exasperation, "It seems to me that the Committee is fast drifting into the position of a society for granting outdoor relief" (Spooner to Phelps, 27 November 1884, Phelps papers). Furthermore, some university representatives faced with the realities of poverty proved unable to resist grants of outdoor relief regardless of their own self-professed principles. In a letter to Phelps of 7 January 1884, A. L. Smith related an incident in which Spooner, having heard of a new case, exclaimed, "Oh let's give her a little out-relief," whereas Marshall argued that the abolition of outdoor relief would only relieve the selfish rich of their responsibilities.
8. *Oxford Times,* 5 November 1881. See also F. C. Montague, *Arnold Toynbee* (Baltimore, 1889), p. 49.
9. C. M. Toynbee, "Poverty and the Poor Law," *Economic Review* (July 1900). See also F. C. Montague, *The Old Poor Law and the New Socialism; or, Pauperism and Taxation* (London, 1886).
10. For the early career of W. Gray, see Fenby, *The Other Oxford; The Life and Times of Frank Gray and His Father* (London, 1970).
11. *Oxford Chronicle*, 5 November 1881. The poll was Gray: 1,053, Simmonds: 1,012, Buckell: 968, Lowe: 935.
12. Ibid., 14 May 1881.
13. Bodleian Library, G. A. Oxon. c. 107 (12), "The List of Persons . . . Guilty of any Bribery, Treating or Personation at an Election Held in the Year 1880 for the Parliamentary Borough of the Said City of Oxford." Buckell was cited in the report for bribery.
14. *Oxford Chronicle*, 14 May 1881.
15. Ibid., 22 October 1881.
16. Ibid., 29 October 1881.
17. *Oxford Times*, 29 October 1881.
18. *Oxford Chronicle*, 29 October 1881.
19. Ibid., 5 November 1881.
20. Ibid., 14 January 1882.
21. Ibid., 11 March 1882. Cf. Toynbee, *Leicester Chronicle* (Supplement), 1 April 1882: "They [the Liberals] had not yet made up their minds whether they should abolish or reform the House of Lords."
22. G. Toynbee, *Reminiscences*, pp. 161–62.
23. Toynbee to Phelps, 8 April 1882, Phelps papers.
24. *Leicester Chronicle* (Supplement), 1 April 1882.
25. *Oxford Chronicle*, 1, 8, and 15 April 1882. The poll was Turner: 1,005, Buckell: 978.
26. Ibid., 12 August 1882.
27. Ibid., 20 May 1882.

28. Ibid., 1 July 1882.
29. Ibid., 12 August 1882. Buckell was to be elected six times mayor (in 1885, 1890, 1896, 1897, 1916, and 1918).
30. Ibid., 7 October 1882.
31. *Oxford Times*, 14 and 21 October 1882.
32. Toynbee to Gell, 5 December 1880, Gell family papers. Toynbee had first come into contact with Buckell toward the end of 1880 while seeking advice on the fomentation of popular support for the NCRU campaign.
33. *Oxford Chronicle*, 21 October 1882.
34. *Oxford Times*, 21 October 1882.
35. *Oxford Chronicle*, 21 October 1882.
36. *Oxford Times*, 28 October 1882; *Jackson's Oxford Journal*, 28 October 1882.
37. Balliol College Ledger, Junior Bursar, 1880–1885, p. 75. "The Stores, 1881–1882" contains the only entry for a purchase made at the co-operative shop on 18 October 1881 for £7.11.5. The rest of the purchases were made mainly with local firms although considerable orders were also placed with the Army and Navy.
38. *Jackson's Oxford Journal*, 28 October 1882.
39. "Mr. Toynbee and Out Door Relief," *Oxford Chronicle*, 28 October 1882. See also *Oxford Times*, 11 November 1882.
40. *Oxford Chronicle*, 28 October 1882.
41. *Oxford Times*, 25 November 1882.
42. For some doubts expressed by R. Ewing in the matter see ibid., 5 November 1881. Toynbee was to conclude that the whole issue of his behavior as a Poor Law Guardian had originated in information leaked by a fellow Guardian (*Oxford Chronicle*, 4 November 1882; *Jackson's Oxford Journal*, 4 November 1882).
43. *Oxford Times*, 28 October 1882.
44. B. Jowett, "Memoir," in Toynbee, *Industrial Revolution* (1884, 1886, 1890), p. xiv.
45. Figures from an estate in Forfare. See Toynbee, *Industrial Revolution*, pp. 123–24.
46. Kenworthy Brown, an ICS candidate, disqualified on medical grounds, stayed on to take a first in modern history.
47. *Oxford Chronicle*, 28 October 1882.
48. *Oxford Times*, 11 November 1882.
49. *Oxford Chronicle*, 4 November 1882.
50. Ibid., 25 November 1882.
51. Ibid., 18 November 1882. See Sir Norman Chester, "The University in the City," in T. Rowley, ed., *The Oxford Region* (Oxford, 1980).
52. *Oxford Chronicle*, 25 November 1882.
53. *Oxford Times*, 25 November 1883.
54. See *Report of the Fourteenth Annual Trades Union Congress* (Manchester, n.d.); and *Report of the Fifteenth Annual Trades Union Congress* (Manchester, n.d.).

55. The question of the standard of housing had become politically sensitive following W. Gray's campaign against the Liberal-controlled Oxford Building and Investment Company. See Fenby, *The Other Oxford*, pp. 62–64.

Chapter 7

1. *Oxford Co-operative and Industrial Society Ltd. An Historical Sketch From 1872 to 1909* (Manchester, 1909), p. 42.
2. *The Fourteenth Annual Co-operative Congress, 1882* (Manchester, 1882), p. 142; A. H. D. Acland, "The Education of Co-operators and Citizens," in *The Co-operative Wholesale Society Ltd. Annual [and] Diary, 1885* (Manchester, 1885).
3. *Oxford Co-operative*, p. 46.
4. Acland, "The Education of Co-operators and Citizens," p. 423.
5. *Fourteenth Annual Co-operative Congress*, p. 22.
6. Ibid., p. 23.
7. Ibid., p. 75.
8. Ibid., p. 23.
9. *Guide to the Co-operative Congress of 1882* (Oxford, 1882), p. 142.
10. Ibid., p. 109.
11. Ibid., p. 184.
12. Reproduced in Toynbee, *Industrial Revolution*, pp. 239–48.
13. Ibid., p. 240.
14. Ibid., p. 241. Toynbee's views were considerably out of fashion within the movement. See S. Pollard, "Nineteenth Century Co-operation: From Community Building to Shopkeeping," in A. Briggs and J. Saville, eds., *Essays in Labour History* (London, 1967).
15. Toynbee, *Industrial Revolution*, p. 243.
16. Ibid., p. 244.
17. Ibid., p. 245.
18. Ibid., p. 246.
19. Ibid. The qualifications enumerated appear to constitute Toynbee's own self-image.
20. Mentioned in Acland's speech, *Fourteenth Annual Co-operative Congress*, p. 23.
21. Toynbee, *Industrial Revolution*, p. 247.
22. *Fourteenth Annual Co-operative Congress*, p. 62.
23. Ibid., p. 61.
24. Ibid., p. 70.
25. Ibid., p. 71.
26. *The Fifteenth Annual Co-operative Congress, 1883* (Manchester, 1883), p. 17.
27. *Co-operative News*, 24 June 1882. See also E. V. Neale, "The Working Man and University Extension," *Co-operative News*, 1 July 1882.
28. *Co-operative News*, 2 September, 21 and 28 October 1882.
29. Ibid., 21 October 1882.

30. Ibid.

31. Ibid., 28 October 1882.

32. Ibid., 4 November 1882.

33. Ibid., 25 November 1882. Acland had also communicated with J. R. Seeley, Regius Professor of Modern History at Cambridge, and co-founder and president (1879–83) of the Social and Political Education League, and with W. Cunningham, who had preceded R. D. Roberts as assistant secretary (1878–81) of the Cambridge Local Lectures and Examinations Syndicate. Toynbee had also corresponded with Seeley about his cooperative education scheme. See Toynbee to Seeley, 3 June 1882, Seeley papers.

34. *Co-operative News*, 2 December 1882.

35. See A. Kadish, *The Oxford Economists in the Late Nineteenth Century* (Oxford, 1982), chap. 2. Also cf. Acland, "The Education of Co-operators and Citizens," and R. D. Roberts, "Culture," in A. H. D. Acland and Ben Jones, eds., *Working Men Co-operators* (London, 1884).

36. *Co-operative News*, 4 November 1882.

37. Dated 30 November in ibid., 16 December 1882.

38. Ibid., 2 December 1882.

39. Ibid., 16 December 1882.

40. Ibid., 17 March 1883.

41. Ibid., 16 December 1882; and *Fifteenth Annual Co-operative Congress*, pp. 21–22.

42. E.g., the exchange between Acland and Jones in *Fifteenth Annual Co-operative Congress*, p. 40.

43. *The Seventeenth Annual Co-operative Congress* (Manchester, 1885).

Chapter 8

1. H. George, *The Land Question* (New York, 1930), p. 62.

2. Ibid., p. 99.

3. J. A. Hobson, "The Influence of Henry George in England," *Fortnightly Review* (December 1897).

4. *Report of the Fourteenth Annual Trades Union Congress* (Manchester, n.d.), p. 33.

5. Ibid., pp. 7–8.

6. Ibid., p. 13.

7. Ibid., p. 17.

8. *Report of the Fifteenth Annual Trades Union Congress* (Manchester, n.d.), p. 15.

9. Ibid., p. 28.

10. Ibid., pp. 35–36.

11. George also stated in *The Land Question*, p. 60, that consequently the "natural allies of the Irish agitators are the English working classes."

12. Milner papers, MS dep. 56, diary entries of 30 March 1882 and 29 April 1882.

13. Michael Davitt, *The Fall of Feudalism in Ireland or the Story of the Land League Revolution* (London, 1904), p. 381.

14. J. L. Joynes, *The Adventures of a Tourist in Ireland* (London, 1882), p. 77.

15. G. Toynbee, *Reminiscences*, p. 162.

16. Ibid., pp. 163–64.

17. Partly described in Joynes, *Adventures of a Tourist in Ireland*.

18. From a speech in the *Newbury Weekly News*, 11 January 1883.

19. Davitt, *Fall of Feudalism*, p. 381.

20. See T. W. Moody, "Michael Davitt and the British Labour Movement 1882–1906," in *Transactions of the Royal Historical Society*, 5th ser., vol. 3 (1953).

21. Rumors that Davitt had been officially invited to address the congress were denied by Broadhurst (*Report of the Fifteenth Congress*, p. 16).

22. Davitt, *Fall of Feudalism*, p. 382.

23. A. Toynbee, *"Progress and Poverty," A Criticism of Mr. Henry George*, galley proofs, LSE, R. (Coll) Misc. 212, p. 24. See also report in the *Daily News*, 19 January 1883.

24. E.g., in Milner's "current affairs" diary, 8 November 1882, Milner papers, MS Milner dep. 58: "Hardly a day passes but one hears of some unexpected person or other giving in his assent to it [land nationalization]." For one such "unexpected" source of support, see Headlam's *The Church Reformer*, no. 11 (November 1882), p. 3.

25. *Co-operative News*, 4 November 1882. It should be noted that the TUC's standard resolution in support of the cooperative movement was changed to include a reproach of societies who sought cheap labor and disregarded the interests of their workers. This must be rectified if the members of the movement "wish to secure the support of the working classes."

26. Balliol College Register (English), 1875–1908. On 13 October 1882, Toynbee was appointed member of a committee set up to consider the bylaws necessitated by the new statutes.

27. See W. J. Ashley, "A Notebook of Arnold Toynbee," *Economic History Review* (January 1927). The notebook's present whereabouts are unknown.

28. Toynbee papers, MS beginning, "I have examined Mr. George's theory," pp. 3–3a.

29. Ibid., p. 29.

30. A. Toynbee, *"Progress and Poverty," A Criticism of Mr. Henry George* (London, 1883), p. 16. The lectures were first published as a pamphlet (cost 1s.) and later as an appendix to the 1894 Longmans edition of the *Industrial Revolution*. Despite a statement to the contrary in the preface, some passages had been deleted as well as the audiences' responses and the discussions, while other passages were added. See the galley proofs and the press reports in the *Bradford Observer*, 13 and 20 January 1883; and the *Daily News* (London), 19 January 1883.

31. George, *Progress and Poverty* (1879; London, 1908), p. 147; Toynbee, *"Progress and Poverty,"* p. 13.

32. Although George rejected the law of diminishing returns his argument concerning the law of increasing returns is confined to systems that combine agricultural and industrial production. See P. H. Wicksteed, "Mr. Toynbee's Lectures on 'Progress and Poverty,' " *Inquirer*, 21 April 1883.
33. George, *Progress and Poverty*, p. 165.
34. Wicksteed, "Mr. Toynbee's Lectures," *Inquirer*, 12 May 1883.
35. Toynbee, "*Progress and Poverty*," p. 14.
36. Ibid., p. 21.
37. Ibid., p. 8. See also pp. 28–31.
38. Ibid., p. 16.
39. Wicksteed, "Mr. Toynbee's Lectures," *Inquirer*, 5 May 1883.
40. George, *Progress and Poverty*, p. 323.
41. Toynbee, "*Progress and Poverty*," p. 20.
42. Ibid., p. 39.
43. Ibid., p. 5.
44. Ibid., p. 6.
45. Ibid., p. 8.
46. Toynbee, *Industrial Revolution*, pp. 6, 87.
47. Toynbee, "*Progress and Poverty*," p. 14.
48. Ibid., p. 22.
49. Ibid., p. 32.
50. Ibid., p. 34.
51. Ibid., pp. 46–48; George, *The Land Question*, pp. 31–32.
52. Toynbee, "*Progress and Poverty*," pp. 48–49.
53. *Newbury Weekly News*, 11 January 1883.
54. The Honorable G. Brodrick, warden of Merton College, addressing the Junior Reform Club on the "Reform of the English Land System," *Oxford Chronicle*, 3 February 1883.
55. Toynbee, *Industrial Revolution*, pp. 122–24. The same had been argued by Alfred Marshall in his criticism of Henry George. See George J. Stigler, "Alfred Marshall's Lectures on Progress and Poverty," *Journal of Law and Economics* (April 1969).
56. Toynbee had been scheduled to address a meeting of the NALU early in February 1883. The meeting, which was chaired by Percival, passed as its main resolution a motion in favor of county franchise (moved in Toynbee's absence by A. Sidgwick) (*Oxford Chronicle*, 10 February 1883).
57. In ibid., Sidgwick expressed his regret for having to move the main resolution instead of Toynbee "who was competent to deal with the subject far more effectually."
58. Cf. Marshall (on *Progress and Poverty*) whose main remedy was to improve the bargaining position of both the agricultural and the industrial laborer.
59. In the galley proofs, p. 34. In the edited version Toynbee's statement was modified to a call for the reform of the House of Lords (p. 46).
60. Toynbee, "*Progress and Poverty*," p. 48.
61. Toynbee to Grey, 18 November 1882, Grey papers.

62. Letter to Henry George, quoted in Charles A. Barker, *Henry George* (New York, 1955), p. 390.
63. Frederick Griffin to Phelps, 20 October 1882, Phelps papers.
64. Ibid., Rev. T. Fowle to Phelps, 12 March 1883.
65. Toynbee to Grey, 21 November 1882, Grey papers.
66. Quoted in Davitt, *Fall of Feudalism*, p. 382, dated 30 December 1882.
67. *Bradford Observer*, 13 January 1883.
68. Pringle to Grey, 6, 15, and 17 January 1883, Grey papers.
69. Galley proofs, p. 1. See also *Times*, 12 January 1883.
70. Toynbee, *"Progress and Poverty,"* p. 7. The same phrase was used in "Ricardo and the Old Political Economy."
71. Ibid., p. 28.
72. Ibid., p. 7.
73. Galley proofs, p. 15.
74. Toynbee, *"Progress and Poverty,"* p. 23.
75. Ibid.
76. Ibid., p. 24.
77. See *Daily News* (London), 19 January 1883: "The interest [in the second lecture] was all the keener because Mr. Toynbee had indicated that he had an alternative to offer to Mr. George's scheme."
78. Toynbee, *"Progress and Poverty,"* p. 25.
79. Ibid.
80. G. Toynbee, *Reminiscences*, p. 165, letter dated 14 January 1883.
81. *Daily News*, 19 January 1883.
82. Toynbee, *"Progress and Poverty,"* pp. 44–45.
83. Ibid., p. 35.
84. Ibid., p. 37.
85. Ibid., p. 35.
86. Ibid., p. 34.
87. Galley proofs, p. 27.
88. Toynbee, *"Progress and Poverty,"* p. 41.
89. Ibid., p. 45.
90. Ibid., p. 42.
91. Ibid., p. 44.
92. Galley proofs, p. 32.
93. Toynbee, *"Progress and Poverty,"* p. 44.
94. Ibid., p. 51.
95. See Toynbee, *Industrial Revolution*, pp. 135, 236.
96. Toynbee, *"Progress and Poverty,"* pp. 52–53.
97. Ibid., pp. 53–54.
98. *Oxford Magazine*, 24 January 1883.
99. *Economist*, 17 March 1883.
100. *Daily News*, 19 January 1883.
101. Galley proofs, pp. 40–41.
102. Ibid., p. 41.
103. Ibid., p. 42.
104. Ibid., p. 43.

105. Ibid.
106. "Death of Mr. Arnold Toynbee," *Oxford Chronicle,* 17 March 1883.
107. Gell to Grey, 10 March 1883, Grey papers.
108. *Economist,* 17 March 1883. See also the review of Toynbee's *Industrial Revolution,* in the *Times,* 6 August 1884: "The last half of the address was the utterance of a man who was evidently suffering from illness, and who had lost command over his words."

Chapter 9

1. Milner papers, MS dep. 56, diary.
2. Printed after Milner's death in the *National Review* (January–June 1931) as "A View of Socialism," "Robert Owen and Socialism," "Socialism and Robert Owen," "German Socialists," "Socialism and State Enterprise," and "Socialism and the Land."
3. The term "breakdown" was used by Charlotte Toynbee in a letter to Phelps, 23 January 1883, Phelps papers.
4. Milner papers, dep. 25, Charlotte Toynbee to Milner, 7 February 1883.
5. Ibid.
6. Charlotte Toynbee to Phelps, 4 March 1883, Phelps papers.
7. Initially for twelve consecutive nights. Charlotte Toynbee to Phelps, 30 January 1883, Phelps papers.
8. Milner papers, dep. 25, Charlotte Toynbee to Milner, 13 February 1883.
9. Ibid. In a letter to Foxwell, Marshall wrote in reference to Toynbee's second London lecture, "I hear Toynbee is not well; so I don't like to write to him." Two days later he added, somewhat obliquely, "I am very sorry for T, I don't admire him any the less for it" (15 and 17 February 1883, Marshall papers, Marshall Library, Cambridge).
10. Toynbee, *"Progress and Poverty,"* p. 34.
11. See G. Toynbee, *Reminiscences,* p. 184; Cecil Headlam, ed., *The Milner Papers, South Africa, 1897–99* (London, 1931), p. 13.
12. Charlotte Toynbee to Phelps, 4 March 1883, Phelps papers.
13. Ibid., 7 March 1883.
14. Milner papers, dep. 25, W. Toynbee to Milner [c. early March 1883].
15. It was also suggested that the doctor treating him "was far from equal for the occasion" (Gell to Grey, 10 March 1883, Grey papers).
16. "Brain fever," in W. A. R. Thomson, *Black's Medical Dictionary* (London, 1974), p. 130.
17. Gell to Grey, 10 March 1883, Grey papers. See also Montague, *Arnold Toynbee,* p. 53.
18. Grey papers, Gell to Grey, 10 March, 1883.
19. F. C. Montague, *Arnold Toynbee* (Baltimore, 1889), pp. 52–53.
20. Charlotte Toynbee to Abbott, 17 April 1895, Jowett papers.
21. Charlotte Toynbee to Phelps, 20 March 1883, Phelps papers.
22. *Oxford Magazine,* 18 April 1883.
23. Charlotte Toynbee to Grey, 30 December 1883, Grey papers.
24. Jer. 20:9. See the review of *Industrial Revolution* in the *Times,* 6

August 1884: "When he died last year a feeling of something like despair settled down upon the minds of many in Oxford, and the question on their lips was the old question, 'Who shall show us any good?' "

25. Mrs. Rundle Charles, *Three Martyrs of the Nineteenth Century, Studies from the Lives of Livingstone, Gordon, and Patteson* (London: Society for Promoting Christian Knowledge, 1891).

26. Frederick Rogers, *Labour, Life and Literature* (London, 1913), p. 77. Edward Denison, son of the bishop of Salisbury and nephew of the speaker of the House of Commons had briefly resided in the East End (1867–68). In 1868 he was elected MP for Newark; he died in 1870. See Baldwyn Leighton, ed., *A Brief Record, Being Selections from Letters and Other Writings of the Late Edward Denison, M.P. for Newark* (London, 1871); and J. R. Green, "Edward Denison—In Memoriam," in *Macmillan's Magazine* (September 1871).

27. *Edward Denison, M.P., Arnold Toynbee, and Social Problems* (London, 1892), a pamphlet published by the Howard Association "for the Promotion of the best Methods of the Treatment and Prevention of Crime, Pauperism, etc."

28. E. E. Green, *Olive Roscoe or the New Sister* (London, 1896), p. 330. I owe this reference to Miss Judith Rowbotham.

29. Ibid., pp. 359–60.

30. *Academy*, 24 March 1883.

31. *Oxford Chronicle*, 17 March 1883.

32. *Oxford Magazine*, 18 April 1883. See also R. L. Nettleship in the *Co-operative News*, 17 March 1883: "he combined the fervour of an apostle with the foresight and method of a statesman"; and A. H. D. Acland in ibid., 31 March 1883.

33. *Oxford Magazine*. "Epicurean indifference" is an allusion to W. Pater's followers.

34. *Inquirer*, 21 April 1883.

35. Albert Mansbridge, *Arnold Toynbee*, no. 5 of *The Pioneer Biographies of Social Reformers* (London and Leicester, n.d.).

36. A. M[ansbridge] "An Oxford Talk about Arnold Toynbee," *Commonwealth* 1, no. 1 (January 1896).

37. G. Toynbee, *Reminiscences*, pp. 102–3.

38. R. R. Marett, *A Jerseyman at Oxford* (Oxford, 1941), p. 79.

39. J. G. Lockhart, *Cosmo Gordon Lang* (London, 1949), pp. 39, 47.

40. Smith to Phelps, 12 April 1883, Phelps papers.

41. *Oxford Magazine*, 18 April 1883.

42. Ibid., 9 May 1883. The fund's committee consisted of W. Byles, E. T. Cook, H. S. Foxwell, Bolton King, W. Markby, A. Milner, R. L. Nettleship, R. Spence-Watson, A. H. D. Acland, and F. C. Montague.

43. "Toynbee Memorial Medallion," Gell papers. The list of contributors included all of Toynbee's friends and associates as well as some of his students, including W. J. Ashley and Bolton King.

44. *Oxford Chronicle*, 1 December 1883; GLC, A/Toy./1, minutes, 31 August 1886. The total amount collected was £615, of which £500 were

invested in the Barrow Hometite Steel Company, 5 percent debentures. In comparison the sum collected for T. H. Green's memorial reached by the end of 1883 £1,175.16s.

45. *Oxford Chronicle*, 28 April 1883. See also John Burrows, *University Adult Education in London, A Century of Achievement* (London, 1976), p. 10.

46. Rogers, *Labour, Life and Literature*, pp. 108–9.

47. Mrs. S. A. Barnett, *Canon Barnett, His Life, Work, and Friends* (London, 1918), 1:308; J. J. Mallon, "The Story of Toynbee Hall," *Social Service Review* (January 1939). Members of the Friary and their associates mentioned by H. O. Barnett included Rev. T. G. Gardiner (Balliol 1871–75 and then curate of Saint Jude's), B. F. C. Costelloe (Balliol 1874–78 and barrister, Lincoln's Inn), James Bonar (Balliol 1873–76 and since 1881 junior examiner, H. M. Civil Service Commission), Rev. C. M. Marson, Rev. Ronald Bayne (who was to succeed Barnett as vicar of Saint Jude's), F. C. Mills (who started the Broad Street Club in 1883), and Dick Frances.

48. *Oxford Magazine*, 23 and 30 May 1883.

49. Barnett, *Canon Barnett* 1:308–9, 2:33–34; H. O. Barnett, "The Beginnings of Toynbee Hall," in S. A. Barnett and H. O. Barnett, *Practicable Socialism*, new ser. (London, 1915).

50. Written around 1883. GLC, A/Toy.

51. According to the Reverend Brooke Lambert, "Jacob's Answer to Esau's Cry," *Contemporary Review* (September 1884), p. 377, John Ruskin convened around 1869 a meeting in his house in Denmark Hill in which the participants, including Edward Denison, Rev. J. R. Green, and possibly Edmund Hollond discussed the idea of a university settlement.

52. Ball to Gell, 5 November [1883], Gell family papers.

53. Ibid., Ball to Barnett, 10 November [1883].

54. Charlotte Toynbee to Phelps, 28 November 1883, Phelps papers.

55. Milner to Gell, [c. November 1883], Gell family papers.

56. Barnett's paper was later reproduced in two slightly different versions: as "University Settlements" in Barnett and Barnett, *Practicable Socialism*, and as "Settlements of University Men in Great Towns," in Barnett and Barnett, *Practicable Socialism*, new ser. See also report in the *Oxford Magazine*, 21 November 1883.

57. See F. Rogers, *The New Movement at the Universities, and What May Come of It* [n.d.], pamphlet in GLC, A/Toy.

58. *Oxford Magazine*, 21 November 1883.

59. Barnett to Gell, [n.d.], Gell family papers.

60. *Oxford Magazine*, 21 November 1883.

61. Ibid., 5 December 1883.

62. Lockhart, *Cosmo Gordon Lang*, p. 39.

63. See A. Kadish, *The Oxford Economists in the Late Nineteenth Century* (Oxford, 1982), pp. 16–17, 25–28.

64. *Oxford Magazine*, 13 February 1884. See ibid., 21 November 1883;

Gell to Grey, [c. early 1884], Grey papers, in which Gell, upon returning from Oxford, reports on having "found young Oxford in the most wholesome state of enthusiasm about the enterprise. . . . so let's back the young ones."

65. See W. R. Anson, "The Oxford House in Bethnal Green," *Economic Review* (1893); Mandy Ashworth, *The Oxford House in Bethnal Green; 100 Years of Work in the Community* (London, 1984); Bodleian Library, G. A. Lond. 4°132, The Oxford House in Bethnal Green.

66. See Henry Jones and J. H. Muirhead, *The Life and Philosophy of Edward Caird* (Glasgow, 1921), pp. 114–15.

67. W. Reason, *University and Social Settlements* (London, 1898). Cf. S. A. Barnett's introduction to C. Russell and H. S. Lewis, *The Jew in London* (London, 1900), p. xx, in which he confirms that Toynbee Hall "received its name not because the founders wished the place to be a memorial of Arnold Toynbee, but because his name seemed to express their hopes of uniting men of culture with men of industry."

68. GLC, A/Toy.

69. Mallon, "The Story of Toynbee Hall."

70. GLC, A/Toy./1. The original committee consisted of the thirteenth earl of Dalhousie (Balliol 1875–76, at the time lord-in-waiting to the queen) as chairman, Milner, H. Sidgwick (later replaced by Marshall), Spence-Watson, Foxwell, Markby, Acland, and Gell. The vacancy created by the earl of Dalhousie's death in 1887 was not filled.

71. L. L. F. R. Price, *Industrial Peace; Its Advantages, Methods, and Difficulties* (London, 1887); "West Barbary or Notes on the System of Work and Wages in the Cornish Mines," *Journal of the Royal Statistical Society* (September 1888); H. Ll. Smith, *Modern Changes in the Mobility of Labour* (London, 1890); and W. R. Sorley, *Mining Royalties and Their Effect on the Iron and Coal Trade* (London, 1889).

72. Gell to Markby, 18 November 1890, GLC, A/Toy./2.

73. See Barnett's introduction to Russell and Lewis, *The Jew in London*, p. xix.

74. Kadish, *Oxford Economists*, chap. 2.

75. *Co-operative News,* 31 March 1883.

76. F. Hall and W. P. Watkins, *Co-operation* (Manchester, 1937), p. 138. See also "Arnold Toynbee," in *Co-operative Yearbook 1902*, pp. 80–82.

77. See M. E. Sadler, "Owen, Lovett, Maurice and Toynbee," *University Review* (July 1907); and Sadler's annual report in the *Extensions Annual Report of the Year 1886–87* (Oxford, 1887).

78. R. Halstead, "Working Men and University Extension," *Oxford University Extension Gazette* (May 1893). See also ibid., March 1893 and February 1891.

79. Ibid., July 1892.

80. G. Toynbee, *Reminiscences,* p. 186.

81. As much was admitted by Grey and Gell in a letter published in the *Church Reformer,* 15 September 1883.

82. *Oxford Chronicle,* 27 October 1883.

83. Following the 1888 Local Government Act the city council was constituted of forty-five councillors and fifteen aldermen. Six of the councillors were appointed by the heads and bursars of the colleges and three by the convocation. These nine councillors were entitled to elect three of the aldermen. See Sir Norman Chester, "The University in the City" in Rowley, ed., *The Oxford Region* (Oxford, 1980).

84. F. Wylie to Robinson, 20 November 1883, A. Robinson papers, New College; Milner papers, dep. 25, R. Buckell to Milner and Milner's reply.

85. William Jaffé, ed., *Correspondence of Leon Walras and Related Papers* (Amsterdam, 1965).

86. See J. M. Keynes, "Herbert Somerton Foxwell, 1849–1936," *Economic Journal* (December 1936).

87. H. S. Foxwell, "The Economic Movement in England," *Quarterly Journal of Economics* (October 1887).

88. J. K. Ingram, *A History of Political Economy* (Edinburgh, 1888), p. 234.

89. In the *Inquirer*, 21 April, 5 and 12 May 1883.

90. "Preface," to Price, *Industrial Peace*, pp. vii–viii.

91. B. Jowett, "Memoir," in Toynbee, *Industrial Revolution* (1884, 1886, 1890).

92. Luigi Cossa, *An Introduction to the Study of Political Economy* (London, 1893), pp. 345–46.

93. L. L. F. R. Price, *A Short History of Political Economy in England from Adam Smith to Arnold Toynbee*, enlarged ed. (London, 1937), p. 188.

94. E.g., his 1895 presidential address to Section F of the British Association for the Advancement of Science: "The Relations of Economic Science to Practical Affairs," reprinted in L. L. F. R. Price, *Economic Science and Practice* (London, 1896).

95. Price, *A Short History*, p. 195.

96. Ibid., p. 190.

97. L. L. F. R. Price, "The Relations between Industrial Conciliation and Economic Theory," read in 1888 to Section F and reprinted in Price, *Economic Science and Practice*.

98. Price, *A Short History*, p. 191.

99. Ibid., pp. 192–93.

100. Ibid., p. 193.

101. Ibid., p. 195. On socialism and individualism as complementary rather than contradictory approaches to social thought, see Milner's lectures on socialism in the *National Review* (1931).

102. W. J. Ashley's review of Montague, *Arnold Toynbee*, in *Political Science Quarterly* (1889).

103. As for the question of the influence of the German school on Toynbee, see "A German Critic on Arnold Toynbee," *Oxford Magazine* (13 May 1885), which treats with justified skepticism the eagerness with which the German economists have tried "to establish a direct influence of German thought upon the new school of English economists." A more likely source of German influence is through history.

278

104. W. J. Ashley, *An Introduction to English Economic History and Theory* (London, 1888), pt. 1.
105. Anne Ashley, *William James Ashley, A Life* (London, 1932), p. 35.
106. H. W. McCready, "Sir William Ashley; Some Unpublished Letters," *Journal of Economic History* (1955).
107. Bodleian Library, 232 c. 641.
108. Charlotte M. Toynbee, "Prefatory Note," in Toynbee, *Industrial Revolution*.
109. Milner was named editor in ibid., which prefaced the first edition. In later editions a different version of the "Note," signed July 1908, was used in which the reference to Milner was omitted.
110. Charlotte Toynbee to Grey, 25 May 1884, Grey papers.
111. For a summary of the debate, see P. Deane, *The First Industrial Revolution* (Cambridge, 1965), pp. 2–3. See also R. M. Hartwell's introduction to Hartwell, ed., *The Causes of the Industrial Revolution in England* (London, 1967), pp. 11–12.
112. W. J. Ashley, *The Economic Organization of England* (London, 1914), p. 141.
113. Deane, *The First Industrial Revolution*, p. 211.
114. G. N. Clark has argued in *The Idea of the Industrial Revolution* (Glasgow, 1970) that economic historians had followed the periodization of A. V. Dicey in his "Lectures on the Relations between Law and Public Opinion in England" (1905).
115. Deane, *First Industrial Revolution*, p. 238; E. P. Thompson, *The Making of the English Working Class* (New York: Penguin, 1980), pp. 213, 229; and Malcolm I. Thomis, *The Town Labourer and the Industrial Revolution* (London, 1974), esp. pp. 3, 8, 16, 151.
116. Hartwell, ed., *Causes of the Industrial Revolution*, p. 7.
117. E.g., Clark, *Idea of the Industrial Revolution*; R. M. Hartwell, "Good Old Economic History," *Journal of Economic History* (March 1973); and Gerard M. Koot, "English Historical Economists and the Emergence of Economic History in England," *History of Political Economy* (Summer 1980).
118. Lord Macaulay, *The History of England from the Accession of James the Second* (London, 1913), p. 1.
119. Ibid., pp. 1311–12.
120. For the reasons for Rogers's limited influence on a younger generation of economic historians, see W. J. Ashley, "James E. Thorold Rogers," *Political Science Quarterly* (1889); W. A. S. Hewins's biography in DNB 17; and Price, *A Short History*, p. 215.
121. In Toynbee's instance this has been stated by Clark, *Idea of the Industrial Revolution*.
122. Reprinted in John Morley, *Critical Miscellanies* (London, 1892).
123. For Cunningham's approach, see his introductory essay to Cunningham, *The Growth of English Industry and Commerce during the Early and Middle Ages* (1882), in which he stated categorically that "politics are more important than economics in English History."

Index

Library of Congress Cataloging-in-Publication Data

Kadish, Alon, 1950–
Apostle Arnold.

Bibliography: p.
Includes index.
1. Toynbee, Arnold, 1852–1883. 2. Historians—Great Britain—Biography.
I. Title.
DA3.T68K33   1986   951'.0072024   [B]   85-25265
ISBN 0-8223-0489-9